THE SIEGE OF VALENCIA

©2002 Susan J. Wolfson and Elizabeth Fay
All rights reserved. The use of any part of this publication reproduced, transmitted in any
form or by any means, electronic, mechanical, photocopying, recording, or otherwise, or
stored in a retrieval system, without prior written consent of the publisher – or in the case
of photocopying, a licence from CANCOPY (Canadian Copyright Licensing Agency), One
Yonge Street, Suite 201, Toronto, ON M5E 1E5 – is an infringement of the copyright law.

National Library of Canada Cataloguing in Publication Data
Hemans, Felicia Dorothea, 1793-1835
The siege of Valencia : a parallel text edition / Felicia Hemans ; edited by Susan J.
Wolfson, Elizabeth Fay.

(Broadview literary texts)
Includes bibliographical references.
ISBN 1-55111-442-9

I. Wolfson, Susan J., 1948- II. Fay, Elizabeth A., 1957- III. Title. IV. Series.

PR4780.S53 2002   821'.7   C2002-902493-5

Broadview Press Ltd. is an independent, international publishing house, incorporated in
1985. Broadview believes in shared ownership, both with its employees and with the gen-
eral public; since the year 2000 Broadview shares have traded publicly on the Toronto
Venture Exchange under the symbol BDP.

We welcome comments and suggestions regarding any aspect of our publications–please
feel free to contact us at the addresses below or at broadview@broadviewpress.com.

North America
PO Box 1243, Peterborough, Ontario, Canada K9J 7H5
3576 California Road, Orchard Park, NY, USA 14127
Tel: (705) 743-8990; Fax: (705) 743-8353
email: customerservice@broadviewpress.com

UK, Ireland, and continental Europe
Thomas Lyster Ltd., Units 3 & 4a, Old Boundary Way
Burscough Road, Ormskirk
Lancashire, L39 2YW
Tel: (01695) 575112; Fax: (01695) 570120
email: books@tlyster.co.uk

Australia and New Zealand
UNIREPS, University of New South Wales
Sydney, NSW, 2052
Tel: 61 2 9664 0999; Fax: 61 2 9664 5420
email: info.press@unsw.edu.au

www.broadviewpress.com

Broadview Press Ltd. gratefully acknowledges the financial support of the Government of
Canada through the Book Publishing Industry Development Program for our publishing
activities.

Series editor: Professor L.W. Conolly
Advisory editor for this volume: Professor Eugene Benson

Text design and composition by George Kirkpatrick

PRINTED IN CANADA

THE SIEGE OF VALENCIA

Felicia Hemans

A Parallel Text Edition

The Manuscript and the Publication of 1823

edited by Susan J. Wolfson & Elizabeth Fay

broadview literary texts

Contents

Acknowledgments

For permission to publish our transcription of the MS, we are most pleased to thank Leslie Morris and the Houghton Library, Harvard University.

For conceptual support for and encouragement of this edition and more particularly for generous permission to rely on some of the annotation in Susan Wolfson's *Felicia Hemans*, we gratefully thank Princeton University Press.

For material support in the preparation of this edition, we are indebted to the generosity of the Department of English, Princeton University.

For intrepid research and technical assistance we are fortunate to have enlisted Andrew Krull of Princeton University. For general support and encouragement, we are happy to thank Stephen Behrendt, Michael Eberle-Sinatra, Paula Feldman, Julia Gaunce, Don Le Pan, Ronald Levao, Peter Manning, Jerome McGann, Anne Mellor, Nanora Sweet, and Duncan Wu.

Introduction

Felicia Hemans

In 1819, after more than a decade of diligent publishing, Felicia Hemans won national fame when the newly founded Royal Society of Literature awarded its competition-prize (£50) to her poem on Scots national heroes William Wallace and Robert the Bruce. It was soon published in a recently founded journal that meant to make its mark as an arbiter of literary value, *Blackwood's Edinburgh Magazine*. In this same issue (September 1819), Hemans read her praises by reviewer John Wilson, who placed her in a pantheon of national female icons: "Scotland has her Baillie—Ireland her Tighe—England her Hemans." The next year, the publisher of her six latest volumes of poetry (all between 1816 and 1820), John Murray, saw to it that "Mrs. Hemans" received a laudatory retrospective in his *Quarterly Review*, the most influential, widely read periodical of the day, with a circulation of 10,000, and many more readers than that. *The Siege of Valencia*, one of the works to title her next major volume (published by Murray in 1823), was conceived and written in the glow of this national emergence.

Hemans was thirty, on the cusp of a decade in which her fame as England's premier "poetess" would swell to trans-Atlantic proportions. Born in Liverpool, in 1793 (the year England launched nearly a quarter of a century of war against France), young Felicia Browne lived in this bustling city until 1800, when her merchant father, suffering reversals, closed up shop and moved the family to a coastal village in North Wales. The family could not afford schooling for her, so her mother undertook her education, teaching her languages and encouraging her to explore their domestic library. Felicia Browne learned quickly and read avidly, among her pleasures, Robert Southey's *Chronicles of the Cid* (1808). This work would inspire and become a frequent point of reference in *The Siege of Valencia* and its accompanying *Songs of the Cid*. Her affection for Spanish chivalry was no antiquarianism, but was charged with contemporary politics, Britain's military support of Spain's resistance to Napoleonic invasion. Two brothers served in the British forces in

Spain, along with Captain Alfred Hemans, her future husband. One of her first poetic efforts, published when she was sixteen, was *England and Spain, or, Valour and Patriotism* (1809), about these nations' alliance against Napoleon, a war charged with chivalric romance. By the time she published this poem, she was well into another long work of seemingly contradictory statement, *War and Peace*. Although this, too, celebrated England's military heroes (especially Nelson and Wellington) and reviled war-mongering Napoleonic ambition, it voiced a pan-national, impassioned plea for peace in an age of war, a plea notably infused with the "feminine"-centered laments over war-ruptured domestic affections.

It was also in 1809 that Felicia Browne, a romantic and a patriot, found a focus for both passions in Captain Hemans. They fell in love when they met. He went back to war, and when he returned in 1811 his body was scarred and his health considerably weakened. They married in 1812, the year the poet turned nineteen and her third volume, *The Domestic Affections* (including *War and Peace*) appeared. In the same year Byron changed the literary landscape with his epic of alienation, *Childe Harold's Pilgrimage*, its first canto including a bitter denunciation of Britain's betrayal of its Spanish allies by assisting the withdrawal of Napoleon's troops from Portugal, in a treaty known as The Convention of Cintra. Hemans's emphasis on the personal and domestic effects of war, in both *The Domestic Affections* and *War and Peace*, was infused not only by the tenor of the times but also by her own domestic affections for her brother and her fiancé. These issues recur in subsequent poems, especially those in *Tales, and Historic Scenes* (1819), and come into dramatic conflict with the imperatives of nation-defining, heart-rending warfare in *The Siege of Valencia*.

Domestic Affections did not attract notice critically or commercially, and when her husband's postwar appointment ended in a discharge without pay, the family, now with a baby boy, joined her mother's household in Wales. Hemans kept writing, her first success coming with a poem keyed to Britain's triumphant emergence as world power after the fall of Napoleon: *The Restoration of the Works of Art to Italy* (1816), on the Regent's financing of the return of some of the plunder Napoleon's armies had brought to Paris to establish the prestige of the French empire. Byron praised it and his publisher John Murray purchased it for a second edition. Soon after, Murray brought out Hemans's *Modern Greece* (1817) and a volume of translations and original poetry (1818). There were four boys by this point, and she was pregnant again. In 1818, just before the birth of a fifth son, the Captain left for Italy. The reasons were unclear; the "story" was a better climate for his poor health, but some sensed that he would have preferred an ordinary domestic care-taker to a "literary lady" for a wife, and was uncomfortable living off her earnings. His departure was all the more painful for Hemans for its repetition of her father's desertion of his family in 1810 for a fresh start in Canada, where he died the year of her marriage. The idealism of hearth and home for which "Mrs. Hemans" would become famous in the 1820s was haunted by these paternal desertions, even as the events sharpened her determination to support her family with her writing.

Raising five boys, ages three to ten, was demanding, but Hemans had a sister, a mother, and brothers to help out and to manage the home while she wrote, and she was now free of a husband's expectations of wifely service and obedience. With discipline and a savvy eye on the literary marketplace, she kept reading and writing, and her career took off. *Tales, and Historic Scenes*, a wide-ranging critical view of politics, was well reviewed and had moderate commercial success, earning about £120 by 1821. She won prize competitions and further favor with the public and the reviewers. New venues for poetry had opened with the founding of *Blackwood's* in 1817 and would dramatically expand with the inauguration of the annuals fad, heralded by *Forget Me Not* in 1822. Throughout the 1820s Hemans profited from these outlets, and her fame was clinched by the volumes that followed *The Siege of Valencia: The Forest Sanctuary* (1825 and 1829), *Records of Woman* (1828, with several editions) and *Songs of the Affections* (1830).

The death of her mother in 1827 was devastating, a loss deepened by the breakup of the household as older sons left for school and siblings married or moved away. To escape the emptiness, Hemans moved with her younger sons to Wavertree, a village near Liverpool, where she found schooling for them and literary and musical society for herself. But her health was weakening from emotional and physical stress, and in 1831 she sent her two oldest boys to their father in Italy and moved to Dublin, to be near her brother George and his wife. Although she again found good society and continued to write and publish, the climate was a disaster. She became very ill, and then bed-ridden in 1834, and died a few months before her forty-second birthday, in 1835, only eight years after her mother—and with regrets about the poetry she never realized: "My wish ever was to concentrate all my mental energy in the production of some more noble and complete work."[1]

The Siege of Valencia, A Dramatic Poem

Such energetic mental concentration had already shaped *The Siege of Valencia*. With a story inspired by sieges from ancient times to recent history, Hemans set her stage in an imaginary thirteenth-century Moorish siege of this Christian city on Spain's Mediterranean coast. Her drama involves the passions of several overlapping but not fully congruent conflicts: Spain versus Africa; Christian versus Islam, with a racial overlay (the manuscript shows a canceled subtitle: *Or, The Race of the Cid*); maternal love versus patriarchal pride; war versus peace; death versus life; noble martyrdom versus dishonorable surrender; the privileges of ruling classes versus the misery of the poor. A summary of the plot delineates the fissures and tensions. Valencia has been under a prolonged and wasting siege by the Moors, led by Abdullah (his name means "servant of God"). In the opening scene, the Governor, a descendant of legendary hero El Cid, conveys news to his wife Elmina that their two young sons have been taken hostage. The boys, "eager to behold / The face of noble war," says the proud father, got too close to the action and were captured. The ransom is the surrender of the city. To avert such national "disgrace," Gonzalez accepts the sons' "noble" martyrdom, on the model of heroic Christian sacrifice. Their daughter, "heroic" Ximena (El Cid's wife is her namesake), agrees, but Elmina pleads in anguish for her sons' lives. Gonzalez berates her, invoking national and dynastic honor, and not hesitating to gender this system of values: honor is male, dishonor female. In anger and despair Elmina seeks out the chief priest Hernandez for counsel, not knowing that in his pre-ecclesiastical, warrior life he had killed a Moor who turned out to be his own son (he deserted his Christian home and faith to be with his

---

1 Letter to Rose Lawrence, 13 February 1835 (private collection, with words missing from damage supplied from Hughes, *Memoir* 296–97).

beloved Moorish maid). Hernandez upbraids Elmina's frailty and counsels to her to accept the glorious martyrdom of her sons. In desperation, Elmina disguises herself to visit the Moors' camp, to see her sons (the elder is brave, the younger terrified) and to make a deal, agreeing to unlock the gates of the city in exchange for their lives. Hemans represents a mother impelled not only by love but also by courage. Is she a hero, or a traitor? When she returns to Valencia, she ruefully confesses her transgression to Gonzalez and Ximena. Gonzalez scorns her, but Ximena (quietly dying in grief for a beloved already fallen in battle), pities her mother and rallies the citizens to save her brothers. When Gonzalez refuses to surrender, Abdullah has his elder son (a willing martyr) slain before his eyes. Gonzalez rushes into battle in a futile attempt to save his remaining son, and receives a fatal wound. Ximena dies of a broken heart, but in faith that she is going to a better world, while Gonzalez lives long enough to behold the King of Castile's army come to the rescue. Abdullah is slain, the Moors are vanquished, Valencia is delivered, and Elmina supervises the funeral of Gonzalez as a noble hero's ascent to "that last home of glory."

The plot's didactic apparatus — the pivotal exhortations of Ximena, the reform of Elmina, and the last-minute rescue of the city by Castile's army of Christian soldiers — argues for steadfast faith amid crisis and would seem to refute any murmurings of dissent. But the programmatic devices and the artifice of rescue seem inadequate to the ruptures these would contain. The chief divorce is between patriarchal honor and maternal affection. Hemans sets this conflict not just in the context of honor joined to faith but also, and with contradictory force, in a social system in which gender subtends a patriarchal pride that would discredit the maternally based values of love and affection. In the maternal view, voiced passionately by Elmina, self-sacrifice makes sense only to nurture the next generation; to sacrifice children to the pride of their fathers seems an inhuman tribute to "glory," "fame," and "honor." National myths, codes of honor, definitions of masculine patriotism, and the priestly sanctions that govern political and domestic life come into continual conflict with the way the military defense (and pursuit, as in the frequent references to the Crusades) of these values fatally overwhelms hearth and home, the entire world sustained by domestic affections. Even in otherwise opposed cultural systems—Moslem Africa and Christian Spain—fathers behave with disturbing consistency, especially in the martyrdom of sons: "the sons of Afric" revere patriarch Abraham, who would sacrifice his son to divine command; the sons of Spain revere the legacy of this prototype in the New Testament, God's sacrifice of his Son. Although Elmina is chastened into this "glory," her final words speak of a "God, / Whose hand around her hath unpeopled earth" (9.224-25), uncreating a world in which a mother's best hope is not for her children's future lives, but for her own death.

Hemans's recognition of the intractability of these conflicting values on the level of historical existence is reflected in her patently romance resolution, a *deus ex machina*. A force of "ten thousand" Castilian soldiers arrives at the last minute to save Valencia with the "flash / Of knightly swords" (9.62-70). This advent would evoke for contemporary readers Edmund Burke's dismay at the failure of chivalry in Marie Antoinette's arrest in October 1789, in the most famous passage of *Reflections on the Revolution in France* (1790): "Little did I dream that I should have lived to see such disasters fallen upon her in a nation of gallant men, in a nation of men of honour, and of cavaliers. I thought ten thousand swords must have leaped from their scabbards to avenge even a look that threatened her with insult. But the age of chivalry is gone." If Hemans's romance resolution calls back the age of chivalry with the rescue of the she-city, its patent artificiality exposes a fictional displacement of persistent ideological conflicts. Out of the tension between romance aesthetics and social process, Hemans (a mother of five "fatherless" boys) shapes the historical meaning and resonance of *The Siege*.

The Romance of Spain and El Cid

In giving dramatic voices to contradictions and conflicts (which extend in scene 6 to class grievances of a kind that finds little sympathy in Edmund Burke's *Reflections on the Revolution in France*), Hemans complicates a lifelong militant patriotism, of domestic affection for brothers and a husband-to-be fighting in Spain against the modern blasphemer Napoleon. The Peninsular Campaign against Napoleon, with Britain allied to Spanish patriotism, was enthusiastically cheered in England as a chivalric revival untainted by the aristocratic decadence that provoked the French Revolution. The events of the War "are so associated in my mind with the most vivid recollections of my early youth," she wrote early in 1823, "that I could almost fancy I had passed that period of my life in the days of Chivalry, so high and ardent were the feelings they excited."[1] The national icon for the days of chivalry in Christian Spain, and an inspiration in the struggle against imperialist invaders, is warrior-hero El Cid, invoked throughout *The Siege* to exhort the honor of Valencia and chastise incipient doubts.

The historical El Cid is a far more problematic figure, a free-lance warrior who adapted his commitments to his employers. The exploits of Rodrigo (or Ruy) Díaz de Vivar (or Bivar, his supposed birthplace) earned him the name "El Cid," from the Arabic *Seid* or *Sidi* ("feudal lord"); he was also called Campeador, from the Latin *Campi doctor* ("battlefield master"). Born around 1043 into an aristocratic family of northern Spain, he fought for King Ferdinand I of Castile, then commanded the forces of Ferdinand's son and successor, Sancho II, against his brothers, the kings of León and Galicia. After Sancho's death, he served Sancho's brother and successor, Alfonso VI of Castile and León, one of the strongest rulers of the period. In 1074 Alfonso arranged El Cid's marriage to Sancho's daughter Ximena Díaz, but suspicious of his popularity and agenda, Alfonso banished him from Castile around 1081. El Cid then turned soldier of fortune, even serving the Muslim Moorish ruler of Saragossa (the most important city of Aragón, in northeastern Spain) against the Christian count of Barcelona. When a zealous force of North African Moors, the Almoravides, invaded Spain, ousting weak Moorish rulers and threatening Christian ones, El Cid was restored to Alfonso's favor—but not for long. Accused of bungling the defense of some territories, he left Alfonso's service in 1089 and resumed his independent career. His conquest of Valencia from the Moors in 1094 was a highlight, a decisive halt of the expanding Almoravid dynasty. El Cid ruled and defended Valencia until his death in 1099; the Moors then besieged the city, forcing Ximena's exit in 1102. She and the entire community of his followers withdrew with El Cid's remains to his lands in native Castile, where his body was interred in

---

1 Chorley, *Memorials* 1.89-90. See her letter to her aunt, 1808, in the Appendix.

the monastery of San Pedro de Cardeña. The monks promoted a cult of sainthood, and even his horse Babieca, reputedly buried at the monastery, became an object of veneration. The oldest source of the Cid legend is *Poema del Cid* (*Song of the Cid*), an anonymous work from the mid-twelfth century. After the expulsion of Moors (by Ferdinand of Castile and Isabella of Aragon) in 1492, ballads flourished, casting El Cid as the loyal servant and chivalric hero of Christian Castile, an opponent of Moorish expansion, Ximena his worthy mate. These "romances," first collected in the sixteenth century, inspired Guillén de Castro's drama *Mocedades del Cid* (1618), the source of Pierre Corneille's *Le Cid* (1637), a European classic. Southey's *Chronicle of the Cid, from the Spanish* (1808) assembled and translated several sources, romances, poems and chronicles, from medieval times through the mid-seventeenth century. All these works have a strong medieval aura (reflected in the antiqued look of Southey's tome), and Hemans was enamored of the legends. "I often think, what a dull, faded thing life,—such life as we lead in this later age,—would appear to one of those fiery knights of old. Only imagine 'My Cid,' spurring the good steed Bavieca through the streets of Liverpool! or coming to pass an evening with me at Wavertree!"[1]

Yet for all its antiquarian flavor, Southey's *Chronicle* had contemporary bearing, as did Hemans's political imagination. The *Chronicle* appeared in 1808, at the outset of England's alliance with Spanish guerillas in the war against Napoleonic France, and was meant to encourage British affection for Spanish (anti-Napoleonic) nationalism. This "Peninsular War" began when Napoleon prohibited Spain's trade with Britain. In June 1808, he replaced King Ferdinand VII with his brother Joseph Napoleon, provoking widespread revolts. France's modern siege of Valencia, a port central to trade, was heroically resisted, with similar reactions throughout the Peninsula. In August 1808, Wellington's British forces landed in Portugal and negotiated the Convention of Cintra, securing the liberation of Lisbon by conveying the French army and its booty in British ships back to France. The treaty outraged many back home, including William Wordsworth and Lord Byron (not inclined to agree on

---

1 Letters 31 January 1823; and later 1828 (Chorley, *Memorials* 1.89-90, 225-56). Hemans lived in Wavertree, a small village near Liverpool, from 1828 to 1831.

much), who viewed the accommodation as a betrayal of Spanish valor and patriotism. Britain soon produced a national hero, Sir John Moore, who commanded the British invasion of Spain. When he died in the retreat to Coruña, he joined Admiral Nelson in the pantheon of British military martyrs. The war concluded in 1814 with the abdication of Napoleon, the British victories in Spain contributing to his downfall (Wellington vanquished him at Waterloo, in 1815), reviving the spirit of chivalry at home, and raising Britain's prestige abroad.

By the time Hemans was at work on *The Siege of Valencia*, however, the romance of Spanish resistance had evolved into a messier civil war. Ferdinand returned to the throne in 1814 (the Bourbon Restoration), with the acclaim of "liberales" and patriots, but his reactionary measures soon alienated this support and fueled an opposition that erupted into a revolution in 1820. To the dismay of many Britons, the insurgents were put down in 1823 by the restored French monarchy, acting on behalf of the Holy Alliance of monarchal powers. What had been a valiant Spanish struggle against a foreign foe in 1808 had become, in 1823, a civil war against a reactionary ruler and his French allies. By these lights, the "romance" of El Cid seems nostalgic rather than prescriptive—at best, a mythologized ghost in the machine of modern warfare.

The Siege of Valencia (1823)

The Siege of Valencia; A Dramatic Poem. The Last Constantine: with other Poems was published in London by John Murray in 1823, in octavo (with eight pages to the printed sheet, more economical than a quarto), and priced at nine shillings, sixpence. *The Last Constantine*, a monologue in 105 Spenserian stanzas (a form associated with epic romance, made spectacularly popular by *Childe Harold*), is about another Christian-"infidel" conflict, this one sited in the last days of the fall of Constantinople to a Moslem siege in the fifteenth century: "its thousand years of christian pomp are o'er" (LXIV). Hemans had written this poem for a competition sponsored by the Royal Society of Literature soliciting entries on the subject, with an advertised prize of 50 guineas (£52.5)—not a spectacular sum, but enough to support her family for many months. Unhappy with the handful of submissions (all anonymous), the Society extended the deadline, and in frustration Hemans withdrew her poem, on which she had expended considerable labor and which she did not want to see deemed unworthy in advance of any publication. It fit thematically with *The Siege*, and led off the 1823 volume.[1] Its monologue form favored a single point of view, animated by fluctuations of hope, despair, and consolation focused on the heroic but doomed resistance of Constantine Paleologus (the last Constantine ruler). This is a story of a Christian city (indeed dynasty) that succumbs to the "Other": an eastern race and empire, the forces of Islam. The poem concludes in the hope of a future triumph and an exhortation to present faith, a "trust / On Him whose ways are dark, unsearchable—but just" (CV).

The Siege is a drama of several voices and points of view. Hemans's concern for a concentration of mental energy led her to identify its genre as "a dramatic poem" in her subtitle. She did not want the work (mis)taken as a script for theatrical production, which in her day favored sensational events and operatic passions, and was tied to a contemporary culture of commercial interest and theatrical vanities:

> When I first entered upon theatrical affairs, I had some idea of writing for the house myself, but soon became a convert to Pope's opinion of that subject. Who would condescend to the drudgery of the stage, and enslave himself to the humours, the caprices, the taste or tastelessness, of the age? Besides, one must write for particular actors, have them continually in one's eye, sacrifice character to the personating of it, cringe to some favourite of the public, neither give him too many nor too few lines to spout, think how he would mouth such and such a sentence, look such and such a passion, strut such and such a scene, Who, I say, would submit to all this?

This is Byron fulminating in 1821 or so; even he couldn't manage a success in this culture.[2] Hemans's subtitle names a non-stage dramatic

---

1 According to Hughes, this order was a printer's error. As the volume title indicates, Hemans meant *The Siege* to be the lead, as chief "in importance and interest" (*Memoir* 68).

2 Thomas Medwin, *Conversations of Lord Byron: Noted During a Residence with His Lordship at Pisa, in the Years 1821 and 1822* (London: Henry Colburn, 1824) 104.

form, with a respectable lineage. "*A Dramatic Poem*" subtitles Milton's *Samson Agonistes* as well as Byron's *Manfred*. This genre is akin to the "closet" drama, a work designed for reading and reflection in the intimacy of one's private room (closet), rather than for staging in a theater. Although playwright-poet Joanna Baillie insisted that her *Plays on the Passions* (1798-1812) were not closet dramas, they were widely admired (by Hemans and Byron among others) as if they were, a literature devoted less to sensational incident than to "delineat[ing] the progress of the higher passions in the human breast," as Baillie wrote in her "Introductory Discourse." (They did not succeed on the stage.) Hemans admired Baillie's achievements, especially her portrayal of women of ideas and of heroic stature.

Hemans's 1823 volume also included *Elysium* (about the virtues of the Christian afterlife as opposed to that of classical religion, in which only heroes are rewarded in the Elysian fields), a set of six *Greek Songs*, about the devastations caused by Greece's wars, invasions, and slaughters, four *Songs of the Cid,* about the hero's exile, death, and miraculous "rising," as well as eleven other poems previously published in magazines and newspapers, among the most well-known, *England's Dead,* a vision of the global empire as global cemetery. The volume was a respectable success, its edition of 1000 selling out, with a profit of £132 for Hemans and Murray to split. Although *The Siege* itself did not have another lifetime printing in England, it was collected in an American volume edited by Andrews Norton: *The League of the Alps, The Siege of Valencia, The Vespers of Palermo, and Other Poems* (Boston, 1826). It was republished in England for the first time, posthumously, in the 1839 *Works of Mrs. Hemans.*

The Houghton Manuscript

Modern literary study has enjoyed two lively developments in textual scholarship: "genetics" (tracking a text from manuscript drafts, to publication, to later revision); and "versioning" (a comparative study of these different texts). Because genetics may tell various stories (improvements, retractions, corruptions, or clarifications), all versions have "legitimacy and interest," contends critic and textual editor Jack Stillinger. Another expert, Donald Reiman, even advocates an editorial practice of "versioning," making available "different *primary* textual documents and states of major texts" to enable comparisons of "ideologies, aesthetic perspectives, or rhetorical strategies."[1] We now recognize two plays called *King Lear* and two endings to *Great Expectations*.[2] Students of Romanticism embrace a number of multiples: Coleridge's *The Rime of the Ancyent Marinere* (1798) and *The Rime of the Ancient Mariner* (1817); Keats's "La Belle Dame sans Mercy" (the ballad published in the *Indicator*) and the long-canonized letter-text titled "La Belle Dame sans Merci"; *Frankenstein*, 1818 and 1831, and the welter of Wordsworth's *Preludes*, from 1798 to 1850.[3]

Hemans's unsigned 191-page manuscript of *The Siege of Valencia*, held in the archives of the Houghton Library at Harvard University since September 1964, was apparently unnoticed by any scholar before late 1999. It is transcribed and published here, in entirety, for the first time.[4] The pages, written recto and verso, in Hemans's hand, fill four uncovered booklets (18.5 x 22.75 cm, approximately 7.3 x 9 inches), the third and fourth sewn together. The first three are of fine rag paper, gilt-edged, of smaller size than foolscap; the fourth is of much cheaper, thinner paper. It is inscribed "To Mr. Mackenzie Bell, with Felicia Hemans [*sic*] compliments / April 1899." (The namesake

---

1   Stillinger, *Multiple Authorship and the Myth of Solitary Genius* (New York: Oxford UP, 1991) 94; Reiman, "'Versioning': The Presentation of Multiple Texts," *Romantic Texts and Contexts* (Columbia: U of Missouri P, 1988) 169.

2   In *Shakespeare's Revision of "King Lear,"* Steven Urkowitz argues for the 1608 first quarto and the 1623 first folio versions of *King Lear* as equivalent "alternative texts created by a revising author" rather than as products of a missing original (Princeton: Princeton UP, 1980) 5. George Bernard Shaw insisted on printing the original and the revised endings of *Great Expectations* in the edition he supervised (Edinburgh: Limited Editions Club, 1937).

3   *The Rime of the Ancyent Marinere, In Seven Parts,* antiqued and unglossed, opened the 1798 *Lyrical Ballads; The Ancient Mariner. A Poet's Reverie,* less antiqued, with some revision appeared in 1800; in 1802 and 1805, the subtitle was dropped and further revisions applied; *The Rime of the Ancient Mariner,* revised, with marginal gloss and a new epigraph, was first issued with Coleridge's name in *Sibylline Leaves* in 1817. For discussions of "La Belle Dame," see Jerome McGann, "Keats and the Historical Method in Literary Criticism" (1979; rpt. *The Beauty of Inflections: Literary Investigations in Historical Method & Theory,* 1985; Oxford: Clarendon, 1988), and David Simpson, *Irony and Authority in Romantic Poetry* (London: Macmillan, 1979) 14-23. Charles E. Robinson's *The "Frankenstein" Notebooks: A Facsimile Edition of Mary Shelley's Manuscript Novel, 1816-17* (New York and London: Garland Publishing, 1996) gives the 1818 and 1831 texts, and the manuscripts. For a brief summary of the situation of Wordsworth's *Prelude,* see Susan J. Wolfson, *Formal Charges: The Shaping of Poetry in British Romanticism* (Stanford: Stanford UP, 1997) ch. 4.

4   Susan J. Wolfson includes a number of the MS variants in her notes to *1823* in her edition of Hemans.

is the poet's granddaughter.)[1] The Houghton purchased it, along with a second short Hemans manuscript, in 1964, for $150, from The Seven Gables Bookshop, 3 West 46th Street, New York City.

Like the 1823 publication, the manuscript has nine distinct scenes, unnumbered, but there is no prefacing "Advertisement" and far fewer notes. Its Dramatis Personae show three variants: the servant "Diego" is listed; the Governor's name is "Gonsalvo"; most strikingly, Ximena is listed as "his daughter" (in *1823*, she is listed as "Her Daughter" — that is, Elmina's). Hemans's equivocation of lineage indexes the agonized commitments that besiege Ximena, ones that play out more fully in the manuscript. In both versions, Ximena is "his" daughter in her embrace of honor in war at all costs, including the lives of her young brothers. She is also "her" daughter in a "female" sensibility (as characterized in the 1820s): heart-broken, self-sacrificing, spiritually faithful, inspirational to others. More than any other figure in the drama, she embodies, suffers, and succumbs to irresolvable conflicts between love and war, wasting away after her beloved is killed in battle. The manuscript heightens these tensions: Ximena is more militant in the cause of Valencia; Elmina is given a fuller, more passionate voice for maternal claims and values, including a sharper critique of the masculine culture of glory; Gonsalvo (Gonzalez in *1823*) is much more anguished about the claims of the heart's affections; the priest Hernandez is at once more blood-thirsty and more heartbroken; the civic dirges gloomier and more fatalistic; the wasting effects of the siege given much fuller, more starkly impressive description.

One of the most remarkable revisions that the MS discloses occurs in the opening debate between Gonsalvo and Elmina about the martyrdom of their sons. Gonsalvo protests her accusations that he has a cold unfeeling heart:

> — Thinkst thou I feel no pangs?
> He, that hath given me sons, doth know the heart
> Whose treasures he recalls. — Of this no more! (MS 1.297-99)

---

1   Mackenzie Bell (1856-1930) was an English poet, biographer (Charles Whitehead; Christina Rossetti), traveler, and imperialist, who was active in liberal and progressive politics. It was through his leadership that a memorial to Hemans was established in Liverpool.

This "He" is divine providence, who giveth and who taketh away, requiring faithful acceptance, heart-pangs notwithstanding. Here Gonsalvo gets to have his heart and his faith; but for *1823*, Hemans shifts the terms, so that the appeal to a divine "He" now involves a contempt for any she-claims from the mother. Gonzalez rebukes her:

— Thinkst thou *I* feel no pangs?
He that hath given me sons, doth know the heart
Whose treasure she recalls. — Of this no more. (1.302-4)

With an italicized "I" to claim his pain, his next lines seem quite cruel to Elmina, for the only female claim they acknowledge is that of his own (feminized) heart of recalling. Elmina is triply excluded, first from the line of child-production that goes from He-god to father, then by her husband's appropriation of the feminine to trope the feeling male heart, and finally by a summary exclusion of any heart-pangs from deciding the civic question. In the first posthumous edition (*1839*), 304 reads (again) "Whose treasure he recalls" (vol. 3, p. 297), as if correcting an erroneous sliding in *1823* of the "s" from "treasures" to "he" (yielding "she"). Hemans's American editor, Andrews Norton, also made this change for his edition. Do these texts correct an error in Murray's printing, or do they interfere with a revision? Whatever one decides, manuscript evidence ("treasures he") is critical.

One of the most impressively sustained manuscript variants is scene 6, which opens with the citizens of Valencia discussing the wasting siege. Focused on the sudden leveling of the aristocratic class to the conditions of ordinary peasants, it is a political enough moment in *1823*, and even more so in the class grievances voiced in the manuscript. "Why, this is just!" says one embittered citizen; "These are the days when pomp is made to feel / Its human mould! (*1823*, 6.26-28). Hemans here echoes the sarcastic retorts to Burke's tragedy of aristocratic fall in *Reflections* (1790), written by Wollstonecraft and Paine, among others. "What is this mighty revolution in property? The present incumbents only are injured," Wollstonecraft writes in *Vindication of the Rights of Men* (1790); "Did the pangs you felt for insulted nobility, the anguish that rent your heart when the gorgeous robes were torn off [...] deserve to be compared with the long-drawn sigh of melancholy reflection, when [...] the sick wretch, who can no longer earn the sour bread of unremitting labour, steals to a ditch to bid the world a long good night." Paine famously sneers in his *Rights of Man* that Burke has bestowed "not one glance of compassion, not one commiserating reflection [...] on those who lingered out the most wretched of lives, a life without hope." It seems a short Paineful step from the voice Hemans gives to one Citizen, "Aye, let the balance be awhile struck even / Between the noble's palace and the hut" (*1823* 6.16-17), to forming the Citizens of Valencia into a counter-insurgent force, or even an organized class that will, beyond the interval of "awhile," claim and press its political rights against the lordly train. The manuscript deepens, extends, and multiplies these voices. Although Hemans writes out the complaint to set the stage for the patriotic rally of a dying Ximena, the dramatic structure does not mute its contemporary rhetoric. And she knows it. Through the heterodox political voice of Citizen-complaints, she addresses the English public of the 1820s with a mordant editorial on the general waste of sons to insure an aristocracy normally indifferent to the laboring classes that sustain their luxury, and she admonishes aristocratic arrogance about the resentment in these classes. Along with Elmina's bitter denunciations and protests in Scene 1, Scene 6 opens up a powerful form of what Jerome McGann has termed "double perspectivism": "two dialectically functioning historical frames of reference," that of the plot or story, and that of the writer's own historical moment.[1]

Reception

Even so, readers in Hemans's day and well into her century tended not to hear a "political" Hemans, except as she seemed to voice orthodoxies of nationalism and patriotism. By 1823 "Mrs. Hemans" had been installed and revered as the culture's icon of "feminine" values (domestic affection, female self-sacrifice), especially their vital role as the spiritual front-guard, the heart and soul, of nationalism and patriotism. Yet like *The Siege,* Hemans's patriotic pieces, from *War and Peace* through *Tales, and Historic Scenes,* betray a death-haunt-

---

1   *The Beauty of Inflections,* 266.

ed consciousness. Another poem in *The Siege* volume, *The Chieftan's Son*, conveys a father's grief for a son fallen in battle. *England's Dead,* also in the volume, ponders the empire not as a realm on which the sun never sets, but as a vast graveyard: "*There* slumber England's dead!" Hemans's most famous poem, *Casabianca* (which appeared in one of the annuals in 1826), may seem a sentimental tribute to a youthful war martyr. Yet a boy's futile call to his dead father ("unconscious of his son") for release from his post on the burning deck is no simple, chivalrous poetry, but a grim meditation on patriotic and patriarchal obligations, at home and abroad, and implicitly everywhere. Hemans decided to make this pathos an event on the French side in Admiral Nelson's first celebrated victory over Napoleon's fleet: the Battle of the Nile, 1798 (Casabianca père was the commander of the Admiral ship, *L'Orient*). It was a bold decision, and most politically so in the way it exposes the sentimentality attached to fatal filial obedience, a patriotism that requires the questionable expense of children's lives. *Casabianca* is neither pro- nor anti-French, and it is certainly not triumphalist about the British victory: the categories of "boy," "Father," "battle," and "post of death," are pan-national, transhistorical. Hemans's exotic historical or cultural displacements, as the stage of medieval Valencia shows, are never romantically distancing and derealizing; their fictionality allows disturbingly familiar issues to emerge, the foreign scene returning a sign of a universal condition.

The sensitivity of Tory reviews to Hemans's emergent critique of military patriotism in post-Napoleonic England is evident both in their refusal to acknowledge this perspective and in the negative rhetoric of their praise for her other virtues. The *British Critic* (Tory and High Church) launched its review of *The Siege* with a diatribe against female pretenses to intellectual authority, and it countered with everything from divine creation to the legacy of forefathers, modern science, Shakespeare, and sneers of ridicule and disgust. "We heartily abjure Blue Stockings," it opened, using Hemans as a welcome contrast, a lady to love: "She is especially excellent in painting the strength, and the weaknesses of her own lovely sex, and there is a womanly nature throughout all her thoughts and her aspirations. [...] There is a fineness of apprehension, and a subtlety of feeling, peculiar to the weaker sex, and perhaps the result of that very weakness. [...] A woman is so much more a creature of passion than man." This praise is everywhere gender-marked: Hemans is liked for what she doesn't do; her attention to weakness is her strength. And she conveys a sense of "woman" that the *British Critic* prefers to view as "natural": she is a "creature" of passion, in whom an indistinguishable blend of "natural qualities" and cultural acquisition simultaneously defines the "woman" and distinguishes her art from "the most powerful productions of men."

Following this praise, where the language of "nature" displaces any political subject, George Gilfillan could say of *The Siege* in the 1840s, it "has stormed no hearts." This may be because the passages favored for admiring quotation in the reviews of 1823 were the songs of consolation, Hemans's own acclaimed genres. *The Monthly Review* admired the "high chivalric poetry," hearing it in the genre of national song, especially as it spoke to "a sentiment of degradation and shame" at the fate of modern Spain.[1] Although the reviews heard Elmina, too, it was through a filter of already codified "feminine" expectation that translated her passion in the genre of female song. They seemed tone-deaf to Elmina's stormy plea to Gonzalez for their sons' lives, a diatribe that Hemans even underscored with a language of gender, especially in her contempt for "man's" values:

ELMINA.   Aye, on the boy he looks,
The bright glad creature springing in his path,
But as the heir of his great name, the young
And stately tree, whose rising strength ere long
Shall bear his trophies well. — And this is love!
This is *man's* love! (*1823*, 1.434-39)

She added these last exclamations for *1823* (cf. MS 1.477ff). Elmina plays out her indictment with an anaphora of what man never does for his children, with this climax:

You ne'er smooth'd
His couch, ne'er sung him to his rosy rest,
Caught his least whisper, when his voice from yours

---

1   Gilfillan, "Female Authors No. I," *Tait's Edinburgh Magazine* ns 14 (1847): 361; *Monthly Review* 102 (1823): 180. Spain had recently restored a repressive monarchy, sparking a futile revolution to restore constitutional liberties. In *The Contours of Masculine Desire*, Marlon Ross discusses Ximena's ballads from this perspective (282).

Had learn'd soft utterance; press'd your lip to his,
When fever parch'd it; hush'd his wayward cries,
With patient, vigilant, never-wearied love!
No! these are *woman*'s tasks! (1.433-54)

For all this, the *Monthly Review* heard a "singularly pleasing passage,"
and the *British Critic* a voice that was "exquisitely beautiful," the
"weaker sex" impelled by "passion" and "affection" into a kind of
Hemans-signature aria: a "deep and passionate strain of eloquence"
that a "mother *only* could have poured forth." The *New European
Magazine* reported it as "sweetly poetical," not only eliding the terms
of Elmina's grievance but even praising "the fair Authoress of this
elegant little volume" for her "purity of taste, a correctness of senti-
ment, and an elegance of expression, truly feminine" — what the
British Review called the "ardent spirit" of Hemans's "elegant pen."[1]
Hemans's memoirist Henry Chorley (a champion of strong-minded
women writers) was alone in reading Elmina as a woman "broken
down but not degraded, by the agony of maternal affection"; it was
"strong, fervid, indignant." He understood the "treachery" such affec-
tion tempted and was shrewd enough to see a drama driven by "a
thrilling conflict between maternal love and the inflexible spirit of
chivalrous honour" — a conflict he preferred to the monotonous
Ximena, "all glowing and heroic" but in sum "too spiritual, too saint-
ly, wholly to carry away the sympathies" (*Memorials* 1.111). "Indig-
nant," "fervid," "conflict," the relative claim of "inflexible [...] hon-
our," the militant authority of "maternal" values: these words might
punctuate praise of Wollstonecraft, but they are quite anomalous in
writing about Hemans.

The reviewers' resistance to hearing an assault on the system of
values for which Gonzalez is exemplar is reflected not only in their
reaction to Elmina but also in their special pleading for him, taking
his voice ("Think'st thou *I* feel no pangs?") as their cue: "Gonzalez is
brave, dignified, faithful, calm, and kind; exhibiting the honour and
integrity of a soldier. [...] Wherever he appears he obtains our love,
esteem, and sympathy," said the *British Review*, admiring the lineage
of this masculine integrity in his eldest son Alphonso, royally named:

1 *Monthly Review* 180-81; *British Critic* 52-53; "Contemporary Poets. No. I," *New Euro-
pean Magazine* 3 (1823): 120-22; *British Review* 31 (August 1823): 201.

"a boy of high, and unbending spirit, full of pride and impetuosity."
The *British Review* managed to be sympathetic to Elmina's anguish,
but not without hinting at something too Wollstonecrafted: "Elmina
principally appears in the character of a distressed mother, over-
whelmed with grief, and losing, in the prevalence of maternal affec-
tion, all sight and sense of rectitude and propriety. But we also see in
her a peculiar spirit of pride and loftiness, even after the death of her
sons, after her own reconciliation with her husband, and his death"
(200). The implication is that she has not been made to suffer
enough, that even her devotion to her husband's honor is releasing
an unfeminine pride, another version of rectitude and propriety
compromised.

This is a failing, they hint, lurking in Hemans herself: "there is too
much vehemence, too much effort in our authoress, especially when
she enters on scenes that require the exhibition of tender or ardent
feeling; [...] she has a strong predilection for warlike affairs, for bold,
fervid, and daring characters. We must, however, remark, that the
military spirit that breathes and glows in many of her pages, does not
add to their real excellence. We do not like Bellona as a Muse" (202).
A "military spirit" emanating from a woman seems a troubling form
of patriotic passion. Bellona as a Muse presents both a gender prob-
lem and, relatedly, a political one. The gender trouble is that her
acolytes are traditionally male erotic subjects, whom she espouses
(Shakespeare's Macbeth is "Bellona's bridegroom" [1.2.54]). What
happens when women turn warlike in their fervor and boldness? A
woman who espouses Bellona may produce a hyper-feminine force
against men altogether. In Hemans's play, "the military spirit," as
Chorley recognized, is less apparent in Ximena's chivalric songs than
in Elmina's critique of "men" and patriarchy. Is it this unpredictable
combination that repels the *British Review*?

W.M. Rossetti (editing Hemans for the 1870s) is the hardest on
Elmina, not liking her insurrection, and quickest to read in her mis-
erable survival an apt retribution and poetic justice:

> As the reader approaches the *dénouement,* and finds the
> authoress dealing death with an unsparing hand to the hero-
> ically patriotic Gonzalez and all his offspring, he may perhaps
> at first feel a little ruffled at noting that the only member of the

family who has been found wanting in the fiery trial—wanting through an excess of maternal love—is also the only one saved alive: but in this also the authoress may be pronounced in the right. Reunion with her beloved ones in death would in fact have been mercy to Elmina, and would have left her undistinguished from the others, and untouched by any retribution: survival, mourning, and self-discipline, are the only chastisement in which a poetic justice, in its higher conception, could be expressed. ("Prefatory Notice," *The Poetical Works of Mrs. Hemans*, 17)

Another way to sort out the evidence, however, would be to say that "the authoress dealing death with an unsparing hand to the heroically patriotic Gonzalez and all his offspring" has been siding with Elmina's critique all along. Elmina lives to bear witness to the world she knew Gonzalez's way of doing things would produce:

> May you live
> To be alone, when loneliness doth seem
> Most heavy to sustain.... (1.466-68)

Manuscript Elmina is more bitter yet, adding, "When failing Age / ... / Would sit beneath his Twilight-star, and look / But upon those whose Past hath been his own!" (1.516-22), and the page shows Hemans's laboring over the indictment. In *1823* she italicized to convey an even more sarcastic tone:

> Aye, then call up
> Shadows—dim phantoms from ancestral tombs,
> But all—all *glorious*—conquerors, chieftains, kings—
> To people that cold void! (1.477-80; cf. MS p. 34)

The "God, / Whose hand ... hath unpeopled earth" (9.224-25) seems, in the memory of these lines, the creator of no more than a cold void shimmering with phantoms tagged "glorious."

If Hemans's nineteenth-century reviewers overlooked this information, it has emerged in our own post-Vietnam skepticism about the sacrifice of sons and daughters to a politically suspect sloganeer-

ing of "national honor." The strongest difference between her histor-
ical moment and our own, at least before September 11, 2001, may
be this skepticism. In the wake of 9/11, the ideological appeal of
going to war against what President George W. Bush defined as the
"axis of evil" has proven a potent rally to patriotic fervor. Hemans's
imaginative power is to push patriotic rallying to a radical but
implicitly logical consequence—the martyrdom of children in filial
obedience to fathers, domestic, national, and religious—and to stage
this consequence in ways that put pressure on the whole system. It's
not that her world valued honor over life, while our post-Vietnam
culture may be inclined to question a "national honor" ransomed by
the lives of children or the non-elite. Hemans shaped this question in
the midst of overt and deeply sentimental commitments to national
honor, but with a sense of growing unease—and not hers alone.
Hers may have been a culture in which every schoolboy idolized
military heroes Nelson, Moore, and Wellington, but this same world
was also quick to memorize a dirge that concluded in a rhyme of
"gory" and "glory"—Charles Wolfe's *The Burial of Sir John Moore at
Corunna* (1817)—the retreat in which one of Hemans's brothers par-
ticipated. And it was a culture that responded to Byron's mordant
critiques of military glory—most famously in *Childe Harold's Pil-
grimage, Cantos I and II* (1812) and continuing to *Don Juan, Canto VII*
(published the same year as Hemans's *Siege,* 1823, by Byron's former
publisher John Murray).

The *Siege* shapes a stage for debates today, not only about Hemans
but also and more extensively about Romantic-era warfare and its
conscription of "feminine" fuel to sanctify its mission. To Marlon
Ross, Hemans serves up a double conservatism: the lesson that Elmi-
na learns about patriotic honor is the same that Hemans transmits to
her readers. Elmina "realizes that her heroic attempt to save her chil-
dren, though empowered by the right affection, has been misplaced.
Her affection is then transferred to the state as she comes to realize
the continuity between political freedom and domestic happiness";
she returns "to domesticity now cognizant of the continuity between
the hearth and the state, between the state the heart." Anne Mellor,
by contrast, sees these linkages strained into a powerful critique:
Elmina is the center of a story of alienated, and ultimately annihilat-
ed, domestic values, and the play "is finally the story of *her* suffering,

her tragedy—the tragedy of a woman whose 'feminine' love and virtue [have] been rejected by a patriarchal state religion."[1] For both critics, domestic affections, in the family and the state, get caught up in national self-determination. Does the symbolic coherence of *The Siege* abide in the rescue of Valencia, or in the ravaged city? Hemans's most important cultural work is no facile elaboration of a nationalist ideology of honor-at-any-and-all-costs. It is her testing of its elements to reveal their interaction with differences of gender, class, race, and religion—issues which the manuscript version deepens and elaborates.

---

1   Ross, *Contours* 275, 282, Mellor, *Romanticism & Gender* 137, 140-41.

Felicia Hemans: A Brief Chronology

[With events pertinent to *The Siege of Valencia*. Adapted from SJW, *Felicia Hemans*]

1793   25 September, Felicia Dorothea Browne, the 5th of 7 children, born in Liverpool. The family's fortunes suffer in the financial panic of that year. Louis XVI and Marie Antoinette executed; Reign of Terror; Britain and France declare war.

1794   FDB's brother Claude Scott born.

1795   Famine in England; Napoleon invades Italy.

1796   Spain shifts allegiance, taking France's side against England.

1798   FDB's sister and future memoirist Harriett-Mary born (d. 1858).

    Lyrical Ballads (Wordsworth and Coleridge); Joanna Baillie, *Plays on the Passions*. Napoleon invades Egypt; the Battle of the Nile (Horatio Nelson's first great victory) claims the lives of the French admiral Louis de Casabianca and his young son, the subject of FH's most famous poem.

1799   His finances suffering, FDB's father closes his Liverpool business; the family moves to North Wales, where they reside for nine years. Napoleon's coup d'état.

1800   FDB's first poems, including *Lines on her Mother's Birthday*. *Lyrical Ballads*, 2nd edition, with Preface; Coleridge's translations of Schiller's *Piccolomini, Death of Wallenstein*. Act of Union with Ireland.

1802   Baillie, *Plays*, vol. 2. Peace of Amiens between England and France.

1803   FDB's elder sister Eliza dies. War resumes with France.

1804   Baillie, *Miscellaneous Plays*. Napoleon becomes Emperor and prepares to invade Britain; Britain declares war on Spain.

1805   Admiral Nelson dies in the British victory over Napoleon's restored fleet at Trafalgar.

1806   FDB's brother Thomas Henry (1787-1855) enlists in the Royal Welsh Fusiliers, and would distinguish himself and be wounded in the war. Napoleon closes Continental ports to British ships and defeats Prussia at Jena.

1807 Wordsworth, *Poems.* France invades Spain and Portugal and the "Peninsular War" begins.

1808 FDB's *Poems*, dedicated to the Prince of Wales, is published in handsome quarto. Captain Alfred Hemans of the 4th or King's Own Regiment orders 3 copies. Robert Southey, *Chronicle of the Cid.* Anti-French uprisings in Spain; British land in Portugal; the Convention of Cintra (August) supervises French withdrawal from Portugal.

1809 Evicted from Gwrych for nonpayment of rent, the Brownes move to St. Asaph, North Wales. FDB completes *England and Spain; or Valour and Patriotism* (in praise of the war against Napoleon). FDB and Captain Hemans (whom she met through her brothers) pledge their love before he returns to Spain. George returns from the wars wounded and disillusioned.

John Murray founds the *Quarterly Review;* edited by William Gifford, it becomes the chief Tory-establishment journal. Wordsworth, *Convention of Cintra.*

Sir John Moore (under whom one of the Browne brothers serves) dies in the retreat at Coruña, Spain; Joseph Bonaparte crowned King in Madrid; Wellesley in command in Portugal.

1810 FDB's father leaves for Quebec "on business," never to return (d. ca. 1812).

1811 Captain Hemans returns. Reginald Heber reads and praises *War and Peace.* May: George Browne in the battle of Albuera (of nearly 60,000 troops, 13,000 were killed). George III is deemed incompetent; the Prince of Wales named Regent.

1812 FDB's *The Domestic Affections* published, to no success. FDB studying Spanish. Shelley writes to her, praising her talents but not liking her enthusiasm for "fatal sanguinary war." George Browne recovers and re-enlists. 30 July: FDB and Captain Hemans marry.

Baillie, *Plays on the Passions*, vol. 3; Byron's, *Childe Harold's Pilgrimage I-II* becomes an overnight sensation. Britain declares war on the U.S.

1813   First son, Arthur Hemans born. When Captain Hemans is discharged, they join her mother's household in St. Asaph. Byron, *The Giaour* and *The Bride of Abydos*, both sensations; Southey, *Life of Nelson*; Mary Russell Mitford, *Narrative Poems on the Female Character*. Southey becomes Poet Laureate. Napoleon suffers several defeats.

1814   Byron, *The Corsair* (10,000 copies sell at once) and *Lara*; Wordsworth, *The Excursion; New Monthly Magazine* founded. The Allies invade France and Paris falls; Napoleon abdicates and is exiled to Elba; the Bourbon restoration brings Louis XVIII to the throne. Treaty of Ghent ends Britain's war with the U.S.

1815   Son George Willoughby born (?). Napoleon escapes from Elba, enters France, is defeated at Waterloo, and exiled to St. Helena; restoration of European monarchies.

1816   Son Claude Lewis born. FH works on *Tales, and Historic Scenes*. May: *The Restoration of the Works of Art to Italy*, "by a Lady," published; Murray issues a second expanded edition under FH's name, her first critical and popular success, with modest profits. Lord and Lady Byron separate, and in the wake of the scandal, he leaves England forever.

1817   Son Henry William born; June: *Modern Greece* published anonymously by Murray. *Blackwood's Edinburgh Magazine* founded.

1818   April: FH's debut in *Blackwood's* with *On the Death of the Princess Charlotte*. Murray publishes her translations of several Romance-language poets. Captain Hemans departs for Rome for "his health," never returns, and ceases to support his wife and sons; after he leaves, FH gives birth to their fifth son, Charles Lloyd, and remains in her mother's household, which she supports by writing.

1819   May: *Tales, and Historic Scenes* published by Murray and is well reviewed. FH wins a £50 prize for *The Meeting of Wallace and Bruce on the Banks of the Carron*; when it appears in *Blackwood's* (September), it receives a warm notice from John Wilson, who places FH in a female pantheon: "Scotland has her Baillie—Ireland her Tighe—England her Hemans." It is republished in London and Edinburgh (by Blackwood) as *Wallace's Invocation to Bruce*.

1820   January: Murray publishes FH's 16-page *Stanzas to the Memory of the Late King* (George III) and *The Sceptic*. FH begins a project "contrasting the spirit and tenets of Paganism with those of Christianity," titled *Superstition and Revelation*. April: *Wallace's Invocation to Bruce* published. Gifford gives a warm retrospective review to several of FH's volumes in the *Quarterly*. Prince Regent becomes George IV; Queen Caroline tried for adultery (FH's brother Thomas Browne is one of George IV's legion of spies); Scott is knighted. Revolutions in Spain, Portugal, and Naples; royalist reactions across Europe.

1821   June: *Superstition and Error* (revised title) published. FH wins a prize of fifty guineas (£52.50, a year's income for many at the time) from the Royal Society of Literature for *Dartmoor*, soon published; second editions (from Murray) of *The Sceptic, Stanzas to the Memory of the Late King,* and *Modern Greece,* bound together. FH begins to contribute to *Blackwood's* and *New Monthly*; writes *The Vespers of Palermo,* a verse tragedy about the "Sicilian Vespers" insurrection against French rule in 1282. FH continues her study of German. Her brother Claude Browne dies in Canada.

1822   FH's *Songs of the Cid* appear in *New Monthly*.

1823   Hereafter, FH's annual earnings average over £200. June: *The Siege of Valencia* published by Murray, 1000 copies; he gives FH £210 for the copyright for *Vespers* (published in November). Though not meant for the stage, Heber and Henry H. Milman recommend the play to Covent Garden; it opens on 12 December but fails immediately, poor work by the lead actress blamed. FH contributing regularly to *New Monthly*.
        Rudolf Ackermann publishes *Forget Me Not*, inaugurating the annuals fad in England. French intervention in Spain, to suppress anti-royalist rebellion.

1824   Hemans begins *De Chatillon, or, The Crusaders.*

1825   After FH's brother marries, she, her three youngest sons, her mother, and her sister Harriett move to a house near St. Asaph; returning from Canada, her second brother and his wife join them. *The Forest Sanctuary* published. FH begins writing for the annuals.

1826 FH's mother's health begins to fail; *Casabianca* and *The Landing of the Pilgrim Fathers*, two of her most popular poems in the nineteenth century, first published.

1827 FH's mother dies, 11 January; FH's offer to join her husband is rejected. FH becomes a regular and paid contributor to *Blackwood's*. She begins to have serious health problems.

1828 FH's sister marries and her brother moves to Dublin. In poor health, FH moves to Wavertree, a village near Liverpool, to seek society, friendship, medical care and opportunities for her younger sons. May: *Records of Woman*, dedicated to Baillie, published, her most successful volume, critically and financially.

1829 Second edition of *The Forest Sanctuary* published to much success. Francis Jeffrey's influential article, praising FH's literary achievements, appears in the *Edinburgh Review*.

1830 June: third edition of *Records*. FH and her younger sons visit the Lake District, and spend time with the Wordsworths. *Songs of the Affections* published in Edinburgh and London; sells well.

1831 FH sends her two oldest sons to live with their father in Italy, leaves England for Dublin, to be near her brother, George Browne, Commissioner of the City Police.

1833 FH's health worsens.

1834 FH's last lifetime volume, *Scenes and Hymns of Life* (dedicated to Wordsworth), published. Her health worsens.

1835 February: Prime Minister Robert Peel gives FH a grant of £100 and arranges a clerkship in the Customs at £80 a year for son Charles. Second edition of *Songs of the Affections*, third edition of *The Forest Sanctuary*. 16 May: death of FH.

Editorial Procedures

For references in the notes by abbreviation or short title, full bibliographic information is in the Bibliography. *1823*, for which Hemans supplied nine scholarly endnotes, is also the anchor for our notes. Hemans's are placed in sequence with ours, distinguished by [FH]. Any commentary on her note follows in a separate paragraph. Notes to the MS are limited to textual matters or information that pertains only to MS readings.

To MS and *1823* we add line numbers and scene numbers, and spell out names of characters in full. Line-numbering is by the convention of metrical line, not page-line; in some cases a metrical line staggers across two or more page-lines. Canceled fragmentary lines in the manuscript are counted. The bracketed line numbers in MS are coordinates to *1823*.

We have set MS stage directions in italics, in order to distinguish these from the emphases of Hemans's underlining. For *1823*, we follow Murray in italicizing these emphases as well as the stage directions.

In the MS transcription we use these following typographical indicators:

{uncanceled alternative readings}	
~~canceled, legible text~~	
~~virgule~~ / ~~slash mark~~	canceled, legible alternative phrasings or words
[?text]	conjectural reading
[?~~text~~]	conjectural reading of canceled text
w[?] / w[?]d / [?]d	word with some letters legible
~~w[~~—?] / w[—?]d / [—?]d	canceled word with some letters legible
[?]	illegible word
[? ... ?]	several illegible words
[?—]	illegible canceled word
[?—?]	several illegible words canceled

Abbreviations

CM   Chorley, Henry F. *Memorials of Mrs. Hemans*

HM   [Hughes, Harriett] *Memoir of the Life and Writings of Felicia Hemans: By Her Sister*, in volume 1 of *Works* (1839)

MS   Houghton Library MS of *The Siege of Valencia*

1823   *The Siege of Valencia*, 1823

1839   *The Works of Mrs. Hemans*. 7 vols. Blackwood/Cadell, 1839

SJW   Wolfson, Susan J. *Felicia Hemans: Selected Poems, Letters, and Reception Materials.*

THE SIEGE OF
VALENCIA

Felicia Hemans

A Parallel Text

The Manuscript
and the Publication of 1823

THE SIEGE OF VALENCIA

~~or the Race of the Cid~~[1]

---

1   Hemans's sense of a racial polarization appears in *The Last Constantine*. Circling and
    besieging the Christian city of Constantinople is a "turban'd race, / The sun, the
    desert, stamp'd in each dark haughty face" (XXI) (1823 volume, p. 13).

THE SIEGE OF VALENCIA:
A DRAMATIC POEM

(London: John Murray, 1823)

Jndicio ha dado esta no vista hazaña
Del valor que en los siglos venideros
Tendrán los Hijos de la fuerte España,
Hijos de tal padres herederos.

Hallo solá en Numancia todo quanto
Debe con justo titulo cantarse,
Y lo que puede dar materia al canto.

Numancia de Cervantes[1]

Advertisement

The history of Spain records two instances of the severe and self-devoting heroism, which forms the subject of the following dramatic poem. The first of these occurred at the siege of Tarifa, which was defended in 1294 for Sancho, King of Castile, during the rebellion of his brother, Don Juan, by Guzman, surnamed the Good.[2] The second

---

1   "This unprecedented deed has given an indication
         Of the valor that in centuries to come
         The sons of mighty Spain will possess,
         Sons of such fathers the heirs.

         I find in Numancia alone all
         That should with just warrant be celebrated in poetry
         And that which can give material for song."

From the voice of "Fame" near the end (act 4) of Cervantes' *El Cerco de Numancia* (ca. 1580-90). The last three lines supply the title-page epigraph for FH's 1823 volume. In later editions, "Jndicio" (or "Indicio") was wrongly read as an erratum, and miscorrected to "Judicio." *El Cerco* treats the Numancians' mass suicide and destruction of their city, in northern Spain, after an eight-month siege in 133 B.C., their action thwarting Scipio Æmilianus's honors in the Roman conquest of Spain. In its heroic repulse of attacks from the time of Cato the Elder's campaign (195 B.C.), Numancia was a rallying point for opposition to Roman imperialism. During the Napoleonic invasion (1807-9), *El Cerco de Numancia* was staged in Spain as an incitement to resistance.

2 See Quintana's 'Vidas de Españoles celebres,' p. 53. [FH]
    Manuel José Quintana (1772-1857), *Lives of Celebrated Spaniards* (1807). This Spanish patriot and poet was famed for his odes, pamphlets, and proclamations against

is related of Alonso Lopez de Texeda, who, until his garrison had been utterly disabled by pestilence, maintained the city of Zamora for the children of Don Pedro the Cruel, against the forces of Henrique of Trastamara.[1]

Impressive as were the circumstances which distinguished both these memorable sieges, it appeared to the author of the following pages that a deeper interest, as well as a stronger colour of nationality might be imparted to the scenes in which she has feebly attempted "to describe high passions and high actions";[2] by connecting a religious feeling with the patriotism and high-minded loyalty which had thus been proved "faithful unto death,"[3] and by surrounding her ideal dramatis personæ with recollections derived from the heroic legends of Spanish chivalry. She has, for this reason, employed the agency of imaginary characters, and fixed upon "*Valencia del Cid*" as the scene to give them

"A local habitation and a name."[4]

Napoleonic occupation. Tarifa, on the Strait of Gibraltar, was the first Roman colony in Spain. Sancho IV (?1257-95), or "Sancho the Brave," King of Castile (1284-95), regained it from the Moors in 1292. Nuño de Guzmán was a controversial Spanish conquistador (d. 1544).

1 See the Preface to Southey's "Chronicle of the Cid." [FH]
   The Preface does not show such an account. During the middle ages, control of the strategically located river city of Zamora in northwestern Spain shifted between Christians and Moors, then in civil war between the Christian kingdoms of León and Castile. Henrique II of Trastámara (?1333-79), illegitimate son of Alfonso XI of Castile (1311-50), waged several unsuccessful revolts against his half brother Don Pedro (1320-67), king of Portugal (1357-67), called "the Cruel" for harsh reprisals against his enemies. Aided by France, Henrique invaded Castile in 1366 and was crowned king, but was dethroned in 1367 by English forces led by Edward, the Black Prince (Pedro's daughter was married to John of Gaunt). Then with French aid, Henrique captured and killed Pedro.

2 Milton's praise of classical Greek tragedians in *Paradise Regained:* "High actions, and high passions best describing" (4.266).

3 Christ says, "be thou faithful unto death, and I will give thee a crown of life" (Revelation 2.10).

4 Theseus's remark on poetic power in *A Midsummer Night's Dream* (5.1.17). Valencia was under Moorish rule from the eighth century to the thirteenth century, except for two brief intervals. El Cid ruled from 1094 until his death in 1099, his conquest of the city the highlight of his career. His widow Ximena endured a three-year siege before withdrawing to Castile in 1102. Hemans makes Gonzalez a descendant of El Cid (1.162, 4.75).

Gonsalvo[1]	Governor of the City
Alphonso	
Carlos,	his Sons
Garcias	an Officer of Gonsalvo's
Hernandez	a Priest
Abdullah	the Moorish Chief
Diego[2]	

Elmina	Wife of Gonsalvo
Ximena	his daughter
Theresa	Attendant

---

1 The name may evoke "the Great Captain" Gonsalvo (or Gonzalo) Fernández de Córdoba (1453-1515) among whose many engagements was the conquest of Granada from the Moors.

2 This servant, who accompanies Elmina into the Moors' camp, is not listed in the 1823 dramatis personae.

DRAMATIS PERSONÆ

ALVAR GONZALEZ,[1]   *Governor of Valencia*
ALPHONSO and CARLOS,[2]   *His Sons*
HERNANDEZ,   *A Priest*
GARCIAS,   *A Spanish Knight*
ABDULLAH,   *A Moorish Prince, Chief of the Army besieging Valencia*
ELMINA,   *Wife to Gonzalez*
XIMENA,[3]   *Her Daughter*
THERESA,   *An Attendant*
Citizens, Soldiers, Attendants, &c.

---

1   This name may evoke Fernán González (d. 970), the first Count of Castile, who established the independence of this kingdom from León. His exploits are recounted in a popular thirteenth-century epic poem. "Alvar" is the name of El Cid's loyal companion in the old legends; see *The Cid's Funeral Procession* (p. 247, note 1).

2   The sons bear the names of former Christian kings. El Cid had served Alfonso VI of Castile and León, one of the strongest rulers of the period. Carlos's namesake may be Charlemagne (Charles I), champion of Christianity, ruler of the western Holy Roman Empire in the 9th century; early in this century he captured Barcelona from the Moors, establishing a Christian frontier in Spain beyond the Pyrenees. Roland, Charlemagne's commander in a retreat from an earlier, unsuccessful assault on Moorish Spain, was killed in an ambush in the Roncesvalles pass, the subject of Ximena's opening ballad.

3   In 1074 Alfonso VI arranged the marriage of his niece Ximena Díaz to El Cid.

[The original MS ballad is less "public" in its theme than the one that opens *1823*, less saturated in the global strife of Christian against "infidel." The loss of a young warrior's life in the campaign to liberate Spain from the Moors is immediate to Ximena: it is her beloved, her hands that have tried to bind his wounds, her consciousness on which this death is seared, her song perpetually devoted to lament. From a later point in *1823*, one may read Ximena's loss back into the terms of the opening ballad, but in the MS ballad this significance is clear from the start. Painfully informed by her own loss, Ximena's subsequent exhortations of her mother's and the citizenry's self-sacrifice thus seem less abstractly idealistic, less susceptible of being read as a romantically hyped patriotism. She is always before us as a character struggling to keep faith in the face of grief, to support a military resistance that has already cost her dearly. The ballad-story she tells of a "youthful Cheftain dying" foreshadows the fate of her brothers, and her grief becomes her parents' anthem as well. Other lines in the ballad also radiate into the play itself: "I have stood when my King hath perished" becomes Elmina's situation in scene 9.]

Scene [1]—*a Room in the Citadel of Valencia*[1]

XIMENA *singing to a Lute.*

The Stars look'd down on the Battle plain,
    Where Night-winds were deeply sighing,
And with shatter'd lance, by his War-steed slain,
    Lay a youthful Chieftain dying.

He had folded ~~his~~ round his gallant heart,
    The Banner once o'er him streaming,
For a noble shroud as he sunk to rest,
    On the couch that knows no dreaming.

Proudly he lay on his broken shield,
    By the rushing Guadalquiver,

10

---

1   Citadel: fortress. This ballad, replaced in *1823*, was never published.

SCENE I

[The opening ballad is a genre song in the voice of a young maid questioning a soldier returned from the field to the festal board to report a slaughter by ambush, from which her beloved did not escape, "in the Roncesvalles' Strait." This pass in the Pyrenees is historically laden, both for Spain's legendary past and the Napoleonic wars. It was here that Roland, the most renowned of Charlemagne's Christian knights, was killed in 778 in an ambush of his army of 20,000 by a band of Basque mountaineers—represented in *Chanson de Roland* (11th c.) as an attack force of 400,000 Muslims, a cultural polarization relevant to the historical situation of *The Siege*. Hemans's delay in disclosing Ximena's particular loss, and hence her affinity for the situation of this ballad, heightens the drama of revelation as Ximena is dying of a broken heart.]

Room in a Palace of Valencia. XIMENA *singing to a Lute.*

BALLAD[1]

"Thou hast not been with a festal throng,
   At the pouring of the wine;
Men bear not from the Hall of Song,
   A mien so dark as thine!
     —There's blood upon thy shield,
     There's dust upon thy plume,
  —Thou hast brought, from some disastrous field,
     That brow of wrath and gloom!"

"And is there blood upon my shield?
   —Maiden! it well may be!   10
We have sent the streams from our battle-field,
   All darken'd to the sea!
     We have given the founts a stain,
     Midst their woods of ancient pine;

---

1   Like the play's other songs, this was a favorite in nineteenth-century anthologies.

While dark with the blood of his last red field,
    Swept on the majestic river.

There were hands which came to bind his wound,
    There were eyes o'er the Warrior weeping,
But he rais'd his head from the dewy ground,
    Where the Land's high hearts were sleeping:

And "Away!" he cried, "your aid is vain,
    My Soul may not brook recalling,
I have seen the stately flower of Spain,
    As the Autumn vine-leaves falling.

I have seen the Moorish Banners wave,
    O'er the Walls where my Youth was cherish'd!
I have drawn a sword that could not save,
    I have stood when my King hath perish'd!

Leave me to die with the free and brave,
    On the bankes of my own proud River,
Ye can give me nought but a Warrior's grave
    By the chainless Guadalquiver!"

20

And the ground is wet — but not with rain,
  Deep-dyed — but not with wine!

The ground is wet — but not with rain —
  We have been in war array,
And the noblest blood of Christian Spain
  Hath bathed her soil to-day.   20
    I have seen the strong man die,
      And the stripling meet his fate,
Where the mountain-winds go sounding by,
    In the Roncesvalles' Strait.

In the gloomy Roncesvalles' Strait
  There are helms and lances cleft;
And they that moved at morn elate
  On a bed of heath are left!
    There's many a fair young face,
      Which the war steed hath gone o'er;   30
At many a board there is kept a place
    For those that come no more!"

"Alas! for love, for woman's breast,
  If woe like this must be!
— Hast thou seen a youth with an eagle crest,
  And a white plume waving free?
    With his proud quick flashing eye,
      And his mien of knightly state?
Doth he come from where the swords flash'd high,
    In the Roncesvalles' Strait?"   40

"In the gloomy Roncesvalles' Strait
  I saw and mark'd him well;
For nobly on his steed he sate,
  When the pride of manhood fell!
    — But it is not *youth* which turns
      From the field of spears again;
For the boy's high heart too wildly burns,
    Till it rests amidst the slain!"

ELMINA *enters.*

ELMINA. Your songs are not as those of other days,
30   Mine own Ximena!—Where is now the young
And buoyant Spirit of the life and hope, which once
Breath'd in your Spring-like Melodies, and woke
Joy's echo from all hearts?
XIMENA.   My Mother, this

[70]   Is not the free air of our Mountain-Wilds,
And these are not the Halls, wherein my Voice
First pour'd those gladdening strains?
ELMINA.   Alas! thy heart
(I see it well,) doth sicken for the pure
And joyous breezes of thy native Hills,
40   Where thy young Brothers, o'er the rock & heath,
~~Sprung~~ Bound in glad boyhood, e'en as torrent-streams
~~As wading in th'exulting fearlessness~~
~~And glow of Boyhood's~~
Leap brightly from the heights. Had we not been
Within these Walls thus suddenly begirt,
Thy fairy step should track, the wild-wood-paths,
With theirs e'en now.

"Thou canst not say that *he* lies low,
　　The lovely and the brave!　　　　　　　　　50
Oh! none could look on his joyous brow,
　　And think upon the grave!
　　　　Dark, dark perchance the day
　　　　Hath been with valour's fate,
But *he* is on his homeward way,
　　　　From the Roncesvalles' Strait!"

"There is dust upon his joyous brow,
　　And o'er his graceful head;
And the war-horse will not wake him now,
　　Tho' it bruise his greensward bed!　　　　60
　　　—I have seen the stripling die,
　　　　And the strong man meet his fate,
Where the mountain-winds go sounding by,
　　　　In the Roncesvalles' Strait!"

　　　　　　　　　　　　　　ELMINA *enters.*

ELMINA. Your songs are not as those of other days,
　　Mine own Ximena!—Where is now the young
　　And buoyant spirit of the morn, which once
　　Breath'd in your spring-like melodies, and woke
　　Joy's echo from all hearts?
XIMENA.　　　　　　　　My mother, this
　　Is not the free air of our mountain-wilds;　　　70
　　And these are not the halls, wherein my voice
　　First pour'd those gladdening strains.
ELMINA.　　　　　　　　　Alas! thy heart
　　(I see it well) doth sicken for the pure
　　Free-wandering breezes of the joyous hills,
　　Where thy young brothers, o'er the rock and heath,
　　Bound in glad boyhood, e'en as torrent-streams
　　Leap brightly from the heights. Had we not been
　　Within these walls thus suddenly begirt,
　　Thou shouldst have track'd ere now, with step as light,
　　Their wild wood-paths.

[80]   XIMENA.   I would not but have shar'd
              These hours of woe and peril, tho' the deep
              And solemn feelings wakening at their Voice,
        50   Claim all the wrought-up Spirit to themselves,
              And will not blend with Mirth! The storm doth hush
              All floating whispery sounds, all ~~joyous Notes~~ Bird-notes wild
              O' th' summer forest, filling Earth and Heaven
              ~~With its own awful music. — And its Heaven!~~
              With its own terrible Music. — And 'tis well!
              Should not a Hero's Child be train'd to hear
              The Trumpet's blast unstartled, and to look
[90]   In the fix'd face of Death without dismay?
        ELMINA. Woe! woe! that aught so gentle and so young
        60   Should thus be call'd to stand i' th' Tempest's path,
              And bear deep ~~the~~ images of Death impress'd
              On a bright Soul so soon! — I had not shrunk
              From mine own lot, but thou, my Child, shouldst move
              As a light breeze of Heaven, thro' Summer bowers,
              And not o'er foaming billows! We are fall'n
              On dark and evil days.
        XIMENA.   Aye, days, the sound
              Of whose far-pealing thunders doth awake
              All to their tasks! — Youth may not loiter now
[100]   Midst the green Walks of Spring; and Womanhood
        70   Is summon'd unto conflicts, heretofore
              The lot of Warrior-souls. But we will take
              Our toils upon us nobly and sustain
              The lofty name we bear! It is for us
              To bind the breastplate on, howe'er the heart
              May bleed beneath.
        ELMINA.   Hast thou some secret grief
              That thus thou speak'st?
        XIMENA.   What sorrow should be mine,
              Unknown to thee?
        ELMINA.   Alas! the baleful air
              Wherewith the Pestilence, walking forth in darkness,
              Wraps our the devoted City, like a blight
        80   [? ~~Touching~~] ~~upon its~~

XIMENA.   I would not but have shared   80
    These hours of woe and peril, tho' the deep
    And solemn feelings wakening at their voice,
    Claim all the wrought-up spirit to themselves,
    And will not blend with mirth. The storm doth hush
    All floating whispery sounds, all bird-notes wild
    O' th' summer-forest, filling earth and heaven
    With its own awful music. — And 'tis well!
    Should not a hero's child be train'd to hear
    The trumpet's blast unstartled, and to look
    In the fix'd face of Death without dismay?   90
ELMINA. Woe! woe! that aught so gentle and so young
    Should thus be call'd to stand i' the tempest's path,
    And bear the token and the hue of death
    On a bright soul so soon! I had not shrunk
    From mine own lot, but thou, my child, shouldst move
    As a light breeze of heaven, thro' summer-bowers,
    And not o'er foaming billows. We are fall'n
    On dark and evil days![1]
XIMENA.   Aye, days, that wake
    All to their tasks! — Youth may not loiter now
    In the green walks of spring; and womanhood   100
    Is summon'd unto conflicts, heretofore
    The lot of warrior-souls. But we will take
    Our toils upon us nobly! Strength is born
    In the deep silence of long-suffering hearts;
    Not amidst joy.
ELMINA.   Hast thou some secret woe
    That thus thou speak'st?
XIMENA.   What sorrow should be mine,
    Unknown to thee?
ELMINA.   Alas! the baleful air
    Wherewith the pestilence in darkness walks
    Thro' the devoted° city, like a blight   doomed, steadfast

---

1   Echoing Milton's description of his peril after the Restoration: "fall'n on evil days, ...
    In darkness, and with dangers compassed round" (*Paradise Lost* 7.25-27). Throughout
    the scene, Hemans echoes Milton to evoke a "fall'n" paradise (cf. 110); Valencia was
    famed as "the garden of Spain."

In Spring-time, o'er thy blossoming hath breath'd,

Effacing its young rose-tints. Thou hast cross'd

The paths of Death, and minister'd to those

O'er whom his shades were falling, till thine eye

Hath changed its glancing sunbeam for a still,

Deep, solemn radiance, and thy brow hath caught

A wild and high expression, which at times,

Fades to desolate calmness, most [?——] unlike

What youth's bright mien should wear. My gentle Child!

90   I look on thee, and tremble! — Can it be,

That thou, in all thy loveliness, art seal'd,

Unto an early doom?

     XIMENA.   Thou hast no cause

To fear for me. When the wild clash of steel,

And the deep tambour, and the heavy step

Of armed Men, break on our Morning dreams;

When, hour by hour, the Noble and the Brave

Are falling round us, and we deem it much

To give them funeral rites, and call them blest

If the good Sword, in its own stormy hour,

100   Hath done its work upon them, ere disease

Had chill'd their fiery blood; ~~when things like these~~ when Men scarce ask

~~For when the~~ [?——] ~~is hung;~~

~~Are~~ [?~~pressing~~] ~~in our paths~~

Who from his place hath sunk; we may not wear

The reckless mien wherewith, in happier times,

We trod the Woodland mazes, when light leaves

Were whispering in the gale, and deep-blue Heavens

Ringing with all glad sounds! — My Father comes —

Oh! speak of me no more. I would not shade

110   His princely aspect with a thought less high

Than his proud Duties claim.

                                        GONSALVO *enters.*

Amidst the rose-tints of thy cheek hath fall'n, 110
And wrought an early withering!—Thou hast cross'd
The paths of Death, and minister'd to those
O'er whom his shadow rested, till thine eye
Hath changed its glancing sunbeam for a still,
Deep, solemn radiance, and thy brow hath caught
A wild and high expression, which at times
Fades unto desolate calmness, most unlike
What youth's bright mien should wear. My gentle child!
I look on thee in fear!
XIMENA.   Thou hast no cause
To fear for me. When the wild clash of steel, 120
And the deep tambour, and the heavy step
Of armed men, break on our morning dreams;
When, hour by hour, the noble and the brave
Are falling round us, and we deem it much
To give them funeral-rites, and call them blest
If the good sword, in its own stormy hour,
Hath done its work upon them, ere disease
Had chill'd their fiery blood;—it is no time
For the light mien wherewith, in happier hours,
We trod the woodland mazes, when young leaves 130
Were whispering in the gale.—My Father comes—
Oh! speak of me no more. I would not shade
His princely aspect with a thought less high
Than his proud duties claim.

GONZALEZ *enters.*

ELMINA.   My noble Lord!
Welcome from this Day's toil! — It is the hour
Whose shadows, as they deepen, bring repose
Unto all weary Men; and wilt not Thou
Free thy mail'd bosom from the corslet's weight,
And doff the helm, and lay the Falchion by,
To rest at fall of Eve?
GONSALVO.   There may be rest
For the tired Peasant, when the Vesper-bell
Doth send him to his Cabin, and beneath
His Vine and Olive, he may sit in peace,
Watching his children's sport; but unto <u>him</u>
Whose place is set upon the Mountain's height,
When Heaven lets loose the storms ~~that~~ which chasten Realms,
Who speaks of Rest?
XIMENA.   My father, shall I fill
The Wine-cup for thy lips, or bring the Lute
Whose sounds thou lov'st?
GONSALVO.   If there be strains, of power
To rouse a Spirit, which in triumphant scorn
May cast off Nature's feebleness, and hold
Its proud career unshackled, dashing down
Tears and fond thoughts, e'en as an Eagle shakes
The rain-drops from his pinion; sing me these!
I have need of such, Ximena! we must hear
No melting music now!
XIMENA.   I know all high
Heroic ditties of the elder time,
Sung by the Mountain Christians, in the holds
Of th' everlasting Hills, whose snows yet bear
The print of Freedom's step; and all wild strains
Wherein the dark Serranos teach the Rocks
And the Pine-forests, deeply to resound
The praise of later Champions. Wouldst thou hear

ELMINA.   My noble lord!
Welcome from this day's toil! — It is the hour
Whose shadows, as they deepen, bring repose
Unto all weary men; and wilt not thou
Free thy mail'd bosom from the corslet's weight,
To rest at fall of eve?
GONZALEZ.   There may be rest
For the tired peasant, when the vesper-bell   140
Doth send him to his cabin, and beneath
His vine and olive, he may sit at eve,
Watching his children's sport: but unto *him*
Who keeps the watch-place on the mountain-height,
When Heaven lets loose the storms that chasten realms
— Who speaks of rest?
XIMENA.   My father, shall I fill
The wine-cup for thy lips, or bring the lute
Whose sounds thou lovest?
GONZALEZ.   If there be strains of power
To rouse a spirit, which in triumphant scorn
May cast off nature's feebleness, and hold   150
Its proud career unshackled, dashing down
Tears and fond thoughts to earth; give voice to those!
I have need of such, Ximena! we must hear
No melting music now.
XIMENA.   I know all high
Heroic ditties of the elder time,
Sung by the mountain-Christians,[1] in the holds
Of th' everlasting hills, whose snows yet bear
The print of Freedom's step; and all wild strains
Wherein the dark serranos[2] teach the rocks
And the pine forests deeply to resound   160
The praise of later champions. Wouldst thou hear

---

1   Mountain Christians, those natives of Spain, who, under their prince, Pelayo, took
    refuge amongst the mountains of the northern provinces, where they maintained their
    religion and liberty, whilst the rest of their country was overrun by the Moors. [FH]
    Southey's *Chronicle* (Introduction xxiii, xv) gives an account of Pelayo, first king of
    Asturias (in northern Spain), whose victory over the Moors at Covadonga (ca. 718-25)
    launched the Christian resistance. Pelayo is Elmina's ancestor (2.156).
2   "Serranos," mountaineers. [FH]

The war-song of thine Ancestor, the Cid?

GONSALVO. Aye, speak of <u>him</u>! for in that name is power,
Such as might rescue Kingdoms! Speak of him!
We are his Children! They that can look back
~~I~~ In th' annals of their House, on such a name,
As on a Landmark, set to bound the sway
Of Ages and Oblivion, may not dare
To take Dishonour by the hand, and o'er
The Threshold of their mighty Father's Halls
150   First lead her, as a Guest, No! rather be
That House the Home of Death!

ELMINA.   ~~What mean thy words~~ Oh, why is this?
[170]   How my heart sinks!

GONSALVO.   It must not fail thee <u>yet</u>,
Daughter of Heroes! — thine inheritance
Is strength to meet all conflicts! Thou canst number
In thy long line of glorious Ancestry
Men, the bright Offering of whose blood hath made
The ground it bath'd e'en as an Altar, whence
High thoughts shall rise for ever. Bore they not,
Midst flames and swords, their Witness of the Cross,
160   With its victorious Inspiration girt
As with a Conqueror's robe, till th' Infidel
By the Commanding Spirit of their Faith
[180]   O'erawed, shrank back before them? — Aye, the Earth
Doth call them Martyrs, but <u>their</u> Agonies
Were of a moment, tortures whose brief aim
Was to destroy, within whose power and scope
Lay nought but dust. — And Earth doth call them <u>Martyrs</u>!
Why, Heaven but claim'd their blood, their lives, and not
The things which grow as tendrils round their hearts,
170   No, not <u>their Children</u>!

ELMINA.   Mean'st thou? — know'st thou aught?
I cannot utter it — my Sons! my Sons!
Is it of them — Oh! wouldst thou speak <u>of them</u>?

[190]   GONSALVO. A Mother's heart divineth but too well.

ELMINA. Speak, I adjure thee! — I can bear it all.
Where are my Children?

The war-song of thine ancestor, the Cid?
GONZALEZ. Aye, speak of him; for in that name is power,
Such as might rescue kingdoms! Speak of him!
We are his children! They that can look back
I' th' annals of their house on such a name,
How should *they* take dishonour by the hand,
And o'er the threshold of their father's halls
First lead her as a guest?
ELMINA.   Oh, why is this?
How my heart sinks!
GONZALEZ.   It must not fail thee *yet*,   170
Daughter of heroes!—thine inheritance
Is strength to meet all conflicts. Thou canst number
In thy long line of glorious ancestry
Men, the bright offering of whose blood hath made
The ground it bathed e'en as an altar, whence
High thoughts shall rise for ever. Bore they not,
Midst flame and sword, their witness of the Cross,
With its victorious inspiration girt
As with a conqueror's robe, till th' infidel
O'erawed, shrank back before them?—Aye, the earth   180
Doth call them martyrs, but *their* agonies
Were of a moment, tortures whose brief aim
Was to destroy, within whose powers and scope
Lay nought but dust.—And earth doth call them *martyrs!*
Why, Heaven but claim'd their blood, their lives, and not
The things which grow as tendrils round their hearts;
No, not their children!
ELMINA.   Mean'st thou?—know'st thou aught?—
I cannot utter it—My sons! my sons!
Is it of them?—Oh! wouldst thou speak of them?
GONZALEZ. A mother's heart divineth but too well!   190
ELMINA. Speak, I adjure thee!—I can bear it all.—
Where are my children?

GONSALVO.   In the Moorish Camp
    Whose lines have girt the City!
XIMENA.   But they live?
    All is not lost, my Mother!
ELMINA.   Say, they live!
GONSALVO. Elmina, still they live.
ELMINA.   But Captives! — they
    Whom my fond soul had imaged ~~within~~ to itself
180   Bounding from Cliff to Cliff, amidst the Wilds
    Where the Rock-Eagle seem'd not more secure
    In its proud Freedom! — On my dreams they rose,
    With the bright Aspect and triumphant step
    Of boundless Liberty, as well beseem'd
    Th' unconquer'd race they sprung from! — And my sons
[200]   Are Captives with the Moor! — Oh! how was this?
GONSALVO. I know not. From Abdullah's Camp e'en now
    A Herald brought the tidings but reveal'd
    Nought, save that they were Prisoners.
ELMINA.   'Twas enough!
190   — And when shall they be ransom'd?
GONSALVO.   There is ask'd
    A ransom far too high!
ELMINA.   What! have we Wealth
    Which might redeem a Monarch, and our Sons
    The while, wear fetters? — Take thou all for them!
[210]   And we will cast our worthless grandeur from us,
    As 'twere a cumbrous garment, which restrain'd
    The heart's impatient throbs! — Why, <u>Thou</u> art one,
    To whose high Nature Pomp hath ever been
    But as the plumage to a Warrior's helm,
    Worn or thrown off as lightly. And for me,
200   Thou knowest not how serenely I could take
    The Peasant's lot upon me, so my heart
    Amidst its deep Affections undisturb'd,
    May dwell in Silence.

GONZALEZ.   In the Moorish camp
Whose lines have girt the city.
XIMENA.   But they live?
—All is not lost, my mother!
ELMINA.   Say, they live.
GONZALEZ. Elmina, still they live.
ELMINA.   But captives!—They
Whom my fond heart had imaged to itself
Bounding from cliff to cliff amidst the wilds
Where the rock-eagle seem'd not more secure
In its rejoicing freedom!—And my boys
Are captives with the Moor!—Oh! how was this?   200
GONZALEZ. Alas! our brave Alphonso, in the pride
Of boyish daring, left our mountain-halls,
With his young brother, eager to behold
The face of noble war. Thence on their way
Were the rash wanderers captured.
ELMINA.   'Tis enough.
—And when shall they be ransom'd?
GONZALEZ.   There is ask'd
A ransom far too high.
ELMINA.   What! have we wealth
Which might redeem a monarch, and our sons
The while wear fetters?[1]—Take thou all for them,
And we will cast our worthless grandeur from us,   210
As 'twere a cumbrous robe!—Why, *thou* art one,
To whose high nature pomp hath ever been
But as the plumage to a warrior's helm,
Worn or thrown off as lightly. And for me,
Thou knowest not how serenely I could take
The peasant's lot upon me, so my heart,
Amidst its deep affections undisturb'd,
May dwell in silence.

---

1 Crusader Richard I of England was ransomed by a huge sum raised by a heavy tax on
   his subjects. FH's "The Troubadour, and Richard Cœur de Lion" (1819) treats the dis-
   covery of his prison.

XIMENA.   And thy Daughter's soul
From the cold glare of Splendor still hath turn'd,
~~Oh~~ My Father! to the soaring Mountain heights
And the deep Forests, as its own free home,
If there be Home on Earth! — Oh, fear thou not
But we will link ourselves to Poverty,
[220]   With ~~an~~ [?ing] glad devotedness, if this, but this,
210   May win our lov'd Ones back! — Thou must not doubt!
We can bear all things!
GONSALVO.   Can ye bear disgrace?
XIMENA. We were not born for this.
GONSALVO.   No, thou sayst well!
Hold to that lofty faith! — My Wife! my Child!
Hath Earth no treasures richer than the gems
Torn from her secret Caverns? — If by these,
Chains may be riven, then let the Captive spring
Rejoicing to the light! — But He for whom
Freedom and Life may but be worn with shame,
[230]   Hath nought to do, save fearlessly to fix
220   His stedfast look on the Majestic Heavens,
And proudly die!
ELMINA.   Gonsalvo! <u>Who</u> must die?
GONSALVO *(hurriedly)*. They on whose lives a fearful price is set,
But to be paid by Treason! — Is't enough?
Or must I yet seek Words?
ELMINA.   My senses fail—
Thou canst not mean——
GONSALVO.   I do! — Why dwells there not
Power in a glance to speak it? — They must die!
They — must their names be told? — <u>Our sons</u> must die,
Unless I yield the City! — Now, be firm
My noble, my beloved!
XIMENA.   Oh look up!
[240]   My Mother, sink not thus! — Until the Grave
230   Have clos'd upon its Victims, there is Hope!
ELMINA. What knell was in the breeze? — No, no, not <u>theirs!</u>
~~What~~ Whose was the blessed Voice that spoke of <u>Hope?</u>
— And there <u>is</u> Hope! — I will not be subdued!

XIMENA.   Father! doubt thou not
But we will bind ourselves to poverty,
With glad devotedness, if this, but this,   220
May win them back. — Distrust us not, my father!
We can bear all things.
GONZALEZ.   Can ye bear disgrace?
XIMENA. We were not *born* for this.
GONZALEZ.   No, thou sayst well!
Hold to that lofty faith. — My wife, my child!
Hath earth no treasures richer than the gems
Torn from her secret caverns? — If by them
Chains may be riven, then let the captive spring
Rejoicing to the light! — But he, for whom
Freedom and life may but be worn with shame,
Hath nought to do, save fearlessly to fix   230
His stedfast look on the majestic heavens,
And proudly die!
ELMINA.   Gonzalez, *who* must die?
GONZALEZ *(hurriedly)*. They on whose lives a fearful price is set,
But to be paid by treason! — Is't enough?
Or must I yet seek words?
ELMINA.   That look saith more!
Thou canst not mean———
GONZALEZ.   I do! why dwells there not
Power in a glance to speak it? — They must die!
They — must their names be told — *Our sons* must die
Unless I yield the city!
XIMENA.   Oh! look up!
My mother, sink not thus! — Until the grave   240
Shut from our sight its victims, there is hope.
ELMINA *(in a low voice)*.
Whose knell was in the breeze? — No, no, not *theirs!*
Whose was the blessed voice that spoke of hope?
— And there *is* hope! — I will not be subdued —

I will not hear a whisper of Despair!
For Nature is all-powerful, and her breath
Moves, like a quickening Spirit o'er the depths
Within a Father's heart! — Thou too, Gonsalvo,
Wilt tell me, there is Hope!

GONSALVO.   Hope but in Him
[250]   Who bade the Patriarch lay his fair young Son
      240   Bound on the Shrine of Sacrifice, and when
                  The bright steel quiver'd in the Father's hand,
                  Just rais'd to strike, sent forth His awful Voice
                  Through the still clouds, and on the breathless air,
                  Commanding to {forbear} withhold! {what?}—Earth has no
                        hope,
                  It rests with Him!

ELMINA.   <u>Thou</u> canst not tell me this!
                  Thou Father of my Sons, within whose hands
                  Doth lie thy Children's fate!

GONSALVO.   If there have been
                  Men in whose bosoms Nature's Voice hath made
[260]   Its accents as the solitary sound
      250   Of an o'erpowering Torrent, silencing
                  The austere and yet divine remonstrances
                  Whisper'd by Faith and Honour, lift thy hands,
                  And, to that Heaven, which arms the Just with strength,
                  Pray, that the Father of thy sons may ne'er
                  Be thus found wanting!

ELMINA.   Then their doom is seal'd!
                  Thou wilt not save thy Children?

GONSALVO.   Hast thou cause
                  Wife of my Youth! to deem it lies within
                  The Bounds of possible things, that I should link
                  My name to that which bitter scorn hath made
[270] 260   Her word to brand with—<u>Traitor?</u>—They that sleep
                  On their proud Battle-fields, thy sires and mine,
                  Died not for this!

ELMINA.   Oh, cold and hard of heart!

I will not hear a whisper of despair!
For Nature is all-powerful, and her breath
Moves like a quickening spirit o'er the depths
Within a father's heart. — Thou too, Gonzalez,
Wilt tell me there is hope!

GONZALEZ *(solemnly).*   Hope but in Him
  Who bade the patriarch lay his fair young son   250
  Bound on the shrine of sacrifice, and when
  The bright steel quiver'd in the father's hand
  Just raised to strike, sent forth his awful voice
  Through the still clouds, and on the breathless air,
  Commanding to withhold![1]— Earth has no hope,
  It rests with Him.

ELMINA.   *Thou* canst not tell me this!
  Thou father of my sons, within whose hands
  Doth lie thy children's fate.

GONZALEZ.   If there have been
  Men in whose bosoms Nature's voice hath made
  Its accents as the solitary sound   260
  Of an o'erpowering torrent, silencing
  Th' austere and yet divine remonstrances
  Whisper'd by faith and honour, lift thy hands,
  And, to that Heaven, which arms the brave with strength,
  Pray, that the father of thy sons may ne'er
  Be thus found wanting!

ELMINA.   Then their doom is seal'd!
  Thou wilt not save thy children?

GONZALEZ.   Hast thou cause,
  Wife of my youth! to deem it lies within
  The bounds of possible things, that I should link
  My name to that word—*traitor?*— They that sleep   270
  On their proud battle-fields, thy sires and mine,
  Died not for this!

ELMINA.   Oh, cold and hard of heart!

---

1 Abraham's near sacrifice of Isaac (Genesis 22.1-18) is typically read as a prefiguration of
    God's sacrifice of his Son. The patriarchal status of Abraham in Judaism, Christianity,
    and Islam bears directly on Hemans's theme of maternal resistance to the sacrifice of
    sons for national glory.

Thou shouldst be born for Empire, since thy soul
Thus lightly from all human bonds can free
Its ~~haughty~~ scornful flight! — Men! Men! too much is yours
Of Vantage, ye, that with a sound, a breath,
A Shadow, thus can fill the desolate ~~Void~~ space
Of rooted-up Affections, o'er whose void
Our yearning hearts must wither! — Of such Mould
270   These should be formed, that mount the lonely steeps
Wherein Dominion sits, and trample down
Ten thousand faithful and devoted ~~hearts~~ breasts,·

[280]
Ere that proud height is gain'd! — Nay
My heart is bursting, and I <u>must</u> be heard!
Heaven hath given power to mortal Agony
As to the Elements in their hour of might
And mastery o'er Creation! — Who shall dare
To mock that fearful strength? — I must be heard!
Give me my Sons!

GONSALVO.   That they may live to hide
280   With covering hands th' indignant blush of shame
On their young brows, when Men shall speak of him
They call'd their Father! — Was the Oath, whereby,
On th' altar of my Faith, and midst the dust
Of noble Men, whose tombs and trophies sent

[290]
Attesting echoes back, I bound myself,
With an unswerving Spirit to defend
This free and Christian City for my God,
And for my King, a Writing traced on sand?
That passionate tears should ~~sweep~~ wash it ~~for~~ from their course,
290   Or e'en the life-drops of a bleeding heart
Erase it, as a billow sweeps away
The last light Vessel's Wake? — Then never more
Let Man's deep vows be trusted! — though enforc'd
By all th' appeals of high remembrances,

[300]
And silent claims o' th' Sepulchres, wherein
His Fathers with their stainless glory sleep,
On their ~~tried~~ good swords! — Thinkst thou I feel no pangs?
He, that hath given me Sons, doth know the heart

Thou shouldst be born for empire, since thy soul
Thus lightly from all human bonds can free
Its haughty flight!—Men! men! too much is yours
Of vantage; ye, that with a sound, a breath,
A shadow, thus can fill the desolate space
Of rooted up affections, o'er whose void
Our yearning hearts must wither!—So it is,
Dominion must be won!—Nay, leave me not—   280
My heart is bursting, and I *must* be heard!
Heaven hath given power to mortal agony
As to the elements in their hour of might
And mastery o'er creation!—Who shall dare
To mock that fearful strength?—I *must* be heard!
Give me my sons!
GONZALEZ.   That they may live to hide
With covering hands th' indignant flush of shame
On their young brows, when men shall speak of him
They call'd their father!—Was the oath, whereby,
On th' altar of my faith, I bound myself,   290
With an unswerving spirit to maintain
This free and christian city for my God,
And for my king, a writing traced on sand?
That passionate tears should wash it from the earth,
Or e'en the life-drops of a bleeding heart
Efface it, as a billow sweeps away
The last light vessel's wake?—Then never more
Let man's deep vows be trusted!—though enforced
By all th' appeals of high remembrances,
And silent claims o' th' sepulchres, wherein   300
His fathers with their stainless glory sleep,
On their good swords! Thinkst thou *I* feel no pangs?
He that hath given me sons, doth know the heart

Whose treasures he recalls.[1]—Of this no more!
300   'Tis vain. — I tell thee that th' ~~eternal~~ inviolate Cross
~~All~~ Still, from our ancient Temples must look up
Thro' the blue Heavens of Spain, tho' at its foot
I perish, with my race! — Thou dar'st not ask
That I, the Son of Warriors — Men who died
[310]   To fix it on that proud Supremacy,
Should tear the Sign of our victorious Faith,
From its ~~bright place in this blessed Firmament~~
— high place of Sunbeams, ~~with the free~~ and free shrine
~~And blessed Firmanent's Infinitude~~
310   For the false Moor to trample!
ELMINA.   Scorn me not
In mine extreme of Misery! —from my soul
Its pressure hath effac'd all images,
All feeling, save o' th' one o'erwhelming woe,
Which weighs me to the Earth! — My brain grows wild;
I know not what I ask! — And yet 'twere but
A few bright days anticipating Fate,
Since it must fall at last, that Cross must fall!
There is no strength within this wasted City,
[320]   To uphold it on her Fanes. — Her sultry air
320   Breathes heavily of the Grave; her Warriors ~~fall~~ sink
Beneath her ancient Banners, ere the Moor
Hath bent his bow against them, for the shaft
Of Pestilence flies with yet more deadly speed,
Than the Arrow of the Desert! Would'st thou seek
Her people, go not to the silent Mart,
Tread not the grass-grown street, their place is now
Beneath thee, not around. Her Sepulchres
Alone are crowded. Ev'n the skies themselves,
O'erhang the desolate splendour of her Domes
330   With an ill omen's Aspect, shaping forth,
From the dull red clouds, wild menacing forms and signs
Foreboding ruin. Man might be withstood,
[330]   But who shall cope with Famine and Disease,
When leagued with armed foes? — Where now the aid,

---

1   *1839*] treasure he

Whose treasure she recalls. — Of this no more.
'Tis vain. I tell thee that th' inviolate cross
Still, from our ancient temples, must look up
Through the blue heavens of Spain, though at its foot
I perish, with my race. Thou *darest* not ask
That I, the son of warriors — men who died
To fix it on that proud supremacy —   310
Should tear the sign of our victorious faith,
From its high place of sunbeams, for the Moor
In impious joy to trample!
ELMINA.   Scorn me not
In mine extreme of misery! — Thou art strong —
Thy heart is not as mine. — My brain grows wild;
I know not what I ask! — And yet 'twere but
Anticipating fate — since it must fall,
That cross *must* fall at last! There is no power,
No hope within this city of the grave,
To keep its place on high. Her sultry air   320
Breathes heavily of death, her warriors sink
Beneath their ancient banners, ere the Moor
Hath bent his bow against them; for the shaft
Of pestilence flies more swiftly to its mark,
Than the arrow of the desert. Ev'n the skies
O'erhang the desolate splendour of her domes
With an ill omen's aspect, shaping forth,
From the dull clouds, wild menacing forms and signs
Foreboding ruin. *Man* might be withstood,
But who shall cope with famine and disease,   330
When leagued with armed foes? — Where now the aid,

Where are the promis'd Lances of Castile?
We are forsaken! think thou but on this!
By Heaven and Earth forsaken in our need,
To stem the current of disastrous days
All vainly and alone!

GONSALVO.¹   If this be so,

340   (And yet I will not deem it) we must fall
As men that in severe devotedness
Have chos'n their part, and bound themselves to death,
Through high conviction that their suffering land,
By the free blood of Martyrdom alone,

[340]   Shall call deliverance down.

ELMINA.   Oh! I have stood
Beside thee thro' the beating Storms of Life,
With the true heart of unrepining Love,
As the poor Peasant's Mate doth cheerily,
In the parch'd Vineyard, or the Harvest-field,

350   ~~I' th'field or Vineyard bear~~[?ing], ~~with him the heat~~
Bearing her part, sustain with him the heat
And burthen of the day!—My Soul hath still
Drawn Courage from thy glance to which it turn'd
~~As flowers unto the Light, this blessed fount~~
~~Of joy and beauty!~~
For Hope and Inspiration, e'en as Thou
Hast turn'd to Glory! But the hour is come,
The dark and heavy hour, when human strength
Sinks down, a toil-worn Pilgrim, in the dust,

360   Owning that Woe is mightier!—Spare me yet

[350]   This bitter cup, my Husband!—Let not Her,
The Mother of the Lovely, sit and mourn
In her unpeopled Home! a broken stem,
O'er its fall'n roses dying!

GONSALVO.   Urge me not,

---

1   A mostly cancelled version of this speech presents the following legibilities: "Oh, free a
[?—]! / When were [?signs] forsaken? [?—?] / This dark our [?—?] / The sky's [?—]
[?~~ages~~,] [?—?] th'shield, / Is the [?—] Monarch still. We shall not fall! / [?—?] faith / [?
] and that shall be Marvels, when M[?—] / Shall [?~~not~~] [?—?] times the [?~~Best~~]

68   THE MANUSCRIPT

Where the long-promised lances of Castile?[1]
— We are forsaken, in our utmost need,
By heaven and earth forsaken!

GONZALEZ.   If this be,
(And yet I will not deem it) we must fall
As men that in severe devotedness
Have chosen their part, and bound themselves to death,
Through high conviction that their suffering land,
By the free blood of martyrdom alone,
Shall call deliverance down.

ELMINA.   Oh! I have stood   340
Beside thee through the beating storms of life,
With the true heart of unrepining love,
As the poor peasant's mate doth cheerily,
In the parch'd vineyard, or the harvest-field,
Bearing her part, sustain with him the heat
And burden of the day;— But now the hour,
The heavy hour is come, when human strength
Sinks down, a toil-worn pilgrim, in the dust,
Owning that woe is mightier! —Spare me yet
This bitter cup, my husband! —Let not her,   350
The mother of the lovely, sit and mourn
In her unpeopled home, a broken stem,
O'er its fall'n roses dying!

GONZALEZ.   Urge me not,

---

1   One of the Christian kingdoms reclaimed from the Moors in the 8th and 9th cen-
turies.

Thou that thro' all sharp conflicts, hast been found
Worthy a brave Man's love, oh! urge me not
To guilt, which thro' the midst of blinding tears,
In its own hues thou see'st not! — Death may scarce
Bring aught like this!

ELMINA.   All, all thy gentle race,

370   The beautiful Beings that around thee grew,

[360]   Creatures of sunshine, by one ~~stroke~~ shaft must fall
Unless thy Soul relent! — She too is ~~morbid~~ struck,
Thy Daughter! — On her fading cheek doth hang
The spoiler's blight, deep shadows o'er her eye,
Are gathering day by day. Th' oppressive cloud
Brooding o'er this pale City of the Dead,
Hath toughed her loveliness, and the face which made
The Summer of our hearts, now doth but speak
A sad prophetic language, in each glance

380   Telling of early Fate.

GONSALVO.[1]   I see a change
Far nobler on her brow of Youth, Elmina,
Than thou hast reck'd of! — She is e'en as One,

[370]   Who at the Trumpet's sudden call hath ris'n
From the gay Banquet, and in scorn cast down
The Wine-cup, and the garland, and the lute,
Of festal hours, for the Helm and Spear, beseeming
The Day's severer tasks! — Her eye hath lost
The beam, that laugh'd upon th' awakening heart
As Dayspring breaks o'er Earth; but far within

390   Its full dark Orb, a light hath sprung, whose source
Lies deeper in the Soul.

XIMENA.   Oh! say not thus!
Think not on me, my Father! — Many a cause
For Youth's untimely withering, walks this Earth,
Besides dull Sickness. When an Empire falls,
~~Let~~ a flower {may} fade unheeded! 'Tis no time
To dwell on aught so light.

GONSALVO.   I see a change

---

1   This speech is lightly crossed out, and seems, with light revisions, to have been tested
for insertion at MS line 396.

Thou that through all sharp conflicts hast been found
Worthy a brave man's love, oh! urge me not
To guilt, which through the midst of blinding tears,
In its own hues thou seest not!—Death may scarce
Bring aught like this!
ELMINA.   All, all thy gentle race,
The beautiful beings that around thee grew,
Creatures of sunshine! Wilt thou doom them all?   360
—She too, thy daughter—doth her smile unmark'd
Pass from thee, with its radiance, day by day?
Shadows are gathering round her—seest thou not?
The misty dimness of the spoiler's breath
Hangs o'er her beauty, and the face which made
The summer of our hearts, now doth but send,
With every glance, deep bodings through the soul,
Telling of early fate.
GONZALEZ.   I see a change

Far nobler on her brow of Youth, ~~Ximena~~ Elmina,
Than thou hast ~~reck'd~~ dreamt of! — She is e'en as One,
400   Who at the Trumpet's sudden call, hath ris'n
From the gay Banquet, and in scorn cast down
The Wine-cup, and the garland, and the lute
Of festal hours, for the good Spear and Helm,
Beseeming sterner tasks! — Her eye hath lost
The beam which laugh'd upon th' awakening heart,
As Dayspring breaks o'er Earth; but far within
Its full dark Orb, a light hath sprung, whose source
Lies deeper in the Soul. — Aye, let the Torch
Which but illum'd the glittering Pageant, fade!
[380] 410 The Altar-flame i' th' Sanctuary's recess,
Burns quenchless, being of Heaven! — She hath put on
Courage and Faith, and generous Constancy,
Ev'n as a breastplate, and her aspect wears
That in its pale, inspired devotedness,
Which calls up lofty thoughts, where'er her glance
Falls brightly on ~~Men's~~ sad hearts — Men look on her,
As she goes forth serenely to her tasks,
(Like a lone Sunbeam o'er a Battle-field)
Unblenching midst all fearful sights and sounds,
420 Binding the Warrior's wounds, and bearing fresh
Cool draughts to fever'd lips; they look on her,
Thus moving in her beautiful array
Of gentle fortitude, and bless the fair
Majestic Vision, and unmurmuring turn
[390] Unto their heavy toils.
ELMINA.   And seest thou not
In that high faith and strong Collectedness,
A fearful Inspiration? — They have cause
To tremble, who behold th' unearthly light
Of high, and, it may be, prophetic thought,
430 Investing Youth with Grandeur! — From the Grave
It rises, on whose shadowy brink thy Child
Waits but a Father's hand to snatch her back
Into the laughing Sunshine! {Let us never} — Kneel with me,
Ximena, kneel beside me, and implore

Far nobler on her brow! —She is as one,
Who, at the trumpet's sudden call, hath risen   370
From the gay banquet, and in scorn cast down
The wine-cup, and the garland, and the lute
Of festal hours, for the good spear and helm,
Beseeming sterner tasks. —Her eye hath lost
The beam which laugh'd upon th' awakening heart,
E'en as morn breaks o'er earth. But far within
Its full dark orb, a light hath sprung, whose source
Lies deeper in the soul. —And let the torch
Which but illumed the glittering pageant, fade!
The altar-flame, i' th' sanctuary's recess,   380
Burns quenchless, being of heaven! —She hath put on
Courage, and faith, and generous constancy,
Ev'n as a breastplate. —Aye, men look on her,
As she goes forth serenely to her tasks,
Binding the warrior's wounds, and bearing fresh
Cool draughts to fever'd lips; they look on her,
Thus moving in her beautiful array
Of gentle fortitude, and bless the fair
Majestic vision, and unmurmuring turn
Unto their heavy toils.

ELMINA.   And seest thou not   390
In that high faith and strong collectedness,
A fearful inspiration? —*They* have cause
To tremble, who behold th' unearthly light
Of high, and, it may be, prophetic thought,
Investing youth with grandeur! —From the grave
It rises, on whose shadowy brink thy child
Waits but a father's hand to snatch her back
Into the laughing sunshine. —Kneel with me,
Ximena, kneel beside me, and implore

[400]   That which a deeper, more prevailing Voice
Than ours doth ask, and will not be denied;
  —His Children's lives!
XIMENA.   Alas! this may not be!
Mother!—I cannot!

                                    Exit XIMENA.

GONSALVO.   My heroic Child!
  —A terrible Sacrifice thou claim'st, O God!
440   From Creatures in whose agonizing hearts
Nature is strong as Death!
ELMINA.   Is't thus in thine?
Away!—what time is given thee to resolve
On—what I cannot utter!—Speak! thou know'st
Too well what I would say!
GONSALVO.   Until—to-morrow!
[410] ELMINA. Until—I heard not right-! Thou saidst—
GONSALVO.   To-morrow!
ELMINA. To-morrow! was it <u>thus</u>!—What! must we tear
All feelings which the growth of Years hath made
Part of our Souls, our Being, with the hand
Of Violence from them?—Must we burst all ties
450   Wherewith the silver chords of Life are twin'd,
And, for this task's fulfilment, can it be
That Man, in his cold heartlessness, hath dar'd
~~To~~ [?—?], ~~briefly number'd~~
To number and to mete us forth the sands
Of hours, nay, Moments?—Why, the sentenc'd Wretch,
Whom from amongst us, to the dark Unknown
We cast, with all his weight of crimes upon him
He on whose Soul doth rest a Brother's blood
Shed in the hour of slumber, hath more space
460   To wean his turbulent passions from the World
[420] His presence doth pollute!—It [?—] is not thus!
We must have Time to school us!—Not To-morrow!
Heaven would but prove, not madden us!

That which a deeper, more prevailing voice   400
Than ours doth ask, and will not be denied;
— His children's lives!
XIMENA.   Alas! this may not be,
Mother! — I cannot.

Exit XIMENA.

GONZALEZ.   My heroic child!
— A terrible sacrifice thou claim'st, O God!
From creatures in whose agonizing hearts
Nature is strong as death!
ELMINA.   Is't thus in thine?
Away! — what time is given thee to resolve
On? — what I cannot utter! — Speak! thou know'st
Too well what I would say.
GONZALEZ.   Until — ask not!
The time is brief.
ELMINA.   Thou saidst — I heard not right —   410
GONZALEZ. The time is brief.
ELMINA.   What! must we burst all ties
Wherewith the thrilling chords of life are twined;
And, for this task's fulfilment, can it be
That man, in his cold heartlessness, hath dared
To number and to mete us forth the sands
Of hours, nay, moments? — Why, the sentenced wretch,
He on whose soul there rests a brother's blood
Pour'd forth in slumber,[1] is allow'd more time
To wean his turbulent passions from the world
His presence doth pollute! — It is not thus!   420
We must have Time to school us.

---

1 A glancing reference to the usurping King Claudio's murder of his elder brother, King
Hamlet, in Shakespeare's play, a crime that reproduces (as Claudio is acutely aware) the
"primal eldest curse" of Cain's murder of Abel. Hemans makes it clear that in the
world of this siege fratricide evokes greater horror than infanticide.

GONSALVO.   We have but
To bow the head in silence, when its Voice
Calls back the things we love!
ELMINA. Love! Love! — there are soft smiles and ~~gentler~~ soothing
    words,
And there are faces, skilful to put on
~~The~~ Looks which may cheat fond bosoms with a show
And promise of Affection, and all this
470 Is but a Mist, a Desert-Vapour, wearing
The brightness of clear Waters, thus to mock
The thirst that semblance kindled! — There is none,
[430] In all this dull and hollow World, no fount
Of deep, strong, deathless Love, save that within
A Mother's heart! — It is but pride, wherewith
To his fair Son the Father's eye doth turn,
Watching his growth. Aye, on the Boy he looks,
The bright, glad creature ~~bounding~~ springing in his path,
But as the heir of his great Name, the young
480 And stately Tree, whose rising strength ere long
Shall bear his trophies well! What Marvel? —<u>You</u> ne'er made
[440] Your breast the pillow of his Infancy,
While to the fulness of your heart's glad heavings
His fair cheek rose and fell, and his bright hair
Wav'd softly to ~~his~~ your breath! —<u>You</u> ne'er kept watch
Beside him, till the last pale star had set,
And Morn all dazzling, as in Mockery, broke
On the dim weary eye that would not close!
'Twas not <u>your</u> hand that rais'd his gentle head
490 When Sickness bow'd it, as the heavy shower
Doth bow the wild-Bird's wing; not <u>yours</u> the face
Which, early faded thro' fond care for him,
Hung o'er his sleep, and duly as Heaven's light
Was there, to greet his Wakening! <u>You</u> ne'er smooth'd
[450] His couch; ne'er sung him to his ~~happy~~ blessed rest,
Caught his least whisper, when his ~~life~~ voice from yours
Had learn'd its utterance; press'd your lip to his,
When Fever parch'd it; hush'd his wayward cries,
With patient, vigilant, never-wearied love!

GONZALEZ.   We have but
    To bow the head in silence, when Heaven's voice
    Calls back the things we love.
ELMINA. Love! love! — there are soft smiles and gentle words,
    And there are faces, skilful to put on
    The look we trust in — and 'tis mockery all!
    — A faithless mist, a desert-vapour, wearing
    The brightness of clear waters, thus to cheat
    The thirst that semblance kindled! — There is none,
    In all this cold and hollow world, no fount   430
    Of deep, strong, deathless love, save that within
    A mother's heart. — It is but pride, wherewith
    To his fair son the father's eye doth turn,
    Watching his growth. Aye, on the boy he looks,
    The bright glad creature springing in his path,
    But as the heir of his great name, the young
    And stately tree, whose rising strength ere long
    Shall bear his trophies well. — And this is love!
    This is *man's* love! — What marvel? —*you* ne'er made
    Your breast the pillow of his infancy,   440
    While to the fulness of your heart's glad heavings
    His fair cheek rose and fell; and his bright hair
    Waved softly to your breath! —*You* ne'er kept watch
    Beside him, till the last pale star had set,
    And morn, all dazzling, as in triumph, broke
    On your dim weary eye; not *yours* the face
    Which, early faded thro' fond care for him,
    Hung o'er his sleep, and, duly as Heaven's light,
    Was there to greet his wakening! *You* ne'er smooth'd
    His couch, ne'er sung him to his rosy rest,   450
    Caught his least whisper, when his voice from yours
    Had learn'd soft utterance; press'd your lip to his,
    When fever parch'd it; hush'd his wayward cries,
    With patient, vigilant, never-wearied love!

500   No! these are woman's tasks! — In these her Youth,
And bloom of cheek, and buoyancy of heart,
Steal from her all unmark'd! — My Boys! my Boys!
Hath vain Affection borne with all, for this?
    — Why were ye given me?

GONSALVO.   Is there Strength in Man

[460]   Thus to endure? — That thou couldst read, thro' all
Its depths of silent Agony, the heart
Thy Voice of Woe doth rend! — Oh! rather aid
Th'o'er wearied to bear on!

ELMINA. Thy heart! — <u>thy</u> heart! — Away! it feels not now!

510   Is't not a Chief's, a Warrior's, mail'd with that,
More proof than steel, unconquerable pride?
    — But an hour comes to tame the mighty Man
Unto the Infant's weakness; nor shall Heaven
Spare you that bitter chastening! — May you live
To be alone, when Loneliness doth seem
Most heavy to sustain, when failing Age
~~Would sit beneath his peaceful Evening-star~~ / ~~Twilight~~
And [?—] ~~meet but kindred faces, on whose brow~~
~~The past hath left its mark~~ / ~~scar,~~ / ~~on whose glance~~
520   ~~Full of young Hopes, would make the future his!~~
Would sit beneath his Twilight-star, and look
But upon those whose Past hath been his own!
    — For me, my voice of weeping shall be soon

[470]   With all forgotten sounds, my quiet-place
Amidst my lovely Ones, and we shall sleep,
Tho' Kings lead Armies o'er us, we shall sleep,
Wrapt in Earth's covering Mantle! — You the while
Shall sit within your vast, forsaken Halls,
And hear the wild and melancholy Winds
530   Moan thro' ~~its~~ their drooping Banners, never more
To wave above your race! Aye, then call up
Shadows — dim phantoms from ancestral tombs,
But all, all glorious! Conquerors, Chieftains, Kings!

[480]   To people ~~this~~ that cold Void! — And when the strength
From your right arm hath melted, when your sword
Hangs on the silent Wall, and your dull'd ear

78 THE MANUSCRIPT

No! these are *woman's* tasks!—In these her youth,
And bloom of cheek, and buoyancy of heart,
Steal from her all unmark'd!—My boys! my boys!
Hath vain affection borne with all for this?
—Why were ye given me?

GONZALEZ.   Is there strength in man
Thus to endure?—That thou couldst read, thro' all   460
Its depths of silent agony, the heart
Thy voice of woe doth rend!

ELMINA. Thy heart!—*thy* heart!—Away! it feels not *now!*
But an hour comes to tame the mighty man
Unto the infant's weakness; nor shall Heaven
Spare you that bitter chastening!—May you live
To be alone, when loneliness doth seem
Most heavy to sustain!—For me, my voice
Of prayer and fruitless weeping shall be soon
With all forgotten sounds; my quiet place   470
Low with my lovely ones, and we shall sleep,
Tho' kings lead armies o'er us, we shall sleep,
Wrapt in earth's covering mantle!—you the while
Shall sit within your vast, forsaken halls,
And hear the wild and melancholy winds
Moan thro' their drooping banners, never more
To wave above your race. Aye, then call up
Shadows—dim phantoms from ancestral tombs,
But all—all *glorious*—conquerors, chieftains, kings—
To people that cold void!—And when the strength   480
From your right arm hath melted, when the blast

Unto your burthen'd heart doth send no thrill
At the proud Clarion's blast, if then you pine
For the glad Voices, and the [?—?]bounding steps,
540   Once thro' your Home [?—] re-echoing, and the Clasp
Of twining arms, and all the joyous light
Of eyes that laugh'd with Youth, and made your board
A place of sunshine—When those days are come,
Then, in your utter desolation turn
[490]   To the cold World, the smiling, faithless World,
Which hath swept past you long, and bid it quench
Your Soul's deep thirst with <u>Fame!</u>—immortal fame!
Fame to the sick of heart!—a gorgeous robe,
A Crown of Victory, unto him that <u>dies</u>
550   I' th' burning Waste, for Water!
GONSALVO.   This from <u>thee!</u>
—Now the last drop of bitterness is pour'd.
Elmina! I forgive thee!———

                                        Exit ELMINA.

                            Aid me, Heaven!
From whom alone is Power!—Oh! thou hast set
Duties, so stern of aspect, in my path,
[500]   They almost, to my fearful gaze, assume
The hue of things less hallow'd! Men have sunk,
Unblam'd, beneath such trials!—Doth not He
Who made us, know the limits of our strength?
My wife! my Sons!—Away! I must not pause
560   To give my heart one Moment's mastery o'er me;
There's Armour that shall press its gaspings down,
E'en if it burst!—Oh! swift and light of foot
Must be the journeyer of the dizzy path
Which winds along the Precipice![1]

                                        Exit GONSALVO.

---

1   The perilous path is a stock metaphor for temptation to sin.

Of the shrill clarion gives your heart no more
A fiery wakening; if at last you pine
For the glad voices, and the bounding steps,
Once thro' your home re-echoing, and the clasp
Of twining arms,[1] and all the joyous light
Of eyes that laugh'd with youth, and made your board
A place of sunshine;—When those days are come,
Then, in your utter desolation, turn
To the cold world, the smiling, faithless world,   490
Which hath swept past you long, and bid it quench
Your soul's deep thirst with *fame! immortal fame!*
Fame to the sick of heart!—a gorgeous robe,
A crown of victory, unto him that dies
I' th' burning waste, for water!
GONZALEZ.   This from *thee!*
Now the last drop of bitterness is pour'd.
Elmina—I forgive thee!

Exit ELMINA.

                    Aid me, Heaven!
From whom alone is power!—Oh! thou hast set
Duties, so stern of aspect, in my path,
They almost, to my startled gaze, assume   500
The hue of things less hallow'd! Men have sunk
Unblamed beneath such trials!—Doth not He
Who made us know the limits of our strength?
My wife! my sons!—Away! I must not pause
To give my heart one moment's mastery thus!

Exit GONZALEZ.

---

1   Affectionate, embracing arms (cf. 4.210), rather than military "arms" (264, 2.313).

SCENE [2]

[The MS scene is much longer, with a much more elaborate discussion of battlefield terrors and confusions, death, civic suffering, fearful omens, and impending doom.]

The Aisle of a Gothic Church. HERNANDEZ, GARCIAS, *and others.*

HERNANDEZ. The rites are clos'd. Now, valiant Men, depart,
Each to his place — I may not say, of rest;
Your faithful Vigils for your Sons may win
What must not be your own. Ye are as those
Who sow, in peril and in pain, the seed
Of the fair Tree, beneath whose stately shade
They may not sit. But bless'd be they who toil
For after-days! — All high and holy thoughts
Be with you, Warriors! thro' the lingering hours
10   Of the Night-watch!
GARCIAS.   Aye, Father! we have need
Of high and holy thoughts, wherewith to fence
Our hearts against Despair! Yet have I been
From Youth, a Son of War. The stars have look'd
A thousand times, ~~in their cold radiance down~~
~~Upon my couch, a Soldier's couch of Heath~~ upon my couch of
      Heath,
Spread midst the wild Sierras, by some stream
Whose dark-red waves look'd e'en as tho' their source
Lay not in rocky caverns, but the veins
Of noble hearts; while many a knightly crest
20   Roll'd with them to the Deep! — And by the Dead
On the torn Banner, or the bloody shield,
I have slept sound, like them. And in the years
[20]   Of my long Exile and Captivity,
With the fierce Arab, I have watch'd beneath
The still, pale shadow of some lonely Palm,
At Midnight, in the Desert, while the Wind
Swell'd with the Lion's roar, and heavily
The fearfulness and might of Solitude
Press'd on my weary heart.

SCENE [2]

The Aisle of a Gothic Church. HERNANDEZ, GARCIAS, *and others.*

HERNANDEZ. The rites are closed. Now, valiant men, depart,
    Each to his place—I may not say, of rest;
    Your faithful vigils for your sons may win
    What must not be your own. Ye are as those
    Who sow, in peril and in care, the seed
    Of the fair tree, beneath whose stately shade
    They may not sit. But bless'd be they who toil
    For after-days!—All high and holy thoughts
    Be with you, warriors, thro' the lingering hours
    Of the night-watch!
GARCIAS.   Aye, father! we have need   10
    Of high and holy thoughts, wherewith to fence
    Our hearts against despair. Yet have I been
    From youth a son of war. The stars have look'd
    A thousand times upon my couch of heath,
    Spread midst the wild sierras, by some stream
    Whose dark-red waves look'd e'en as tho' their source
    Lay not in rocky caverns, but the veins
    Of noble hearts; while many a knightly crest
    Roll'd with them to the deep. And in the years
    Of my long exile and captivity,   20
    With the fierce Arab, I have watch'd beneath
    The still, pale shadow of some lonely palm,
    At midnight, in the desert; while the wind
    Swell'd with the lion's roar, and heavily
    The fearfulness and might of solitude
    Press'd on my weary heart.

HERNANDEZ *(thoughtfully).* Aye, they that dwell
30   Amidst their Groves of Citron, lull'd, when e'er
They list to catch the Voices of the Earth
With all her Woods and Streams; by whispering leaves
And the cool dash of fountains, little dream
Of what is Solitude!—I too have trod
In Pilgrimage, the solemn Wastes, of old
Travers'd by Israel's Sons, and I have felt
How this, our social Nature, clinging still
To all the bonds of its Mortality,
Doth sink o'erburthen'd by th'oppressive sense
40   Of utter loneliness, whose attribute
Is that of Death—deep Silence!
GARCIAS.   But never yet
Hath aught weigh'd down my Spirit to a mood
Of almost boding Sadness, unto which
No breath of air but teems with Auguries,
Like this our heavy task, the Midnight watch
On these devoted ramparts. Fearful things
Are brooding round us. Death upon the Earth,
Omens in Heaven! The summer night hath lost
Its music and its loveliness; the Skies,
50   The clear deep Sapphire Skies of this bright Spain
Put forth the tremulous Stars, but [?~~shroud~~] wrap themselves,
In [?] brooding clouds, which angrily dilate
[50]   Into gigantic Phantoms, and at times
Catching a wild and fiery hue of Wrath
From some fierce Comet, marshal their dense files
To Armies by ten thousands, traversing
Heaven with the rush of Meteor-steeds; ~~dark manes~~
~~Flash, in their course, like torrents, and~~ th'array
Of Spears and Banners, tossing like the Pines
60   Of Pyrenean forests, when the Storm
Doth sweep the Mountains! But last Night these things
And more were seen on high.
HERNANDEZ.   Far more! I too
Kept Vigil, gazing on the wrathful Heavens,

HERNANDEZ *(thoughtfully).*   Thou little know'st
    Of what is solitude! — I tell thee, those
    For whom — in earth's remotest nook — howe'er
    Divided from their path by chain on chain
    Of mighty mountains, and the amplitude   30
    Of rolling seas — there beats one human heart,
    There breathes one being unto whom their name
    Comes with a thrilling and a gladdening sound
    Heard o'er the din of life! are not alone!
    Not on the deep, nor in the wild, alone;
    For there is that on earth with which they hold
    A brotherhood of soul! — Call *him* alone,
    Who stands shut out from this! — And let not those
    Whose homes are bright with sunshine and with love,
    Put on the insolence of happiness,   40
    Glorying in that proud lot! — A lonely hour
    Is on its way to each, to all; for Death
    Knows no companionship.
GARCIAS.   I have look'd on Death
    In field, and storm, and flood.[1] But never yet
    Hath aught weigh'd down my spirit to a mood
    Of sadness, dreaming o'er dark auguries,
    Like this, our watch by midnight. Fearful things
    Are gathering round us. Death upon the earth,
    Omens in Heaven! — The summer-skies put forth
    No clear bright stars above us, but at times,   50
    Catching some comet's fiery hue of wrath,
    Marshal their clouds to armies, traversing
    Heaven with the rush of meteor-steeds, the array
    Of spears and banners, tossing like the pines
    Of Pyrenean forests, when the storm
    Doth sweep the mountains.
HERNANDEZ.   Aye, last night I too
    Kept vigil, gazing on the angry heavens;

---

1 An echo of Shakespeare's Othello (the Moorish general of Christian Venice's military
   forces), as he recounts his adventures "of most disastrous chances; / Of moving acci-
   dents by flood and field" (*Othello* 1.3.133–34); like Garcias, Othello had been an enemy
   captive.

And I beheld the Meeting and the Shock
Of those wild Hosts i' th' air, when, as they clos'd,
[60] A red and sultry mist, like that which mantles
The Thunder's path, fell o'er them. ~~Then enduced~~ Then were
flung
~~A whirl, a mighty G[―?] t[―?] things,~~
Thro' the dull glare, broad cloudy Banners forth,
70 ~~Yet [?-] appalling [?―] the [?―] death steep~~
Like the dark smoke-wreaths of a burning City,
~~Where with thy min'd before. From these shall glow~~
[?―――――――――――――――――?] ~~Banners~~
[?――――――――――――――――?] ~~burning City,~~
[?――――――――――――――?] ~~Then were flung~~
~~Thro' the dull glarey broad cloudy [?―] [?―] ascend forth~~
And chariots seem'd to whirl, and steeds to sink,
~~With their high crested Helms!~~
Bearing down crested Warriors! But all this
80 Was dim, and [?―] [?―] shadowy, fearfully confus'd,
As a strange dream's tumultuous imagery;
Till—'twas an awful Moment!—Darkness rush'd
Down on the unearthly Battle, as the Deep
Swept o'er th' Egyptian Armament.—I look'd,
And all that fiery field of crests and spears
Was blotted from Heaven's face!—I look'd again,
[70] And from the gather'd mass of cloud leap'd forth,
With swift flash, one sword, one blazing sword,
Which to and fro shook o'er the reddening Sea,
90 With a wild Motion, such as th'Earthquake gives
Unto a rocking Citadel!—I beheld,
And yet my Spirit sunk not.

GARCIAS.   Neither deem
That mine hath blench'd!—But these are sights and sounds
To awe the firmest.—Know'st thou what we hear
At Midnight, from the Walls?—Were't but the deep
Barbaric horn, or Moorish tambour's peal,
Thence might the warrior's heart catch impulses,
[80] Quickening its fiery currents!—But our ears
Are pierced by other tones, wherein there breathes

And I beheld the meeting and the shock
Of those wild hosts i' th' air, when, as they closed,
A red and sultry mist, like that which mantles   60
The thunder's path, fell o'er them. Then were flung
Thro' the dull glare, broad cloudy banners forth,
And chariots seem'd to whirl, and steeds to sink,
Bearing down crested warriors. But all this
Was dim and shadowy;—then swift darkness rush'd
Down on th' unearthly battle, as the deep
Swept o'er the Egyptian's armament.[1]—I look'd—
And all that fiery field of plumes and spears
Was blotted from heaven's face!—I look'd again—
And from the brooding mass of cloud leap'd forth   70
One meteor-sword, which o'er the reddening sea
Shook with strange motion, such as earthquakes give
Unto a rocking citadel!—I beheld,
And yet my spirit sunk not.
GARCIAS.   Neither deem
That mine hath blench'd. —But these are sights and sounds
To awe the firmest. —Know'st thou what we hear
At midnight from the walls?—Were't but the deep
Barbaric horn, or Moorish tambour's peal,
Thence might the warrior's heart catch impulses,
Quickening its fiery currents. But our ears   80
Are pierced by other tones. We hear the knell

---

1 Exodus 14.23-28. Hemans may also have been influenced in some of these nightmare
details by DeQuincey's battle-nightmare in "The Pains of Opium" in *Confessions of an
English Opium Eater* (1821-22), a work she read.

100 ~~The chilling~~ [?—] The chill solemnity of Death, unmix'd
With aught of Glory's Voice! We hear the knell
For brave Men, in their Noon of Strength cut down;
The wail from [?—] Houses, ~~wherein their bright Dead are born~~
o'er whose threshold floor [?—] ~~their~~ [?crests] ~~are borne~~;
The dead in Youth are borne; the chaunted Dirge
Faint swelling thro' the Streets, like the last moan
Of Tempests as they sink. And these are all
A regal City's accents! — Then the Air
Hath strange and fitful murmurs of Lament,
110 As if the viewless Watchers of the Land
Sigh'd heavily upon its hollow Winds,
Their prophecies of Ruin! — To my Soul,
The ~~mighty~~ torrent rush of Battle, with its din
Of trampling Steeds and ringing panoply,
[90] Were, after these, faint sounds of drooping Woe,
As the free Sky's glad Music unto him
Who leaves a Couch of Sickness.
HERNANDEZ.   If to plunge
In the mid-waves of Combat, as they bear
Chargers and spearmen onwards, and to make
120 A reckless bosom's front the buoyant mark
On that wild current, for ten thousand arrows;
If <u>thus</u> to dare, were Valour's noblest aim,
Lightly might Fame be won! — But there are things
Which ask a Spirit of more exalted pitch,
[100] And Courage temper'd with a holier fire.
Well mayst thou say, that these are fearful Times,
Therefore be ~~strong~~ firm, be patient! — There is strength,
And a fierce instinct, e'en in common Souls,
To bear up Manhood with a stormy joy,
130 When red swords meet in lightning! — But our task
Is more, and nobler! — We have to endure,
And to keep watch; and to arouse a Land,
And to defend an Altar! — If we fall,
So that our blood make but the millionth part
Of Spain's great ransom, hastening by one hour,
Aye, by one moment,—the ~~majestic~~ triumphant dawn

For brave men in their noon of strength cut down,
And the shrill wail of woman, and the dirge
Faint swelling thro' the streets. Then e'en the air
Hath strange and fitful murmurs of lament,
As if the viewless watchers of the land
Sigh'd on its hollow breezes! — To my soul,
The torrent-rush of battle, with its din
Of trampling steeds and ringing panoply,
Were, after these faint sounds of drooping woe,   90
As the free sky's glad music unto him
Who leaves a couch of sickness.
HERNANDEZ *(with solemnity).*   If to plunge
In the mid-waves of combat, as they bear
Chargers and spearmen onwards; and to make
A reckless bosom's front the buoyant mark
On that wild current, for ten thousand arrows;
If *thus* to dare were valour's noblest aim,
Lightly might fame be won! — but there are things
Which ask a spirit of more exalted pitch,
And courage temper'd with a holier fire!   100
Well mayst thou say, that these are fearful times,
Therefore be firm, be patient! — There is strength,
And a fierce instinct, e'en in common souls,
To bear up manhood with a stormy joy,
When red swords meet in lightning! — But our task
Is more, and nobler! — We have to endure,
And to keep watch, and to arouse a land,
And to defend an altar! — If we fall,
So that our blood make but the millionth part

Of her deliverance — we may count it joy
To die upon her bosom, and beneath
The Banner of her Faith! — Think but on this,
140 And gird your hearts with silent fortitude,
Suffering, yet hoping all things. Fare ye well.
GARCIAS. Father, farewell.

Exeunt GARCIAS *and followers.*

HERNANDEZ *(alone).*   These men have earthly ties
Cumbering their Natures, therefore to the cause
Of God and Spain's Revenge, they bring but half
Their energies and hopes. But He whom Heaven
Hath call'd to be th' Awakener of a Land,
Should have his Soul's Affections all absorb'd
In that majestic purpose, and press on
To its fulfilment, as a mountain-born
150 And mighty Stream, with all its vassal-rills
Sweeps proudly to the Ocean, pausing not
To dally with the flowers.
                    Hark! What quick step
Comes hurrying thro' the gloom at this lone hour?

ELMINA *enters.*

ELMINA. Are not all hours as one to Misery? — Why
Should <u>she</u> take note of time, for whom the Day
And Night have lost their blessed attributes
Of sunshine and repose? — I come to thee
In mine affliction, which doth little reck
How Stars may rise and wane.
HERNANDEZ.   I know thy woes.
160 But there are trials for the noble heart
Wherein its own deep fountains must supply
All it can hope of comfort. Pity's Voice
Comes with vain sweetness to th' unheeding ear
Of ~~Misery~~ Anguish, e'en as Music heard afar
On the green shore, by him who perishes

Of Spain's great ransom, we may count it joy 110
To die upon her bosom, and beneath
The banner of her faith! — Think but on this,
And gird your hearts with silent fortitude,
Suffering, yet hoping all things — Fare ye well.
GARCIAS. Father, farewell.

Exeunt GARCIAS *and his followers.*

HERNANDEZ.   These men have earthly ties
And bondage on their natures! — To the cause
Of God, and Spain's revenge, they bring but half
Their energies and hopes. But he whom Heaven
Hath call'd to be th' awakener of a land,
Should have his soul's affections all absorb'd 120
In that majestic purpose, and press on
To its fulfilment, as a mountain-born
And mighty stream, with all its vassal-rills
Sweeps proudly to the ocean, pausing not
To dally with the flowers.
                         Hark! What quick step
Comes hurrying through the gloom at this dead hour?

ELMINA *enters.*

ELMINA. Are not all hours as one to misery? — Why
Should *she* take note of time, for whom the day
And night have lost their blessed attributes
Of sunshine and repose?
HERNANDEZ.   I know thy griefs; 130
But there are trials for the noble heart
Wherein its own deep fountains must supply
All it can hope of comfort. Pity's voice
Comes with vain sweetness to th' unheeding ear
Of anguish, e'en as music heard afar
On the green shore, by him who perishes

Midst rocks and eddying Waters.

ELMINA. Think thou not
I sought thee but for Pity! — I am come
For that which 'tis the privilege Heaven hath made
[140]   Grief's charter, to demand from all whose form,
170   Whose human form, doth seal them unto Suffering!
Father! I ask thine <u>aid</u>.

HERNANDEZ. There is no aid
For thee or for thy Children, but with Him
Whose presence is around us in the cloud,
As in the Guiding and the glorious light.

ELMINA. There is no aid! — Art thou a Man of God?
Art thou a Man of Sorrow, (for the World
Doth call thee such,) and hast thou not been taught
By God and Sorrow — mighty as they are!
[150]   To own the claims of Misery?

HERNANDEZ. Is there power
180   With me to save thy Sons? — Implore of Heaven!

ELMINA. Doth not Heaven work its purposes by Man?
I tell thee, <u>thou</u> canst save them! — Art thou not
Gonsalvo's Counsellor? — Unto him thy words
Are e'en as Oracles. He turns to thee
As Men, i' th'elder Time, were wont to seek
Beneath their shadowing Palms, the gifted seers
Upon whose lips hung Prophecy. The key
To his deep Soul is there —

HERNANDEZ. And therefore? — Speak!
The noble Daughter of Pelayo's line
190   Hath nought to ask, unworthy of the name
Which is a Nation's heritage. — Dost thou shrink?

ELMINA. Have pity on me, Father! — I must speak
[160]   That, from the thought of which, but yesterday,
With an indignant eye and burning cheek,
I had recoil'd, in Scorn! — But this is past.
Oh! we grow humble in our Agonies,
And cast the crown of glory from our heads,
To soil their pride with ashes! — I am weak;
My chastening is far more than I can bear!

200 HERNANDEZ. These are no times for Weakness! On our Hills

Midst rocks and eddying waters.

ELMINA.   Think thou not
I sought thee but for pity. I am come
For that which grief is privileged to demand
With an imperious claim, from all whose form,   140
Whose human form, doth seal them unto suffering!
Father! I ask thine *aid*.

HERNANDEZ.   There is no aid
For thee or for thy children, but with Him
Whose presence is around us in the cloud,
As in the shining and the glorious light.

ELMINA. There is no aid! — Art thou a man of God?
Art thou a man of sorrow —(for the world
Doth call thee such)—and hast thou not been taught
By, God and sorrow — mighty as they are,
To own the claims of misery?

HERNANDEZ.   Is there power   150
With me to save thy sons? — Implore of Heaven!

ELMINA. Doth not Heaven work its purposes by man?
I tell thee, *thou* canst save them! — Art thou not
Gonzalez' counsellor? — Unto him thy words
Are e'en as oracles———

HERNANDEZ.   And therefore? — Speak!
The noble daughter of Pelayo's line
Hath nought to ask, unworthy of the name
Which is a nation's heritage. — Dost thou shrink?

ELMINA. Have pity on me, father! — I must speak
That, from the thought of which, but yesterday,   160
I had recoil'd in scorn! — But this is past.
Oh! we grow humble in our agonies,
And to the dust — their birth-place — bow the heads
That wore the crown of glory! — I am weak —
My chastening is far more than I can bear.

HERNANDEZ. These are no times for weakness. On our hills

The ancient Cedars, in their ~~strength and~~ [?—] gather'd strength,
Are battling with the Tempest; and the flower
Which cannot meet its driving blast, must die.

But thou hast drawn thy Nurture from a Stem
Unwont to bend or break. Lift thy proud head!
Daughter of Spain! What wouldst thou with thy Lord?

ELMINA. Look not upon me thus! — I have no words
To tell thee! — Take thy keen, disdainful eye
Off from my soul! — What! am I sunk to this?

210   I, that have been a Hero's lofty Mate
In danger and in suffering! — How my Sons
Will scorn the Mother that would bring disgrace
On their majestic line! — My Sons! my Sons!
Now is all else forgotten. — I had once

A Babe that in the early Spring-time lay
Sickening upon my bosom, till at last,
When all young flowers were opening to the Sun,
Death sunk on his meek eyelid, and I deem'd
All Sorrow light to mine! — But I have learn'd

220   [?—] [~~will~~] Since then how much more heavily may the hand
Of God be laid upon us; for the fate
Of all my Children ~~now seems brooding over me,~~ seems to brood
     above me
In the dark thunder-clouds! — Thou dar'st not scorn
Mine Anguish, for 'tis fearful! — I have power
And voice unfaltering now to speak my prayer
And my last lingering hope, that thou shouldst win
The Husband of my Youth to save his Sons!

HERNANDEZ. By yielding up the City?

ELMINA.   Rather say
By meeting that which gathers close upon us

230   Perchance one day the sooner! — Is 't not so!
Must we not yield at last? — How long shall Man
Array his single breast against Disease,
And famine, and the sword?

HERNANDEZ.   How long? — While He,
Who shadows forth his power more gloriously
In the high deeds and sufferings of the Soul,
Than in the circling Heavens, with all their Stars,

The ancient cedars, in their gather'd might,
Are battling with the tempest; and the flower
Which cannot meet its driving blast must die.
—But thou hast drawn thy nurture from a stem   170
Unwont to bend or break. —Lift thy proud head,
Daughter of Spain! —What wouldst thou with thy lord?
ELMINA. Look not upon me thus! —I have no power
To tell thee. Take thy keen disdainful eye
Off from my soul! —What! am I sunk to this?
I, whose blood sprung from heroes! —How my sons
Will scorn the mother that would bring disgrace
On their majestic line! —My sons! my sons!
—Now is all else forgotten! —I had once
A babe that in the early spring-time lay   180
Sickening upon my bosom, till at last,
When earth's young flowers were opening to the sun,
Death sunk on his meek eyelid, and I deem'd
All sorrow light to mine! —But now the fate
Of all my children seems to brood above me
In the dark thunder-clouds! —Oh! I have power
And voice unfaltering now to speak my prayer
And my last lingering hope, that thou shouldst win
The father to relent, to save his sons!
HERNANDEZ. By yielding up the city?
ELMINA.   Rather say   190
By meeting that which gathers close upon us
Perchance one day the sooner! —Is 't not so?
Must we not yield at last? —How long shall man
Array his single breast against disease,
And famine, and the sword?
HERNANDEZ.   How long? —While he,
Who shadows forth his power more gloriously
In the high deeds and sufferings of the soul,
Than in the circling heavens, with all their stars,

Or the far-sounding and mysterious Deep;

[200]   Doth send abroad a Spirit, which weds itself

To all Affliction, in the righteous cause,

240   With an austere and solemn joy! — How long?

— And who art thou, that in the littleness

Of thine own selfish purpose, would'st set bounds

To the free current of all noble thought

And generous action, bidding its bright waves

Be stayed, and flow no further? — But that Heaven

Whose interdict is laid upon the Seas,

And on the rolling Spheres, that from their path

On high they swerve not; wills ~~that there be none~~ there to be

none,

No limits unto that which Man's high strength,

250   Shall, thro' its aid, achieve! — So Earth shall know

The Chasteness of Oppression! ~~, when her realms~~

~~Lie trampled, as~~ [?——] [?——ness]

[210] ELMINA.   There are times,

When all that hopeless Courage can perform,

But sheds a mournful beauty on the fate

Of those that die in vain.

HERNANDEZ.   <u>Who</u> dies in vain,

Upon his Country's War-fields, and beneath

The shadow of her Altars? — Feeble heart!

I tell thee that the Voice of noble blood,

Thus shed for Faith and Freedom, hath a tone

260   Which, from the Night of Ages, from the Gulphs

Of Death, shall burst, and make its high appeal

[220]   Sound unto Earth and Heaven! Aye, let the Land,

Whose toiling Generations of the Brave

Thro' centuries of Woe, have proudly striven,

And perish'd by her Temples; sink awhile,

Worn by the conflict! — But immortal seed

Deep, by heroic suffering, hath been sown

On all her ancient Hills, and generous Hope

Knows that the soil, in its good time, shall yet

270   Bring forth a glorious Harvest! — Earth receives

Not one red drop from faithful hearts in vain.

Or the far-sounding deep, doth send abroad
A spirit, which takes affliction for its mate,   200
In the good cause, with solemn joy! — How long?
— And who art *thou*, that, in the littleness
Of thine own selfish purpose, would'st set bounds
To the free current of all noble thought
And generous action, bidding its bright waves
Be stay'd, and flow no further? — But the Power
Whose interdict is laid on seas and orbs,
To chain them in from wandering, hath assign'd
No limits unto that which man's high strength
Shall, through its aid, achieve!

ELMINA.   Oh! there are times,   210
When *all* that hopeless courage can achieve
But sheds a mournful beauty o'er the fate
Of those who die in vain.

HERNANDEZ.   *Who* dies in vain
Upon his country's war-fields, and within
The shadow of her altars? — Feeble heart!
I tell thee that the voice of noble blood,
Thus pour'd for faith and freedom, hath a tone
Which, from the night of ages, from the gulf
Of death, shall burst, and make its high appeal
Sound unto earth and heaven! Aye, let the land,   220
Whose sons, through centuries of woe, have striven,
And perish'd by her temples, sink awhile,
Borne down in conflict! — But immortal seed
Deep, by heroic suffering, hath been sown
On all her ancient hills; and generous hope
Knows that the soil, in its good time, shall yet
Bring forth a glorious harvest! — Earth receives
Not one red drop, from faithful hearts, in vain.[1]

---

1 An echo of Milton's sonnet "On the Late Massacre in Piedmont": "Their moans / The
vales redoubled to the hills, and they / To Heaven. Their martyred blood and ashes
sow / O'er all th' Italian fields ... / ... that from these may grow / A hundredfold" (8-
12).

ELMINA. Then it must be!— Those young, bright Lives ~~which drew~~
Their nurture from this bosom, of whose pangs
Man knows not, recks not, must be offer'd up,
[230]   — Heaven! Heaven! is there no Mercy?— to retard
Our doom one day!
HERNANDEZ.   The Mantle of that day
May wrap the Fate of Spain!— He that call'd up
Earth's Kingdoms with a breath, doth ask brief time
To work his awful changes on their face.
280 ELMINA. Why did I turn to thee in my despair?
Thou'rt like them all!— What recks the Conqueror's heart
Although his Car, in its triumphal course,
Crush the poor insect, which perchance had yet
Some few brief hours to glitter in the Sun?
Woman must love, and suffer, and be still
~~Before Affliction~~ In Sorrow's presence![1]— But for you, ye rush
[?~~In~~] ~~the completion of some haughty aim,~~
~~Careless of what ye trample;~~
To gain some night of glory, shaking off
290 Affection's hold, if on your fiery ~~course~~ speed
It hang too closely; and your Slave, Renown,
Doth blazon forth your Victories, tolling nought
Of the fond hopes that died; the gentle hearts
That broke obscurely, when ye burst the ties
Whereby they clung to yours!— No, we but hear
Of Kingdoms won, not of their Vines and flowers
Crush'd by the March of Hosts!— But what had I
To hope from <u>thee</u>, thou lone and childless Man!
Go to thy silent Home! there no young Voice
300 Hath learn'd its utterance, no light step shall bound
O'er the void Threshold at the sound of thine!
Why did I turn to thee?
HERNANDEZ. Woman! how dar'st thou mock me with my woes?
[240]   <u>Thy</u> Children too shall perish, and I say
It shall be well!— Why tak'st thou thought for them?

---

1 "Suffer, and be still," a phrase Hemans would repeat memorably in "Madeline" (one of
the *Records of Woman*, line 62), would become a standard prescription for the domestic
heroism of the Victorian woman. See, for example, Sarah Stickney Ellis's popular and
influential conduct manual, *The Daughters of England* (London: Fisher & Son, 1843) 73.

ELMINA. Then it must be!—And ye will make those lives,
    Those young bright lives, an offering—to retard   230
    Our doom one day!
HERNANDEZ.   The mantle of that day
    May wrap the fate of Spain!
ELMINA.   What led me here?
    Why did I turn to *thee* in my despair?
    Love hath no ties upon thee; what had I
    To hope from *thee*, thou lone and childless man!
    Go to thy silent home!—there no young voice
    Shall bid thee welcome, no light footstep spring
    Forth at the sound of thine!—What knows thy heart?
HERNANDEZ. Woman! how dar'st thou taunt me with my woes?
    Thy children too shall perish, and I say   240
    It shall be well!—Why tak'st thou thought for them?

Wearing thy heart, and wasting down thy life
Unto ~~the~~ its dregs, and making Night thy time
Of yet more watchful care, and casting Health,
As 'twere th'Egyptian's pearl, to melt, unpriz'd,[1]
310   I' th'bitter cup thou drink'st? — Why, what hath ~~Life~~ Earth
To yield for this? — Fond Dupe! — Shall they not live,
(If the sword spare them now,) to prove how soon
All Love may be forgotten? — Years of thought,
[250]   Long faithful watchings, looks of tenderness,
That chang'd not, tho' to change be this World's law?
Shall they not flush ~~with~~ thy cheek with shame, whose blood
Doth mark, e'en like branding iron? to thy sick heart
Make Death a want, as Sleep to Weariness?
Anticipate the tardy hand of Time
320   Upon thy temples, strewing them with snow,
And scorning their own work? Or e'en at best,
Will they not leave thee? — far from thee seek room
For th' overflowings of their fiery Souls,
On Life's wide Ocean? — Give the bounding Steed,
Or the wing'd Bark to Youth, that his free course
[260]   May be o'er Seas and Hills, and weep thou not
In thy forsaken Home, for the bright World
Lies all before him, and be sure, he wastes
No thought on thee!

ELMINA.   Not so! it is not so!
330   Thou dost but torture me! —<u>My</u> sons are kind,
And brave, and gentle!

HERNANDEZ.   Others too have worn
The Aspect of all good. — Nay, stay thee yet;
I will be calm, and thou shalt learn how Earth,
The fruitful in all Agonies, hath woes,
[? ~~Hath~~]Which far outweigh thine own.

ELMINA.   It may not be!

---

1   Compare Othello's indictment of himself as "one whose hand, / Like the base Judean, threw a pearl away / Richer than all his tribe" (5.2.342-45)—the "pearl" being his Venetian wife, whom he has murdered on misplaced suspicion of infidelity; "base Judean" is a Christian epithet for an infidel, or unbeliever, of a piece with the way the Christians of Spain talk about the Moorish and Muslim antagonists.

Wearing thy heart, and wasting down thy life
Unto its dregs, and making night thy time
Of care yet more intense, and casting health,
Unpriz'd, to melt away, i' th' bitter cup
Thou minglest for thyself? — Why, what hath earth
To pay thee back for this? — Shall they not live,
(If the sword spare them now) to prove how soon
All love may be forgotten? — Years of thought,
Long faithful watchings, looks of tenderness,   250
That changed not, though to change be this world's law?
Shall they not flush thy cheek with shame, whose blood
Marks, e'en like branding iron? — to thy sick heart
Make death a want, as sleep to weariness?
Doth not all hope end thus? — or e'en at best,
Will they not leave thee? — far from thee seek room
For th' overflowings of their fiery souls,
On life's wide ocean? — Give the bounding steed,
Or the wing'd bark to youth, that his free course
May be o'er hills and seas; and weep thou not   260
In thy forsaken home, for the bright world
Lies all before him,[1] and be sure he wastes
No thought on thee!
ELMINA.   Not so! it is not so!
Thou dost but torture me! — *My* sons are kind,
And brave, and gentle.
HERNANDEZ.   Others too have worn
The semblance of all good. Nay, stay thee yet;
I will be calm, and thou shalt learn how earth,
The fruitful in all agonies, hath woes
Which far outweigh thine own.
ELMINA.   It may not be!

---

1   A sarcastic allusion to Adam and Eve's exit from Eden at the end of Milton's *Paradise
Lost:* "The World was all before them ..." (12.646).

There is not Sorrow like a Mother's Sorrows,
[270] When mourning for her Sons, because they are not!
HERNANDEZ. My son lay stretch'd upon his Battle-bier,
And there were hands wrung o'er him, which had caught
Their hue from his young blood.
340 ELMINA.   What tale is this?
HERNANDEZ *(wildly)*. Read you no records, in this mien, of things
Whose traces on Man's aspect are not such
As the Breeze leaves on Water? — Lofty birth,
War, Peril, Power? — Affliction's hand is strong,
But not to erase the haughty characters
They grave so deep! — I have not always been
[280] That which I am. — It naught avails to tell
How proud a name I bore; that sound shall live
Amidst my Country's Olive-hills, i' th' songs
350 Of Muleteer and Shepherd, when the last
That answered to its thrilling call hath given
His dust to blend with Spain's. I was once a Chief,
A Warrior! — there's a dearer name than those —
A Father — and 'twas mine.
ELMINA.   Then thy heart canst <u>feel!</u>
Thou wilt have pity!
HERNANDEZ.   Should I pity <u>thee?</u>
Thy sons will perish gloriously. Their blood —
ELMINA. Their blood! My Children's blood! — Thou speak'st as
        'twere
Of casting down a Wine-cup, in the Mirth
And wantonness of feasting. — My fair boys!
360   — Man! hast <u>thou</u> been a Father?
HERNANDEZ.   Let them die!
[290] Let them die <u>now</u>, thy Children! — So thy heart
Shall wear their beautiful image all undimm'd,
Within it, to the last! Nor shalt thou learn
The bitter lesson, of what worthless dust
Are fram'd the Idols, whose false glory binds
Earth's fetter on our Souls! — Thou think'st it much
To mourn the early Dead; but there are tears
Heavy with deeper Anguish! — We endow
Those whom we love, in our fond passionate worship,

Whose grief is like a mother's for her sons?   270
HERNANDEZ. *My* son lay stretch'd upon his battle-bier,
     And there were hands wrung o'er him, which had caught
     Their hue from his young blood!
ELMINA.   What tale is this?
HERNANDEZ. Read you no records in this mien, of things
     Whose traces on man's aspect are not such
     As the breeze leaves on water? — Lofty birth,
     War, peril, power? — Affliction's hand is strong,
     If it erase the haughty characters
     They grave so deep! — I have not always been
     That which I am. The name I bore is not   280
     Of those which perish! — I was once a chief—
     A warrior! — nor as now, a lonely man!
     I was a father!
ELMINA.   Then thy heart can *feel!*
     Thou wilt have pity!
HERNANDEZ.   Should I pity *thee?*
     Thy sons will perish gloriously — their blood—
ELMINA. Their blood! my children's blood! — Thou speak'st as
          'twere
     Of casting down a wine-cup, in the mirth
     And wantonness of feasting! — My fair boys!
     — Man! hast *thou* been a father?
HERNANDEZ.   Let them die!
     Let them die *now*, thy children! so thy heart   290
     Shall wear their beautiful image all undimm'd,
     Within it, to the last! Nor shalt thou learn
     The bitter lesson, of what worthless dust
     Are framed the idols, whose false glory binds
     Earth's fetter on our souls! — Thou think'st it much
     To mourn the early dead; but there are tears
     Heavy with deeper anguish! We endow
     Those whom we love, in our fond passionate blindness,

370   With power upon our Souls, too absolute

     To be a Mortal's trust! ~~They are merciful~~ Within their hands
     {We lay the flaming sword, whose stroke alone
     Can reach our hearts,—and <u>they</u> are merciful,}[1]
     As they are strong, that wield it not to ~~crush~~ pierce us!
     But when doth Man show Mercy?—Had I wept
     O'er my Son's grave, as o'er a Babe's, where tears
     Are but Spring dew-drops, glittering in the sun
     And brightening the young Verdure, I might still
     Have lov'd and trusted!

ELMINA *(disdainfully).*   But he fell in <u>War!</u>

380   And hath not Glory medicine in her cup

     For the brief pangs of Nature?

HERNANDEZ.   Glory!—Peace!
     And listen!—By my side the stripling grew,
     Last of my race. I rear'd him to take joy
     I' the blaze of arms, as Eagles train their Young
     To look upon the Day-King!—His quick blood
     E'en to his boyish cheek would mantle up,
     When the heavens rung with Trumpets, and his eye
     Flash with the spirit of a race whose deeds—
     —But this availeth not!—Yet he <u>was</u> brave!

390   I've seen him clear himself a path in fight

     As lightning thro' a Forest, and his plume
     Wav'd like a Torch, above the Battle-storm,
     The Soldier's guide, when princely crests ~~have~~ had sunk,
     And Banners were struck down. — Around my steps
     Floated his fame, like Music, and I liv'd
     But in the lofty sound. — But when my heart
     In one frail Ark had ventur'd all, when most
     He seem'd to stand between my Soul and Heaven,
     —Then came the thunder-stroke!

ELMINA.   'Tis ever thus!

400   And the unquiet and foreboding sense

     That thus 'twill ever be, doth link itself
     Darkly, with all deep Love! — He died?

---

1   These bracketed lines, appearing in a different medium from the rest of the manu-
script, may be a later addition.

With power upon our souls, too absolute
To be a mortal's trust! Within their hands   300
We lay the flaming sword, whose stroke alone
Can reach our hearts, and *they* are merciful,
As they are strong, that wield it not to pierce us!
— Aye, fear them, fear the loved! — Had I but wept
O'er my son's grave, as o'er a babe's, where tears
Are as spring dew-drops, glittering in the sun,
And brightening the young verdure, *I* might still
Have loved and trusted!
ELMINA *(disdainfully).*   But he fell in war!
And hath not glory medicine in her cup
For the brief pangs of nature?
HERNANDEZ.   Glory! — Peace,   310
And listen! — By my side the stripling grew,
Last of my line. I rear'd him to take joy
I' th' blaze of arms, as eagles train their young
To look upon the day-king! — His quick blood
Ev'n to his boyish cheek would mantle up,
When the heavens rang with trumpets, and his eye
Flash with the spirit of a race whose deeds —
— But this availeth not! — Yet he *was* brave.
I've seen him clear himself a path in fight
As lightning through a forest, and his plume   320
Waved like a torch, above the battle-storm,
The soldier's guide, when princely crests had sunk,
And banners were struck down. — Around my steps
Floated his fame, like music, and I lived
But in the lofty sound. But when my heart
In one frail ark had ventur'd all, when most
He seem'd to stand between my soul and heaven,
— Then came the thunder-stroke!
ELMINA.   'Tis ever thus!
And the unquiet and foreboding sense
That thus 'twill ever be, doth link itself   330
Darkly with all deep love! — He died?

HERNANDEZ.   Not so!
Death! Death! — Why, Earth should be a Paradise,
To make that name so fearful! — Had he died,
With his young fame about him for a shroud,
I had not learn'd the Might of Agony,
To bring proud Natures low! — No! — he fell off —
— Why do I tell thee this? — What right hast <u>Thou</u>
To ~~know~~ learn how pass'd the Glory from my House?
Yet listen! — He forsook me! — He, that was
As mine own Soul, forsook me! — trampled o'er
The ashes of his Sires! — Aye, leagued himself
E'en with the Infidel, the [?—] curse of Spain,
And, for the dark eye of a Moorish Maid,
Abjured his faith, his God! — Now, talk of death!
ELMINA. Oh! I can pity thee ——
HERNANDEZ *(gloomily).*   There's more to hear.
I brac'd the corslet o'er my heart's deep wound,
And cast my troubled Spirit on the tide
Of War and high events, whose stormy waves
Might bear it up from sinking: ————
ELMINA.   And ye met
No more?
HERNANDEZ. Be still! — We did! — we met <u>once</u> more.
God had his own high purpose to fulfil,
Or think'st thou that the Sun in his bright Heaven
Had look'd upon such things? — We met <u>once more.</u>
— That was an hour to leave its lightning-mark
Sear'd upon brain and bosom! — There had been
Combat on Ebro's banks, and when the Day
Sank in red clouds, it faded from a field
~~Still by the Moor disputed~~. Still held by Moorish Lances. Night
     clos'd round,
A night of sultry darkness, in the shadow,
Of whose broad Wing, ev'n unto death I strove
Long with a turban'd Champion; but my Sword

410

[340]

420

[350]

430

[360]

HERNANDEZ.   Not so!
—Death! Death!—Why, earth should be a paradise,
To make that name so fearful!—Had he died,
With his young fame about him for a shroud,
I had not learn'd the might of agony,
To bring proud natures low!—No! he fell off
—Why do I tell thee this?—What right hast *thou*
To learn how pass'd the glory from my house?
Yet listen!—He forsook me!—He, that was
As mine own soul, forsook me! trampled o'er   340
The ashes of his sires!—Aye, leagued himself
E'en with the infidel, the curse of Spain,
And, for the dark eye of a Moorish maid,
Abjured his faith, his God!—Now, talk of death![1]
ELMINA. Oh! I can pity thee——
HERNANDEZ.   There's more to hear.
I braced the corslet o'er my heart's deep wound,
And cast my troubled spirit on the tide
Of war and high events, whose stormy waves
Might bear it up from sinking;————
ELMINA.   And ye met
No more?
HERNANDEZ. Be still!—We did!—we met *once* more.   350
God had his own high purpose to fulfil,
Or think'st thou that the sun in his bright heaven
Had look'd upon such things?—We met *once more.*
—That was an hour to leave its lightning-mark
Sear'd upon brain and bosom!—there had been
Combat on Ebro's banks, and when the day
Sank in red clouds, it faded from a field
Still held by Moorish lances. Night closed round,
A night of sultry darkness, in the shadow
Of whose broad wing, ev'n unto death I strove   360
Long with a turban'd champion; but my sword

---

1   A lover turned infidel is the hero of Hemans's *The Abencerrage* (*Tales, and Historic Scenes*,
    1819) and of Byron's *Siege of Corinth* (1816). This embedded story received very
    different assessments in the nineteenth century, for which see Delta, Butler, and
    Williams (Appendix G, nos. 8, 10, 11).

Was heavy with God's Vengeance — and prevail'd.
He fell — my heart exulted — and I stood
In gloomy triumph o'er him — Nature gave
No sign of horror, for 'twas Heaven's decree!
He strove to speak — but I had done the work
Of wrath too well — yet in his last deep moan
A dreadful something of familiar sound
440   Came o'er my shuddering sense. The Moon look'd forth,
And I beheld — speak not! — I will not bear
[370] The Mockery of thy pity! — 'twas — my Son!
My Boy lay dying there — he raised one glance,
And knew me — for he sought with feeble hand
To cover his glaz'd eyes — a darker Veil
Sank o'er them soon. — I will not have thy look
Fix'd on me thus — Away!

ELMINA.   Thou hast seen this,
Thou hast <u>done</u> this — and yet thou liv'st?

HERNANDEZ.   I live!
And know'st thou wherefore? — On my Soul there fell
450   A horror of great darkness, which shut out
All Earth, and Heaven, and Hope. I cast away
[380] The Spear and Helm, and made the Cloister's shade
The Home of my despair. — But a deep Voice
Came to me thro' the gloom, and sent its tones
Far thro' my Bosom's depths. And I awoke,
Aye, as the Mountain Cedar doth shake off
Its weight of wintry snow, e'en so I shook
Despondence from my heart, and knew myself
Seal'd by that blood wherewith my hands were dyed,
460   And set apart, and fearfully mark'd out
Unto a mighty task! — to rouse the Soul
[390] Of Spain, as from the Dead; and to lift up
The Cross, her sign of Victory, on the Hills,
Gathering her Sons to Battle! — And my Voice
Must be as Freedom's Trumpet on the Winds,
O'er the Sierras and the Cities ~~borne~~ bore
And the proud fields of sainted Chivalry,
From Roncesvalles to the blue Sea-waves
Where Calpe looks on Afric; till the Land

Was heavy with God's vengeance—and prevail'd.
He fell—my heart exulted—and I stood
In gloomy triumph o'er him—Nature gave
No sign of horror, for 'twas Heaven's decree!
He strove to speak—but I had done the work
Of wrath too well—yet in his last deep moan
A dreadful something of familiar sound
Came o'er my shuddering sense. —The moon look'd forth,
And I beheld—speak not!—'twas he—my son!   370
My boy lay dying there! He raised one glance,
And knew me—for he sought with feeble hand
To cover his glazed eyes. A darker veil
Sank o'er them soon. —I will not have thy look
Fix'd on me thus!—Away!
ELMINA.   Thou hast seen this,
Thou hast *done* this—and yet thou liv'st?
HERNANDEZ.   I live!
And know'st thou wherefore?—On my soul there fell
A horror of great darkness, which shut out
All earth, and heaven, and hope. I cast away
The spear and helm, and made the cloister's shade   380
The home of my despair. But a deep voice
Came to me through the gloom, and sent its tones
Far through my bosom's depths. And I awoke,
Aye, as the mountain cedar doth shake off
Its weight of wintry snow, e'en so I shook
Despondence from my soul, and knew myself
Seal'd by that blood wherewith my hands were dyed,[1] ∽
And set apart, and fearfully mark'd out
Unto a mighty task!—To rouse the soul
Of Spain, as from the dead; and to lift up   390
The cross, her sign of victory, on the hills,
Gathering her sons to battle!—And my voice
Must be as freedom's trumpet on the winds,
From Roncesvalles to the blue sea-waves
Where Calpe[2] looks on Afric; till the land

---

1 This blood seal evokes both Abraham's near-sacrifice of Isaac (Genesis 22.1-13) and
   God's sacrifice of his Son.
2 Part of the Gibraltar headland; for Roncesvalles, see Ximena's opening ballad (p. 45).

470 Have fill'd her cup of Vengeance, and her Soil
~~Drawn~~ Drunk deep—but not of Wine!—I live, to wage
Heaven's War against the Moslem!—Ask me now
To yield the Christian City, that its fanes
May rear the Minaret in the face of Heaven!
—But Death shall have a bloodier Vintage-feast
[400] Ere that Day come!—

ELMINA.   I ask thee this no more;
For I am hopeless now, as one who sees
The sword, awhile suspended o'er his head,
Flash in its fierce descent.—But yet one boon—
480 Hear me, by all thy Woes!—Thy Voice hath power
Throu' the wide city—here I cannot rest—
Aid me to pass the Gates!

HERNANDEZ.   And wherefore?

ELMINA.   Thou,
That <u>wert</u> a Father, and art now—alone!
Canst thou ask <u>this?</u>—Go, ask the Wretch, whose sands
Have not an hour to run, whose failing limbs
Have but one earthly journey to perform,
Why, on his pathway to the place of death,
[410] Aye, when the very Axe is glistening cold
Upon his dizzy sight, his pale, parch'd lip
490 Implores a cup of Water?—Why, the stroke
Which trembles o'er him, in itself shall bear
Oblivion of all wants; yet who denies
Nature's last prayer?—I tell thee that the thirst
Which burns my Spirit up, is Agony
To be endured no more! and I must look
Upon my Children's faces, I must hear
Their accents, ere they perish!—But hath Heaven
[420] Decreed that they <u>must</u> perish?—Who shall say,
If in yon Moslem camp there beats no heart
500 Which prayers and tears may melt?

HERNANDEZ.   There! With the Moor!
Let him fill up the measure of his guilt!
Till Earth's loud cry shall wake th'Avenger!—hence!
'Tis madness all!—How wouldst thou pass th' array
Of armed foes?

Have fill'd her cup of vengeance! — Ask me *now*
To yield the Christian city, that its fanes
May rear the minaret in the face of Heaven!
— But death shall have a bloodier vintage-feast
Ere that day come!

ELMINA.   I ask thee this no more,   400
For I am hopeless now. — But yet one boon —
Hear me, by all thy woes! — Thy voice hath power
Through the wide city — here I cannot rest: —
Aid me to pass the gates!

HERNANDEZ.   And wherefore?

ELMINA.   Thou,
That *wert* a father, and art now — alone!
Canst *thou* ask "wherefore?" — Ask the wretch whose sands
Have not an hour to run, whose failing limbs
Have but one earthly journey to perform,
Why, on his pathway to the place of death,
Aye, when the very axe is glistening cold   410
Upon his dizzy sight, his pale, parch'd lip
Implores a cup of water? — Why, the stroke
Which trembles o'er him in itself shall bring
Oblivion of all wants, yet who denies
Nature's last prayer? — I tell thee that the thirst
Which burns my spirit up is agony
To be endured no more! — And I *must* look
Upon my children's faces, I must hear
Their voices, ere they perish! — But hath Heaven
Decreed that they *must* perish? — Who shall say   420
If in yon Moslem camp there beats no heart
Which prayers and tears may melt?

HERNANDEZ.   There! — with the Moor!
Let him fill up the measure of his guilt!
— 'Tis madness all! — How wouldst thou pass th' array
Of armed foes?

ELMINA.   Oh! free doth Sorrow pass,
Free and unquestion'd, thro' a suffering World!
HERNANDEZ.
This must not be!—Enough of Woe is laid
E'en now, upon thy Lord's heroic Soul,
For man to bear, unsinking. Press thou not
[430]   Too heavily th' o'erburthen'd heart!—Away!
510   And bow the knee, and send thy prayers for strength
Up to Heaven's gate! So shalt thou rise, and gird
Thy Husband's armour on, and send him forth
With a prevailing Spirit, to fulfil
The Day's allotted Work.

                                        Exit HERNANDEZ.

ELMINA.   Are all Men thus?
—Why, wer't not better they should fall e'en now
Than live to shut their hearts, in haughty scorn,
Against the ~~suffering~~ Sufferer's pleadings?—But no, no!
Who can be like <u>this</u> Man, that slew his Son,
Yet wears his Life still proudly, and a Soul
520   Untam'd upon his brow?
(*After a pause.*)   There's One, whose arms
Have borne my Children in their infancy,
[440]   And on whose knees they sported, and whose hand
Hath led them oft—a Vassal of their Sire's,
And I will seek him; he may lend me aid
When all beside pass on.

ELMINA.   Oh! free doth sorrow pass,
Free and unquestion'd, through a suffering world!¹
HERNANDEZ.

This must not be. Enough of woe is laid
E'en now, upon thy lord's heroic soul,
For man to bear, unsinking. Press thou not
Too heavily th' o'erburthen'd heart. — Away!   430
Bow down the knee, and send thy prayers for strength
Up to Heaven's gate. — Farewell!

                                        Exit HERNANDEZ.

ELMINA.   Are all men thus?
— Why, wer't not better they should fall e'en now
Than live to shut their hearts, in haughty scorn,
Against the sufferer's pleadings? — But no, no!
Who can be like *this* man, that slew his son,
Yet wears his life still proudly, and a soul
Untamed upon his brow?
(After a pause)   There's one, whose arms
Have borne my children in their infancy,
And on whose knees they sported, and whose hand   440
Hath led them oft — a vassal of their sire's;
And I will seek him: he may lend me aid,
When all beside pass on.

---

1   Frey geht das Unglück durch die ganze Erde.
                            Schiller's Death of Wallenstein, act iv, sc. 2. [FH]
Thekla's remark (paraphrased by Elmina) on her daring to go through enemy lines to
seek the grave of her beloved, slain in battle. Friedrich von Schiller's *Wallensteins Tod* is
the last of his trilogy, *Wallenstein* (1798-9), about the fall of Thekla's father, Count von
Wallenstein, a seventeenth-century Bohemian general celebrated for his victories on
behalf of Ferdinand II but subsequently tempted by personal ambition. Thekla's sor-
row haunted Hemans: she frequently alludes to her suffering in the epigraphs and
notes to her poems; she translated a poem that Schiller wrote for a friend who won-
dered about her fate after her resolve to visit her lover's grave, *Thekla's Song; or, the Voice
of Spirit,—from the German of Schiller* (*New Monthly Magazine* 13, January 1825; rpt.
Forest Sanctuary &c 2d ed., 1829), and she shaped her own fantasy, *Thekla at Her Lover's
Grave* (*Songs of the Affections,* 1830).

DIRGE HEARD WITHOUT.

Thou to thy rest art gone,
High Heart! and what are We,
While o'er our heads the storm sweeps on,
That we should mourn for thee?

530

Free Grave and peaceful bier
To the buried Son of Spain!
[450] To those that live the Lance and Spear,
And well if not the chain!

Be theirs to weep the Dead
As they sit beneath their Vines,
Whose Land hath borne no Spoiler's tread
No Trampler o'er its shrines!

Thou hast thrown off the load
Which we must yet sustain,
540 And pour our blood where thine hath flowed,
Too blest if not in vain!

[460] We give thee holy rite,
~~Loud~~ Slow knell and chaunted strain:
— For those that fall to-morrow night,
May be left no Funeral train.

Again, when Trumpets wake,
We must brace our Armour on;
But a deeper note thy sleep must break,
— Thou to thy rest art gone!

550

Happier in this than all,
That, now thy race is run,
[470] Upon thy name no stain may fall,
Thy work hath well been done!

Thou to thy rest art gone,
High heart! and what are we,
While o'er our heads the storm sweeps on,
That we should mourn for thee?

Free grave and peaceful bier
To the buried son of Spain!
To those that live, the lance and spear,   450
And well if not the chain!

Be *theirs* to weep the dead
As they sit beneath their vines,
Whose flowery land hath borne no tread
Of spoilers o'er its shrines!

Thou hast thrown off the load
Which we must yet sustain,
And pour our blood where *thine* hath flow'd,
Too blest if not in vain!

We give thee holy rite,   460
Slow knell, and chaunted strain!
— For those that fall to-morrow night,
May be left no funeral-train.

Again, when trumpets wake,
We must brace our armour on;
But a deeper note *thy* sleep must break—
— Thou to thy rest art gone!

Happier in *this* than all,
That, now thy race is run,
Upon thy name no stain may fall,   470
Thy work hath well been done!

ELMINA. "Thy work hath well been done!" — So thou mayst rest!
   — There is a solemn lesson in those words —
   But now I may not pause!
   Oh, happy Slumberer! — Thou art where no eye
   Can wound thee with its scorn, no Voice can send
   The sting of its upbraidings thro' thy Soul!
560   Would it were thus with me!

Exit ELMINA.

SCENE [3]

Street in the City. GONSALVO, HERNANDEZ.

HERNANDEZ. Would they not hear?
GONSALVO.   They heard, as one that stands
   By the cold grave which hath but newly clos'd
   O'er his last friend, doth hear some Passer-by,
   Bid him take comfort! — Aye, as sick Men hear
   Of Festivals and Triumphs,[1] which but seem
   To mock the sense of pain. — Their hearts have died
   Within them! — We must perish, not as Those
   That fall when Battle's Voice doth shake the Hills,
   And peal thro' Heaven's great Arch, but silently,
10   And with a wasting of the Spirit down,
   A quenching, day by day, of some ~~bright~~ faint spark,
   Which lit us on our toils! — Reproach me not;
   My Soul is darken'd with a heavy cloud,
   The billows of conflicting thought are on me!
   — Yet fear not I shall yield.
HERNANDEZ.   Breathe not the word,
   Save in proud scorn! — Each bitter day, o'erpass'd
   By slow endurance is a triumph won
   For Spain's red Cross! — Doth not the struggling Land
   From the protraction of our Sufferings gain

[10]

---

1 *Festivals*: feast days, public celebrations; *Triumphs:* victory parades

ELMINA. "Thy work hath well been done!" — so thou mayst rest!
— There is a solemn lesson in those words — ⟨⟩
But now I may not pause.

Exit ELMINA.

SCENE [3]

A Street in the City. HERNANDEZ, GONZALEZ.

HERNANDEZ. Would they not hear?
GONZALEZ.   They heard, as one that stands
    By the cold grave which hath but newly closed
    O'er his last friend doth hear some passer-by,
    Bid him be comforted! — Their hearts have died
    Within them! — We must perish, not as those
    That fall when battle's voice doth shake the hills,
    And peal through Heaven's great arch, but silently,
    And with a wasting of the spirit down,
    A quenching, day by day, of some bright spark,
    Which lit us on our toils! — Reproach me not;   10
    My soul is darken'd with a heavy cloud —
    — Yet fear not I shall yield!
HERNANDEZ.   Breathe not the word,
    Save in proud scorn! — Each bitter day, o'erpass'd
    By slow endurance, is a triumph won
    For Spain's red cross.¹ And be of trusting heart!
    A few brief hours, and those that turn'd away

---

1   The emblem of Christian Spain, but the sanguinary connotation is relevant. Cf. 6.153.

20   The time she needed to arouse her Sons,
And gather all her might? — And take good heart!
A few brief hours, and those that turn'd away
In faint despondence, shrinking from your Voice,
May crowd around their Leader, and demand
To be array'd for Battle. Know you not
That they, or Men ~~on~~ in Multitudes, are but
The Slaves of impulse? — We must wait their hour,
As the Bark waits the Sea's; and then bear on,
Making their passions as the subject waves

[20]   30   O'er which we ride in triumph. You have chos'n
To kindle up their Souls, an hour, perchance,
When they were weary; they had cast aside
The helm to slumber; or a knell, just then,
With its deep hollow sound had made the blood
Creep shuddering thro' their veins; or they had caught
A glimpse of some new Meteor, and shap'd forth
Strange Omens from its blaze. Night is the time
Which makes all Phantoms powerful on the Earth,
All glooming thoughts, and bodings, and wild fears,

40   On human souls.

    GONSALVO.   Alas! a deeper cause
Lies in their Misery. I have seen to-night,

[30]   In my sad course thro' this beleaguer'd City,
Things, whose remembrance doth not pass away
As vapours from the Mountains! — There were some,
That sat beside their dead, with eyes, wherein
Grief had ta'en place of Sight; and shut out all
But its own ghastly object. To my words
Some answer'd with a fierce and bitter laugh,
As Men whose Agonies were made to pass

50   The bounds of sufferance, by the reckless looks,
Or the cold questionings of One, to whom
Life hath yet spar'd her lessons. Others lay —

[40]   — Why should I tell thee, Father! how Despair
Can bring the lofty brow of Manhood down
Unto the very dust? — They <u>have</u> striven well,
But Nature's strength hath limits. Yet for this,
Fear not that I embrace my doom — Oh God!

In cold despondence, shrinking from your voice,
May crowd around their leader, and demand
To be array'd for battle. We must watch
For the swift impulse, and await its time,   20
As the bark waits the ocean's. You have chosen
To kindle up their souls, an hour, perchance,
When they were weary; they had cast aside
Their arms to slumber; or a knell, just then
With its deep hollow tone, had made the blood
Creep shuddering through their veins; or they had caught
A glimpse of some new meteor, and shaped forth
Strange omens from its blaze.

GONZALEZ.   Alas! the cause
Lies deeper in their misery!—I have seen,
In my night's course through this beleaguer'd city   30
Things, whose remembrance doth not pass away
As vapours from the mountains. —There were some,
That sat beside their dead, with eyes, wherein
Grief had ta'en place of sight, and shut out all
But its own ghastly object. To my voice
Some answer'd with a fierce and bitter laugh,
As men whose agonies were made to pass
The bounds of sufferance, by some reckless word,
Dropt from the light of spirit. —Others lay —
—Why should I tell thee, father! how despair   40
Can bring the lofty brow of manhood down
Unto the very dust?—And yet for this,
Fear not that I embrace my doom—Oh God!

That 'twere <u>my</u> doom alone! —with less of fix'd
And solemn fortitude. —Lead on, prepare
60 The holiest rites of Faith, that I by them
Once more may consecrate my sword, my life—
—But what are these? —Who hath not dearer lives
Twined with his own? —I shall be lonely soon—
[50] Childless! —Heaven wills it so! —Let us away—
Perchance before the shrine my heart may beat
With a less troubled motion.[1]
HERNANDEZ.   Doubt thee not
But we shall yet prevail. Thick clouds may heap
Their dark embattled masses, and shut out
The Heaven's clear azure, but the Sun, tho' veil'd,
70 Is there, a Monarch still.[2] We shall not fall!
That Spirit is on us, whose prevailing Might
Works deeds that shall ~~not~~ be marvels, when Mankind
Shall call our times, the Past.
GONSALVO.   It is on <u>thee</u>.
—But we will die in honour, tho' our fate
Grant us not victory.

SCENE [4]

The Moorish Camp.

ABDULLAH— ALPHONSO—CARLOS.

ABDULLAH. These are bold words: but hast thou look'd on death,
Fair stripling? —Has thou set thy daring breast
Against the shock of spears, or with strong hand
Borne on, thro' flashing steel and arrowy shower,
The Banner of a Host? —On thy smooth cheek
Scarce fifteen Summers of their laughing course
Have left light traces. If thy shaft hath pierc'd
The [?—] Ibex of the Mountains, if thy step
Hath climb'd some Eagle's cliff, and thou hast made

---

1 Five pages, with writing, appear to be cut out of booklet 2 at this point.
2 The metaphor of the veiled sun, aided by the sound of "Son," implies Christian providence.

That 'twere *my* doom alone!—with less of fix'd
And solemn fortitude.—Lead on, prepare
The holiest rites of faith, that I by them
Once more may consecrate my sword, my life,
—But what are these?—Who hath not dearer lives
Twined with his own?—I shall be lonely soon—
Childless!—Heaven wills it so. Let us begone.   50
Perchance before the shrine my heart may beat
With a less troubled motion.

Exeunt GONZALEZ *and* HERNANDEZ.

SCENE [4]

A Tent in the Moorish Camp. ABDULLAH, ALPHONSO, CARLOS.

ABDULLAH. These are bold words: but hast thou look'd on death,
   Fair stripling?—On thy cheek and sunny brow
   Scarce fifteen summers of their laughing course
   Have left light traces. If thy shaft hath pierced
   The ibex of the mountains, if thy step
   Hath climb'd some eagle's nest, and thou hast made

10   His nest thy spoil, 'tis much! — And dost thou brave
The leader of the Mighty? — Fear'st thou not
The power whose stroke may crush thee?

ALPHONSO.   I have been
Rear'd amongst fearless Men; and midst the rocks
[10]   And the wild Hills, whereon my Fathers fought
And won their Battles. There are glorious tales
Told of their deeds, and I have learn'd them all.
How should I fear thee, Moor?

ABDULLAH *(scornfully)*.   So, thou hast seen
Fields, where the Combat's roar hath died away
Into the whispering breeze, and where wild flowers
20   Bloom o'er forgotten graves, and quiet flocks
Feed on the grassy Mounds which hide perchance,
The dust of Heroes! — Aye, but know'st thou aught
Of those where sword from crossing sword strikes fire,
And Leaders are ~~struck~~ borne down, and rushing steeds
Trample the life from out the mighty hearts
[20]   That rul'd the storm so late? — Speak not of death,
Till thou hast look'd on such.

ALPHONSO.   I was not born
A Shepherd's Son, to dwell with pipe and crook,
And peasant-Men, amidst the lowly Vales
30   Instead of [?—] ringing clarions, and bright spears,
And crested Knights. — I am of princely race;
And, if my Father would have heard my suit,
I tell thee, Infidel! that long ere now,
I should have seen how Warriors quit themselves
When their good mail is on, and how red swords
Do the field's work.

ABDULLAH.   Boy! know'st thou there are sights
[30]   A thousand times more fearful? — Men may die
Full proudly, when the Skies and Mountains ring
To Battle-horn and Tecbir. — But not all
40   So pass away in glory! There are those,
Midst the dead silence of pale Multitudes,
Led forth in fetters — dost thou mark me, Boy?
To take their last look of th' all gladdening Sun,
And bow, perchance, the stately Head of Youth,

His nest thy spoil, 'tis much! — And fear'st thou not
The leader of the mighty?

ALPHONSO.   I have been
Rear'd amongst fearless men, and midst the rocks
And the wild hills, whereon my fathers fought   10
And won their battles. There are glorious tales
Told of their deeds, and I have learn'd them all.
How should I fear thee, Moor?

ABDULLAH.   So, thou hast seen
Fields, where the combat's roar hath died away
Into the whispering breeze, and where wild flowers
Bloom o'er forgotten graves! — But know'st thou aught
Of those, where sword from crossing sword strikes fire,
And leaders are borne down, and rushing steeds
Trample the life from out the mighty hearts
That ruled the storm so late? — Speak not of death,   20
Till thou hast look'd on such.

ALPHONSO.   I was not born
A shepherd's son, to dwell with pipe and crook,
And peasant-men, amidst the lowly vales;
Instead of ringing clarions, and bright spears,
And crested knights! — I am of princely race,
And, if my father would have heard my suit,
I tell thee, infidel! that long ere now,
I should have seen how lances meet; and swords
Do the field's work.

ABDULLAH.   Boy! know'st thou there are sights
A thousand times more fearful? — Men may die   30
Full proudly, when the skies and mountains ring
To battle-horn and tecbir.[1] — But not all
So pass away in glory. There are those,
Midst the dead silence of pale multitudes,
Led forth in fetters — dost thou mark me, boy?
To take their last look of th' all gladdening sun,
And bow, perchance, the stately head of youth,

---

1   *Tecbir*, the war-cry of the Moors and Arabs. [FH]

Unto the death of shame. — Hadst thou seen this ———

ALPHONSO (*to* CARLOS).
　　Sweet Brother! God is with us — fear thou not!
[40]　We have had Heroes for our Sires; this Man
　　Should not behold us tremble.

ABDULLAH.　　　　　　　　There are means
　　To tame the loftiest Natures. Yet again,
50　I ask thee, wilt thou, from beneath the Walls,
　　Sue to thy Sire for life, or wouldst thou die,
　　With this, thy Brother?

ALPHONSO.　　　　　　Moslem! on the Hills,
　　Around my Father's Castle, I have heard
　　The Mountain-Peasants, as they dress'd the Vines,
　　Or drove the Goats, by rock and torrent, home,
　　Singing their ancient songs, and these were all
[50]　Of the Cid Campeador; and how his sword
　　Tizona clear'd its way through turban'd Hosts,
　　And captur'd Afric's Kings, and how he won
60　Valencia from the Moor; and in good hour
　　Still ~~fought~~ arm'd for Spain. — He was mine Ancestor —
　　I will not shame his blood.

A Moorish Soldier enters

SOLDIER.　　　　　　　　Valencia's lord
　　Sends Messengers, my Chief.

ABDULLAH.　　　　　　　Conduct them hither.

(*The Soldier departs and returns with* ELMINA
disguised, and DIEGO)

Unto the death of shame!—Hadst thou seen this—

ALPHONSO (*to* CARLOS).

Sweet brother, God is with us—fear thou not!
We have had heroes for our sires—this man   40
Should not behold us tremble.

ABDULLAH.   There are means
To tame the loftiest natures. Yet again,
I ask thee, wilt thou, from beneath the walls,
Sue to thy sire for life; or wouldst thou die,
With this, thy brother?

ALPHONSO.   Moslem! on the hills,
Around my father's castle, I have heard
The mountain-peasants, as they dress'd the vines,
Or drove the goats, by rock and torrent, home,
Singing their ancient songs; and these were all
Of the Cid Campeador; and how his sword   50
Tizona[1] clear'd its way through turban'd hosts,
And captured Afric's kings, and how he won
Valencia from the Moor.[2]——I will not shame
The blood we draw from him!

(A *Moorish Soldier enters*).

SOLDIER.   Valencia's lord
Sends messengers, my chief.

ABDULLAH.   Conduct them hither.

The Soldier goes out, and re-enters with ELMINA,
disguised, and an Attendant.

---

1 Tizona, the fire-brand. The name of the Cid's favourite sword, taken in battle from the
   Moorish king Bucar. [FH]
   See Southey, *Chronicle*, Bk.8.VIII (259); cf. *The Cid's Funeral Procession* 82.
2 Valencia, which has been repeatedly besieged, and taken by the armies of different
   nations, remained in the possession of the Moors for an hundred and seventy years
   after the Cid's death. It was regained from them by King Don Jayme of Aragon, sur-
   named the Conqueror; after whose success I have ventured to suppose it governed by a
   descendant of the Campeador. [FH]
   After its conquest by James I in 1238, the city rose to cultural and commercial promi-
   nence.

CARLOS (*springing forward to* DIEGO).

Oh! take me hence, Diego, take me hence
With thee, that I may see my Mother's face
At Morning, when I wake. Here dark-brow'd Men
Frown strangely, with their cruel eyes, upon us!
[60]   Take me with thee, for thou art good and kind,
And well I know, thou lov'st me!
70 ABDULLAH. Peace, Boy!—What tidings, Christian, from thy Lord?
Fate hath a power in her all-conquering hands
To bow the Mightiest—hath it work'd with him?
Is he grown humble?— doth he set the lives
Of these fair Nurslings at a City's worth?
ALPHONSO (*rushing forward impetuously*).

Say not, he doth!—Yet wherefore art thou here?
If it be so—I could weep burning tears
For very shame!—If this <u>can</u> be, return!
Tell him, of all his Wealth, his battle-spoils,
[69]   I will but ask a War-horse and a sword,
80   And in his Halls and at his stately feasts,
And by his side when girding on the mail,
~~My heart~~ [?—'d] ~~far~~ [?—] ~~to behold~~
Which with rejoicing heart, I have borne him oft;
My place shall be no more!—but no! I wrong,
My Father!—he hath taught me nobler things—
He is a Champion ~~on~~ of the Cross and Spain!
Sprung from the Cid!—And I too—I can die,
As a Warrior's high-born Child!
ELMINA. Alas! Alas! And wouldst thou die, fair Boy?
90   What hath Life done to thee, that thou shouldst cast
Its flower away, in very scorn of heart,
[80]   Ere yet the blight be come?
ALPHONSO.   That voice doth sound———
ABDULLAH. Stranger, who art thou?—this is mockery, speak!
ELMINA (*throwing off a mantle and helmet, embraces her Sons*).

My Boys! whom I have rear'd thro' many hours
Of silent joys and sorrows, and deep thoughts
Untold and unimagined; let me die
With you, now I have held you to my heart,

CARLOS (*springing forward to the Attendant*).
Oh! take me hence, Diego; take me hence
With thee, that I may see my mother's face
At morning, when I wake. Here dark-brow'd men
Frown strangely, with their cruel eyes, upon us.
Take me with thee, for thou art good and kind,   60
And well I know, thou lov'st me, my Diego!
ABDULLAH. Peace, boy!—What tidings, Christian, from thy lord?
Is he grown humbler, doth he set the lives
Of these fair nurslings at a city's worth?
ALPHONSO (*rushing forward impatiently*).
Say not, he doth!—Yet wherefore art thou here?
If it be so—I could weep burning tears
For very shame!—If this *can* be, return!
Tell him, of all his wealth, his battle-spoils,
I will but ask a war-horse and a sword,
And that beside him in the mountain-chase,   70
And in his halls and at his stately feasts,
My place shall be no more!—but no!—I wrong,
I wrong my father!—Moor! believe it not!
He is a champion of the cross and Spain,
Sprung from the Cid;—and I too, I can die
As a warrior's high-born child!
ELMINA.   Alas! Alas!
And wouldst thou die, thus early die, fair boy?
What hath life done to thee, that thou shouldst cast
Its flower away, in very scorn of heart,
Ere yet the blight be come?
ALPHONSO.   That voice doth sound——   80
ABDULLAH. Stranger, who art thou?—this is mockery! speak!
ELMINA (*throwing off a mantle and helmet, and embracing her sons*).
My boys! whom I have rear'd through many hours
Of silent joys and sorrows, and deep thoughts
Untold and unimagined; let me die
With you, now I have held you to my heart,

And seen once more the faces, in whose light
My soul hath liv'd for years!

CARLOS.   Sweet Mother! now
100   Thou shalt not leave us more.

ABDULLAH *(sternly)*.   Enough of this!
Woman! what seek'st thou here? — How hast thou dar'd
[90]   To front the Mighty thus amidst his Host?

ELMINA. Think'st thou there dwells no Courage, but that which
           makes
Its breast a sheath for hostile swords? — No Strength,
Save in the mail-girt arm, whose withering stroke
Is felt thro' desolate Houses, unto which
Their Sons return no more? — Thou little know'st
Of Nature's marvels! — ~~Chief!~~ Moor! my heart is nerv'd
To make its way through things which Warrior-Men,
110   — Aye, they that master Death by field and flood,
Would look on, ~~their~~ ere they brav'd! — I have no thought,
No sense of fear. Thou'rt Mighty! but a Soul
Wound up like mine, is mightier, in the power
[100]   Of that one feeling, pour'd thro' all its depths,
Than Monarchs with their Hosts! — Am I not come
To die with these, my Children?

ABDULLAH.   Doth thy faith
Bid thee do this, fond Christian? — Hast thou not
The means to save them?

ELMINA.   I have prayers, and tears,
And agonies! And He, my God — the God,
120   Whose hand, or soon or late, doth find its hour
To bow the crested head; hath made these things
Most powerful in a World where all must learn
That lone deep language, by the Storm call'd forth,
[110]   From the bruised reeds of Earth! — For thee, perchance,
Affliction's chastening lesson hath not yet
Been laid upon thy heart, and thou mayst love
To see the Creatures, by its might brought low,
Humbled before thee! Conqueror! I can kneel;

She throws herself at his feet.

And seen once more the faces, in whose light
  My soul hath lived for years!
CARLOS.   Sweet mother! now
  Thou shalt not leave us more.
ABDULLAH.   Enough of this!
  Woman! what seek'st thou here? — How hast thou dared
  To front the mighty thus amidst his hosts?   90
ELMINA. Think'st thou there dwells no courage but in breasts
  That set their mail against the ringing spears,
  When helmets are struck down? — Thou little know'st
  Of nature's marvels! — Chief! my heart is nerved
  To make its way through things which warrior-men,
  — Aye, they that master death by field or flood,[1]
  Would look on, ere they braved! — I have no thought,
  No sense of fear! — Thou'rt mighty! but a soul
  Wound up like mine is mightier, in the power
  Of that one feeling, pour'd through all its depths,   100
  Than monarchs with their hosts! — Am I not come
  To die with these, my children?
ABDULLAH.   Doth thy faith
  Bid thee do this, fond Christian? — Hast thou not
  The means to save them?
ELMINA.   I have prayers, and tears,
  And agonies! — and he — my God — the God
  Whose hand, or soon or late, doth find its hour
  To bow the crested head — hath made these things
  Most powerful in a world where all must learn
  That lone deep language, by the storm call'd forth
  From the bruised reeds of earth! — For thee, perchance,   110
  Affliction's chastening lesson hath not yet
  Been laid upon thy heart, and thou may'st love
  To see the creatures, by its might brought low,
  Humbled before thee.

                    She throws herself at his feet.

---

1   Another echo of Othello's story of his life (*Othello* 1.3.133-34).

I, that drew birth from Princes, bow myself
130   E'en to thy feet!—Despair may well cast off
The robe of pride!—Call in thy Chiefs, thy Slaves,
If this will swell thy triumph, to behold
The blood of Kings, of Heroes, thus abas'd!
Do this, but spare my Sons!

ALPHONSO *(attempting to raise his Mother).*
                 Thou shouldst not kneel

[120]   Unto this Infidel!—Rise, rise, My mother!
This sight doth shame our House.

ABDULLAH.   Thou daring Boy!
They that in arms have taught thy Father's Land
How chains are worn, shall school that haughty mien
Unto another language.

ELMINA.   Peace, my Son!
140   Have pity on my heart!—Oh, pardon, Chief!
He is of warrior-blood.—Hear, hear me yet!
Are there no lives, thro' which the shafts of Heaven
May reach your Soul?—He that loves aught on Earth,

[129]   Dares far too much, if he be merciless!
Doth he, in his mortality, think to stand
Seal'd for exemption from the mighty Law
Whose worth is Retribution?—Is't for those,
That one day, in their feebleness, must strive
Alone with God and Death, to bar their Souls,
150   Against th' appeal of Nature, in the hour
Of her extremest misery?—Warrior! Man!
To you too, aye, and haply with your Host
By thousands and ten thousands marshall'd round,
And your strong armour on, shall come that stroke
Which the Lance wards not!—Where shall your proud Heart
Find refuge then, if in the day of ~~power~~ might,
Woe hath lain prostrate, bleeding at your feet,

[140]   And you have pitied not?

ABDULLAH.   These are vain words.
Think'st thou to make me tremble at the thought
160   Of Death?—His power is not o'er Kingly hearts.

ELMINA. Have you no Children?—fear you not to bring

Conqueror! I can kneel!
I, that drew birth from princes, bow myself
E'en to thy feet! Call in thy chiefs, thy slaves,
If this will swell thy triumph, to behold
The blood of kings, of heroes, thus abased!
Do this, but spare my sons!
ALPHONSO *(attempting to raise her).*
                              Thou shouldst not kneel
Unto this infidel!—Rise, rise, my mother!   120
This sight doth shame our house!
ABDULLAH.   Thou daring boy!
They that in arms have taught thy father's land
How chains are worn, shall school that haughty mien
Unto another language.
ELMINA.   Peace, my son!
Have pity on my heart!—Oh, pardon, Chief!
He is of noble blood!—Hear, hear me yet!
Are there no lives through which the shafts of Heaven
May reach your soul?—He that loves aught on earth,
Dares far too much, if he be merciless!
Is it for those, whose frail mortality   130
Must one day strive alone with God and death,
To shut their souls against th' appealing voice
Of nature, in her anguish?—Warrior! Man!
To you too, aye, and haply with your hosts,
By thousands and ten thousands marshall'd round,
And your strong armour on, shall come that stroke
Which the lance wards not!—Where shall your high heart
Find refuge then, if in the day of might
Woe hath lain prostrate, bleeding at your feet,
And you have pitied not?
ABDULLAH.   These are vain words.   140
ELMINA. Have you no children?—fear you not to bring

The Lightning on their heads? Oh, far less guilt
Hath oft suffic'd for this!—In your own Land
Doth no fond Mother, from the tents, beneath
Your native Palms, look ~~on~~ o'er the Deserts out,
To greet your homeward step?—You have not yet
Forgot so utterly the patient love—
Wherewith she nurtur'd you;—(for Woman's heart
Doth, in all climes, alike devote itself,)
170 That you should scorn <u>my</u> prayer!—Oh Heaven! his eye
Doth wear no Mercy!
    ABDULLAH.   Then it mocks you not.
Think you, if hearts were not of sterner Mould
Than to be borne away by Woman's tears,
From their high place, that Kingdoms would be won,
And Nations change their Lords?— I have swept o'er

[150] The Mountains of your Country, leaving there,
My traces, as the visitings of Storms
Which upon Earth make Æras; and to me
It were no more to quench your Children's lives,
180 In this, my path of conquest, than to one
Who journeys through a Forest, 'tis to break
The young green branches that obstruct his way,
With their light sprays and leaves.
    ELMINA.   Are there such hearts
Amongst thy works, Oh God?
    ABDULLAH.   Kneel not to me.
My course is to Dominion, and I pass
~~In my lone Spirit's triumphant recklessness~~
O'er all that stands between me and the goal
Of that proud March; ~~as in the fiery clime~~ e'en as the Desert-
    winds
~~Which gives me~~ [?—], ~~the winds,~~ [?—] ~~whirl~~
190 In mine own clime go forth, and ~~o'er the waste~~ scatter [?death]
~~The Desert~~ [?————————?]
From their fire-wings, and pause not for the moan
~~Check not their wings' fleet rushing;~~
Rush on their course, {and pause not for the Moan}
Made above that they slay. Kneel not to me!
Kneel to your Lord! On his resolves doth hang

The lightning on their heads?—In your own land
Doth no fond mother, from the tents, beneath
Your native palms, look o'er the deserts out,
To greet your homeward step?—You have not yet
Forgot so utterly her patient love—
—For is not woman's, in all climes, the same?—
That you should scorn *my* prayer!—Oh Heaven! his eye
Doth wear no mercy!
ABDULLAH.   Then it mocks you not.
I have swept o'er the mountains of your land,   150
Leaving my traces, as the visitings
Of storms, upon them!—Shall I now be stay'd!
Know, unto me it were as light a thing,
In this, my course, to quench your children's lives,
As, journeying through a forest, to break off
The young wild branches that obstruct the way
With their green sprays and leaves.
ELMINA.   Are there such hearts
Amongst thy works, oh God?
ABDULLAH.   Kneel not to me.
Kneel to your lord! on his resolves doth hang

[160]   His Children's doom. He may be lightly won
         By a few bursts of [?——] passionate words and tears.
       ELMINA *(rising indignantly).*
         Speak not of noble Men!—He bears a soul
200   Stronger than Love or Death!
       ALPHONSO *(exultingly).*   I knew 'twas thus!
         He could not fail!
       ELMINA.   There is no mercy, none,
         On this cold Earth!—Vice is too hard of heart,
         And Virtue, in her calm austerity,
         Too lofty, to relent!—We will go hence,
         My children, we are summon'd! Lay your heads,
         In [?——] their young glorious beauty once again
         To rest upon this bosom!—He that dwells
[170]   Beyond the clouds which press us darkly round,
         Will yet have pity! And before his face
210   We three will stand together!—Moslem, now
         Let the stroke fall, [?——] that we ~~will~~ may taste of death
         Thus mingled, and at once!
       ABDULLAH.   'Tis thine own will.
         These might e'en yet be spar'd.
       ELMINA.   <u>Thou</u> wilt not spare!
         And He beneath whose eye their Childhood grew,
         And ~~on~~ in whose ~~knees~~ paths they sported, and whose ear
         From their first lisping accents caught the sound
         Of that word—<u>Father</u>—once a name of Love—
         Is——Men shall call him <u>stedfast</u>!
       ABDULLAH.   Hath the note
         Of sudden Trumpet's ne'er, at dead of Night,
220   When the Land's Watchers fear'd no hostile step,
         Startled the Slumberers from their dreamy World,
         In Cities, whose heroic Lords have been
         <u>Stedfast</u> as thine?
       ELMINA.   There's meaning in thine eye,
         More than thy Words.
       ABDULLAH *(pointing to the City).*
                 Look to yon towers and walls!
          Think you their limits girds ~~in~~ no pining hearts,
         Weary of ~~hoping~~ hopeless Warfare, and prepar'd

His children's doom. He may be lightly won

By a few bursts of passionate tears and words.

ELMINA *(rising indignantly)*. Speak not of noble men!—he bears a
    soul

Stronger than love or death.

ALPHONSO *(with exultation)*.   I knew 'twas thus!
  He could not fail!

ELMINA.   There is no mercy, none,

  On this cold earth!—To strive with such a world,

  Hearts should be void of love!—We will go hence,

  My children! we are summon'd. Lay your heads,

  In their young radiant beauty, once again

  To rest upon this bosom. He that dwells

  Beyond the clouds which press us darkly round,

  Will yet have pity, and before his face

  We three will stand together! Moslem! now

  Let the stroke fall at once!

ABDULLAH.   'Tis thine own will.

  These might e'en yet be spared.

ELMINA.   *Thou* wilt not spare!

  And he beneath whose eye their childhood grew,

  And in whose paths they sported, and whose ear

  From their first lisping accents caught the sound

  Of that word—*Father*—once a name of love—

  Is——Men shall call him *stedfast*.

ABDULLAH.   Hath the blast

  Of sudden trumpets ne'er at dead of night,

  When the land's watchers fear'd no hostile step,

  Startled the slumberers from their dreamy world,

  In cities, whose heroic lords have been

  Stedfast as thine?

ELMINA.   There's meaning in thine eye,

  More than thy words.

ABDULLAH *(pointing to the city)*.

                Look to yon towers and walls!

  Think you no hearts within their limits pine,

  Weary of hopeless warfare, and prepared

160

170

180

To burst the feeble links which bind them yet
Unto endurance?

ELMINA.   Well I know it doth.
But what of this?

[190] ABDULLAH.   Then there are those, to whom
230   The Prophet's Armies not as foes would pass
Yon Gates, but as Deliverers! — Might they not,
In some still hour, when Weariness takes rest,
Be won to welcome us? — Your Children's steps
May yet bound lightly thro' their Father's Halls!

ALPHONSO *(indignantly)*.
Thou treacherous Moor!

ELMINA.   Let me not thus be tried
Beyond all strength, Oh Heaven!

ABDULLAH.   Now, 'tis for <u>thee,</u>
Thou Christian Mother! on thy Sons ~~would~~ to pass
The sentence — Life or Death! — The price is set
[200]   On their young lives, and rests within thy hands.

240 ALPHONSO. Mother! thou tremblest!

ABDULLAH.   Hath thy heart resolv'd?

ELMINA *(covering her face with her hands)*.
My Boy's proud eye is on me, and the things
Which rush, in stormy darkness, o'er my soul,
Shrink from his look! — I cannot answer <u>here.</u>

ABDULLAH. Come forth! We'll commune elsewhere.

CARLOS *(to his Mother)*.   Wilt thou go?
Oh! let me follow thee!

ELMINA.   Mine own fair Child!
Now that thine eyes have pour'd once more on mine
The light of their young smile, and thy sweet Voice
Hath sent its gentle music through my heart,
[210]   And I have felt the twining of thine arms —
250   How shall I leave thee?

ABDULLAH.   Leave him, as 'twere but
For a brief slumber, to behold his face
At Morning, with the Sun's.

ALPHONSO.   Thou hast no look
For me, my Mother!

To burst the feeble links which bind them still
Unto endurance?
ELMINA.   Thou hast said too well.
  But what of this?
ABDULLAH.   Then there are those, to whom   190
  The Prophet's armies not as foes would pass
  Yon gates, but as deliverers. Might they not
  In some still hour, when weariness takes rest,
  Be won to welcome us? — Your children's steps
  May yet bound lightly through their father's halls!
ALPHONSO *(indignantly)*.
  Thou treacherous Moor!
ELMINA.   Let me not thus be tried
  Beyond all strength, oh Heaven!
ABDULLAH.   Now, 'tis for *thee*,
  Thou Christian mother! on thy sons to pass
  The sentence — life or death! — the price is set
  On their young blood, and rests within thy hands.   200
ALPHONSO. Mother! thou tremblest!
ABDULLAH.   Hath thy heart resolved?
ELMINA *(covering her face with her hands)*.
  My boy's proud eye is on me, and the things
  Which rush, in stormy darkness, through my soul,
  Shrink from his glance. I cannot answer *here*.
ABDULLAH. Come forth. We'll commune elsewhere.
CARLOS *(to his mother)*.   Wilt thou go?
  Oh! let me follow thee!
ELMINA.   Mine own fair child!
  — Now that thine eyes have pour'd once more on mine
  The light of their young smile, and thy sweet voice
  Hath sent its gentle music through my soul,
  And I have felt the twining of thine arms —   210
  — How shall I leave thee?
ABDULLAH.   Leave him, as 'twere but
  For a brief slumber, to behold his face
  At morning, with the sun's.
ALPHONSO.   Thou hast no look
  For me, my mother!

ELMINA *(embracing him).* Oh! that I should live
    To say, I <u>dare</u> not look on thee!—farewell!
    My first born, fare thee well!
ALPHONSO.   Yet, yet beware!
    It were a grief more heavy on thy Soul,
    That I should blush for thee, than o'er my grave
    That thou shouldst proudly weep!
ABDULLAH *(impatiently).*
[220]   Away! we trifle here. The Night wanes fast.
260   I will not thus be mock'd.

                    (Exit, ELMINA *& her Attendant)*

ALPHONSO. Hear me once more, my Mother!—art thou gone?
    But one word more!

                He rushes out, followed by CARLOS.

SCENE [5]

The Garden of a Palace in Valencia—Morning.

XIMENA—THERESA

THERESA. Stay yet awhile. A purer air doth rove
    Here thro' the myrtles whispering, and the limes,
    And shaking sweetness from the Orange-boughs,
    Than waits you in the City.
XIMENA.   There are those
    In their last need, and on their bed of death,
    At which no hand doth minister but mine
    That wait me in the City. Let us hence.
THERESA. Doth not enough of Sorrow load your heart,
    But on its burden'd strength you still must lay
10   The woes of others?
XIMENA.   These are idle words!
    We have no thoughts, no use, <u>until</u> our hearts,

ELMINA.   Oh! that I should live
     To say, I *dare* not look on thee! — Farewell,
     My first born, fare thee well!
ALPHONSO.   Yet, yet beware!
     It were a grief more heavy on thy soul,
     That I should blush for thee, than o'er my grave
     That thou shouldst proudly weep!
ABDULLAH. Away! we trifle here. The night wanes fast.   220
     Come forth!
ELMINA.   One more embrace! My sons, farewell!

          Exeunt ABDULLAH *with* ELMINA *and her Attendant.*

ALPHONSO. Hear me yet once, my mother!
                              Art thou gone?
     But one word more!

          He rushes out, followed by CARLOS.

                    SCENE [5]

          The Garden of a Palace in Valencia. XIMENA, THERESA

THERESA. Stay yet awhile. A purer air doth rove
     Here through the myrtles whispering, and the limes,
     And shaking sweetness from the orange boughs,
     Than waits you in the city.
XIMENA.   There are those
     In their last need, and on their bed of death,
     At which no hand doth minister but mine
     That wait me in the city. Let us hence.
THERESA. You have been wont to love the music made
     By founts, and rustling foliage, and soft winds,
     Breathing of citron-groves. And will you turn   10
     From these to scenes of death?
XIMENA.   To me the voice
     Of summer, whispering through young flowers and leaves,

Have felt Life's pressure on them. While we sleep,
Fann'd by soft winds, on rose-leaves, human Grief,
Hath little place or share i' the sunny World
Of human dreams! — I have linger'd here too long.
We must begone.

THERESA.   You have been wont to love
Young flowers and verdure, and music made
By founts, and rustling foliage, and light gales
That breath of Citron-groves. ~~Now grow all these,~~ And will you
[10]   turn
20   ~~You turn~~ From these to scenes of death?

XIMENA.   To me these things
~~Mantled now with sadness / Are fraught with deep sadness;~~
Now breathe mysterious sadness; for they seem
As made for, and with all the secret Soul
Which murmurs in their dreaming melodies,
From some far World invoking that, whose place
Is not amongst us — Happiness! — My heart
Now finds no room, save where high thoughts and powers
Are call'd from its deep places.

THERESA.   Yet, e'en yet,
All may be well! — Alas! the time hath been
30   When Hope look'd forth, like Spring-time, from your eye,
And shone thro' all dark bosoms!

XIMENA.   I have felt
That summons thro' my Spirit, after which
The hues of Earth are chang'd! — Aye, there is cause,
That I should bend my footsteps to the Scenes
[20]   Where Death is busy, taming steel-clad hearts,
And pouring Winter thro' the fiery blood,
And fettering the strong arm! — For now no sound
In the dull air, nor floating cloud in Heaven,
No, not the lightest whisper of a leaf,
40   But of his Angel's silent coming bears
Some token to my Soul. But nought of this
Unto my Mother! — These are awful hours!
And on their heavy steps Afflictions crowd
With such dark pressure, there is left no room
[30]   For one grief more!

Now speaks too deep a language! and of all
Its dreamy and mysterious melodies,
The breathing soul is sadness! — I have felt
That summons through my spirit, after which
The hues of earth are changed, and all her sounds
Seem fraught with secret warnings. — There is cause
That I should bend my footsteps to the scenes
Where Death is busy, taming warrior-hearts,   20
And pouring winter through the fiery blood,
And fettering the strong arm! — For now no sigh
In the dull air, nor floating cloud in heaven,
No, not the lightest murmur of a leaf,
But of his angel's silent coming bears
Some token to my soul. — But nought of this
Unto my mother! — These are awful hours!
And on their heavy steps, afflictions crowd
With such dark pressure, there is left no room
For one grief more.

THERESA.   Sweet Lady, talk not thus!
Your eye this Morn doth wear a calmer light,
There's more of life in its clear tremulous brightness
Than I have mark'd of late. Nay, go not yet.
Rest by this fountain, where the laurels dip
50   Their glossy leaves. A fresher breeze doth ~~play~~ spring
~~Still o'er the bubbling waters~~
From the transparent waters, dashing round
~~Their bright spray with a sweet~~ [?tone], 'twill call up
Their silvery spray, with a sweet voice of coolness,
O'er the pale glistening marble; 'twill call up
Faint bloom, if but a Moment's, to your Cheek.
[40]   Rest here, ere you go forth, and I will sing
The melody you love.

THERESA *sings.*

Why is the Spanish Maiden's grave
60   So far from her own bright Land?
The sunny flowers that o'er it wave
Were sown by no kindred hand!

'Tis not the Orange-bough that sends
Its breath on the sultry air;
'Tis not the myrtle-stem that bends
To the breeze of Evening there!

[50]   But the Rose of Sharon's eastern bloom
O'er the Desert's ~~sleep~~ Slumberer fades,
And none but Strangers pass the tomb
70   Which the Palm of Judah shades!

And why hath Sculpture on the stone,
Which guards that place of rest,

THERESA.   Sweet lady, talk not thus!   30
Your eye this morn doth wear a calmer light,
There's more of life in its clear tremulous ray
Than I have mark'd of late. Nay, go not yet;
Rest by this fountain, where the laurels dip
Their glossy leaves. A fresher gale doth spring
From the transparent waters, dashing round
Their silvery spray, with a sweet voice of coolness,
O'er the pale glistening marble. 'Twill call up
Faint bloom, if but a moment's, to your cheek.
Rest here, ere you go forth, and I will sing   40
The melody you love.

THERESA *sings.*[1]

Why is the Spanish maiden's grave
    So far from her own bright land?
The sunny flowers that o'er it wave
    Were sown by no kindred hand.

'Tis not the orange-bough that sends
    Its breath on the sultry air,
'Tis not the myrtle-stem that bends
    To the breeze of evening there!

But the Rose of Sharon's eastern bloom[2]   50
    By the silent dwelling fades,
And none but strangers pass the tomb
    Which the Palm of Judah shades.

The lowly Cross, with flowers o'ergrown,
    Marks well that place of rest;

---

1   The scene of this song, during the medieval Crusades against Arab "infidels," reflects
     the strife between Christian Spaniard and Muslim Moor. It also involves heroic female
     martyrdom, in the person of a warrior Spanish maiden, a twin to Ximena's longings.
2   A showy flower, named for the Plain of Sharon in Palestine. The Palm of Judah (53)
     is named for the son of Jacob, tribal patriarch of Israel. Myrtle (48) is an emblem of
     love.

Blunt with the Cross o'er a grave unknown,
A sword, a helm, a crest?

These are the trophies of a Chief,
A Lord of the Axe and Spear!
[60] Some broken flower, some faded leaf,
Should mark a Maiden's bier.

Scorn not her tomb!—Deny not Her,
80 The emblems of the Brave!
O'er that forsaken Sepulchre,
Banner and Plume might wave.

She bound the steel, in Battle tried,
Her Woman's heart above,
And stood with brave Men, side by side,
In the strength and faith of Love!

[70] That strength prevail'd—that faith was blest!
—True was the Javelin thrown,
Yet pierc'd it not her Warrior's breast,
90 She made it sheath her own.

And there she won, where Heroes fell
In arms for the Holy Shrine,
A Death which sav'd what she lov'd so well,
And a grave in Palestine.

Then let the rose of Sharon spread
Its breast to the silent air,
[80] And the Palm of Judah lift its head,
Green and immortal there!

And let that grey stone, undefac'd,
100 With its trophy mark the Scene,

But who hath graved, on its mossy stone,
A sword, a helm, a crest?

These are the trophies of a chief,
A lord of the axe and spear!
—Some blossom pluck'd, some faded leaf,   60
Should grace a maiden's bier!

Scorn not her tomb—deny not her
The honours of the brave!
O'er that forsaken sepulchre,
Banner and plume might wave.

She bound the steel, in battle tried,
Her fearless heart above,
And stood with brave men, side by side,
In the strength and faith of love![1]

That strength prevail'd—that faith was bless'd!   70
True was the javelin thrown,
Yet pierced it not her warrior's breast,
She met it with her own!

And nobly won, where heroes fell
In arms for the holy shrine,
A death which saved what she loved so well,
And a grave in Palestine.

Then let the Rose of Sharon spread
Its breast to the glowing air,
And the Palm of Judah lift its head,   80
Green and immortal there!

And let yon grey stone, undefaced,
With its trophy mark the scene,

---

1 The maiden disguised as page or soldier in order to join her beloved in wartime is a
literary convention at least as old as Sidney's *Arcadia*; it was romanticized in Hemans's
day by Byron's *Lara* (1814).

Telling the pilgrim of the Waste,
Where Love and Death have been.

XIMENA. Those notes were wont to make my heart beat quick,
As ~~without~~ at a Voice of triumph, but to-day
The Spirit of the Song is chang'd, and seems
All mournful. Oh! that ere my early grave
[90]   Shuts out the sunbeam, I might hear one blast
Of the Castilian Trumpet, peeling forth,
Beneath my Father's Banner! — In that sound
110   Were Life to you, Sweet Brothers! — But for me —
— Come on — our tasks await us. They who know
Their hours are number'd forth, have little time
To give the vague and slumberous languor way,
Which doth steal o'er them in the breath of flowers,
And whisper of soft winds.

ELMINA *enters hurriedly.*

ELMINA. This air may calm my Spirit, ere yet I meet
[100]   <u>His</u> eye, which must be met. — Thou here, Ximena!

She starts back on seeing XIMENA.

XIMENA. Alas! My mother! In that troubled glance
And hurrying step I read —
ELMINA *(wildly).*   Thou read'st it not!
120   Why, who would live, if unto mortal eye
The things lay glaring, which within our hearts,
~~La~~ Locking the sunbeam from their fastnesses
We treasure up for God's? — Thou read'st it not!
I say, thou canst not! — There's not one on Earth,
Shall know the thoughts which for themselves have found
And kept dark places, in the very breast
Whereon he hath laid his slumber, till the day
[110]   When the Graves open!
XIMENA.   Mother! what is this?
~~Alas!~~ Alas! your eye is wandering, and your cheek
130   Flush'd, as with fever! To your woes the Night

Telling the pilgrim of the waste,
　　Where Love and Death have been.

XIMENA. Those notes were wont to make my heart beat quick,
　　As at a voice of victory; but to-day
　　The spirit of the song is changed, and seems
　　All mournful. Oh! that ere my early grave
　　Shuts out the sunbeam, I might hear one peal   90
　　Of the Castilian trumpet, ringing forth
　　Beneath my father's banner! — In that sound
　　Were life to you, sweet brothers! — But for me —
　　Come on — our tasks await us. They who know
　　Their hours are number'd out, have little time
　　To give the vague and slumberous languor way,
　　Which doth steal o'er them in the breath of flowers,
　　And whisper of soft winds.

　　　　　　　　　　　　　　　ELMINA *enters hurriedly.*

ELMINA. This air will calm my spirit, ere yet I meet
　　His eye, which must be met. — Thou here, Ximena!   100

　　　　　　She starts back on seeing XIMENA.

XIMENA. Alas! my mother! In that hurrying step
　　And troubled glance I read —
ELMINA *(wildly).*　　　　　　Thou read'st it not!
　　Why, who would live, if unto mortal eye
　　The things lay glaring, which within our hearts
　　We treasure up for God's? — Thou read'st it not!
　　I say, thou canst not! — There's not one on earth
　　Shall know the thoughts, which for themselves have made
　　And kept dark places in the very breast
　　Whereon he hath laid his slumber, till the hour
　　When the graves open!
XIMENA.　　　　　　Mother! what is this?   110
　　Alas! your eye is wandering, and your cheek
　　Flush'd, as with fever! To your woes the night

Hath brought no rest.

ELMINA.   Rest! — who should rest? — not He
That holds one earthly blessing to his heart,
Nearer than Life! — No! — if this world have aught
Of bright or precious, let not Him who calls
Such things his own, take rest! — Dark Spirits keep watch,
And they to whom fair honour, chivalrous fame,
Were as Heaven's air, the vital element,
[120]   Wherein they breath'd, may wake, and find their Souls
Made marks for human Scorn, i' th' very quick
140   Of Passionate feeling and proud thought to try
The temper of its ~~m~~ shafts! — Will they bear on
With Life struck down, and thus disrobed of all
Its glorious drapery? — Who shall tell us this?
— Will he so bear it?

XIMENA.   Mother! let us kneel,
And ~~blent~~ blend our hearts in prayer! — What else is left
To Mortals when the dark hour's might is on them?
— Leave us, Theresa! — Grief like this doth find
Its balm in Solitude. — My mother! Peace

                                        Exit THERESA.

Is heaven's benignant answer to the cry
[130] 150   Of troubled Spirits. — Wilt thou kneel with me?
ELMINA. Away! — 'tis but for Souls unstain'd to wear
Heaven's tranquil image on their calmness, as a Stream
Pure thro' its depths! — The current of my thoughts
All darkly toss'd and broken by the storm,
Reflects but clouds and lightnings! — Didst thou speak
Of Peace? — 'tis fled from Earth! — but there is Joy,
Wild, troubled Joy! And who shall know, my Child,
It is not Happiness? — Why, our own hearts
Will keep the Secret close! — Joy! Joy! — if but
160   To leave this desolate [?~~fallen~~] City, with its dull
[140]   Slow knells and dirges, and to breathe again
Th' untainted Mountain Winds! — But hush! The Trees,
The flowers, the Waters, must hear nought of this!,
They are full of Voices, and will whisper things ——

Hath brought no rest.

ELMINA.   Rest! — who should rest? — not he
That holds one earthly blessing to his heart
Nearer than life! — No! if this world have aught
Of bright or precious, let not him who calls
Such things his own, take rest! — Dark spirits keep watch,
And they to whom fair honour, chivalrous fame,
Were as heaven's air, the vital element
Wherein they breathed, may wake, and find their souls   120
Made marks for human scorn! — Will they bear on
With life struck down, and thus disrobed of all
Its glorious drapery? — Who shall tell us this?
— Will *he* so bear it?

XIMENA.   Mother! let us kneel,
And blend our hearts in prayer! — What else is left
To mortals when the dark hour's might is on them?
— Leave us, Theresa. — Grief like this doth find
Its balm in solitude.

                              Exit THERESA.

                    My mother! peace
Is heaven's benignant answer to the cry
Of wounded spirits. Wilt thou kneel with me?   130

ELMINA. Away! 'tis but for souls unstain'd to wear
Heaven's tranquil image on their depths. — The stream
Of my dark thoughts, all broken by the storm,
Reflects but clouds and lightnings! — Didst thou speak
Of peace? — 'tis fled from earth! — but there is joy!
Wild, troubled joy! — And who shall know, my child!
It is not happiness? — Why, our own hearts
Will keep the secret close! — Joy, joy! if but
To leave this desolate city, with its dull
Slow knells and dirges, and to breathe again   140
Th' untainted mountain-air! — But hush! the trees,
The flowers, the waters, must hear nought of this!
They are full of voices, and will whisper things——

—We'll speak of it no more!

XIMENA.   Oh! pitying Heaven!
This grief doth shake her reason!

ELMINA *(starting)*.   Hark! a step!
~~It is~~ 'Tis—'tis thy Father's!—come away!—not now—
He must not see us now!

XIMENA.   Why should this be?

ELMINA. I may not meet my trial unprepar'd.

GONZALEZ *enters, and detains her.*

170 GONZALEZ. Elmina, dost thou shun me?—Have we not,
E'en from the hopeful and the sunny time,
[150]   When Youth was as a glory ~~on~~ round our brows,
Held on thro' Life together?—And is this,
When Eve is gathering o'er us, with the gloom
Of ~~heavy~~ stormy shadows, and the angry moan
Of rising blasts, a time to part our steps
Upon the darkening Wild?

ELMINA *(coldly)*.   There needs not this.
Why shouldst thou think I shunn'd thee?

GONZALEZ.   Should the love
That shone o'er many years, th' unfading love,
180 Whose only change hath been from gladdening smiles,
To mingling Sorrows and sustaining strength;
Thus lightly be forgotten?

ELMINA.   Speak'st <u>thou</u> thus?
[160]   —I have knelt before thee with that holy plea,
When it avail'd me not!—But there are things
Whose ~~breathings~~ very breathings on the Spirit erase
All record of past love, save the chill sense,
Th' unquiet memory of its wasted faith,
And vain devotedness!—Aye, they that fix
Affection's perfect trust on aught of Earth,
190 Have many a dream to start from!

GONZALEZ.   This is but
The ~~sternness~~ wildness and the bitterness of grief,
Ere yet th' unsettled heart hath closed its long
[170]   Impatient conflicts with a mightier Power,

150 THE MANUSCRIPT

We'll speak of it no more.

XIMENA.   Oh! pitying heaven!
This grief doth shake her reason!

ELMINA *(starting)*.   Hark! a step!
'Tis—'tis thy father's!—come away—not now—
He must not see us now!

XIMENA.   Why should this be?

GONZALEZ *enters, and detains* ELMINA.

GONZALEZ. Elmina, dost thou shun me?—Have we not,
    E'en from the hopeful and the sunny time
    When youth was as a glory round our brows,   150
    Held on through life together?—And is this,
    When eve is gathering round us, with the gloom
    Of stormy clouds, a time to part our steps
    Upon the darkening wild?

ELMINA *(coldly)*.   There needs not this.
    Why shouldst thou think I shunn'd thee?

GONZALEZ.   Should the love
    That shone o'er many years, th' unfading love,
    Whose only change hath been from gladdening smiles
    To mingling sorrows and sustaining strength,
    Thus lightly be forgotten?

ELMINA.   Speak'st *thou* thus?
    —I have knelt before thee with that very plea,   160
    When it avail'd me not!—But there are things
    Whose very breathings on the soul erase
    All record of past love, save the chill sense,
    Th' unquiet memory of its wasted faith,
    And vain devotedness!—Aye! they that fix
    Affection's perfect trust on aught of earth,
    Have many a dream to start from!

GONZALEZ.   This is but
    The wildness and the bitterness of grief,
    Ere yet th' unsettled heart hath closed its long
    Impatient conflicts with a mightier power,   170

Which makes all conflict vain.

Hark! was there not
A sound of distant Trumpets, far beyond
The Moorish tents, and of another tone
Than th' Afric horn, Ximena?

XIMENA.   Oh! my Father,
I know that Horn too well! —'tis but the Wind,
Which, with a sudden rising, bears its deep
200 And savage war-note from us, wafting it
O'er the far Hills.

GONZALEZ *(mournfully).* Alas! this woe must be!
I do but shake my Spirit from its height,
[180] So startling it with Hope! —But the dread hour
Shall be met bravely still. I can keep down
Yet, for a little while—and Heaven will ask
No more—the passionate workings of my heart;
And thine—Elmina?

ELMINA *(confused).*   'Tis—I am prepared,
I have prepar'd for all.

GONZALEZ.   Oh, well I knew
Thou wouldst not fail me! Not in vain my Soul,
210 Upon thy Faith and Courage, hath rear'd up
Unshaken trust.

ELMINA.   Away!—thou know'st me not!
Man dares too far, his rashness would invest
[190] This our Mortality with an attribute
Too high and awful for the grasp of aught
So feelingly gifted, boasting that he knows
One human heart!

GONZALEZ.   These are wild words, but yet
I will not doubt thee!—Hast thou not been found
Noble in all things, pouring thy Soul's light
Undimm'd o'er every trial?—And, as our fates,
220 So must our names be, undivided!—Thine,
I' the record of a Warrior's life shall find
Its place of stainless honour. —By his side——

ELMINA. May this be borne?—How much of Agony
[200] Hath the heart room for?—Speak to me in wrath
Call up the Kingly Anger of thy brow

Which makes all conflict vain.
                            —Hark! was there not
A sound of distant trumpets, far beyond
The Moorish tents, and of another tone
Than th' Afric horn, Ximena?
XIMENA.   Oh, my father!
I know that horn too well. —'Tis but the wind,
Which, with a sudden rising, bears its deep
And savage war-note from us, wafting it
O'er the far hills.
GONZALEZ.   Alas! this woe must be!
I do but shake my spirit from its height
So startling it with hope!—But the dread hour   180
Shall be met bravely still. I can keep down
Yet for a little while—and Heaven will ask
No more—the passionate workings of my heart;
—And thine—Elmina?
ELMINA.   'Tis—I am prepared.
I *have* prepared for all.
GONZALEZ.   Oh, well I knew
Thou wouldst not fail me!—Not in vain my soul,
Upon thy faith and courage, hath built up
Unshaken trust.
ELMINA *(wildly).*   Away!—thou know'st me not!
Man dares too far, his rashness would invest
This our mortality with an attribute   190
Too high and awful, boasting that he knows
One human heart!
GONZALEZ.   These are wild words, but yet
I will not doubt thee!—Hast thou not been found
Noble in all things, pouring thy soul's light
Undimm'd o'er every trial?—And, as our fates,
So must our names be, undivided!—Thine,
I' th' record of a warrior's life, shall find
Its place of stainless honour.—By his side——
ELMINA. May this be borne?—How much of agony
Hath the heart room for?—Speak to me in wrath—   200

And I can bear it!—But no gentle words!
No words of love! no praise!—Thy sword might slay,
And be more merciful!

GONZALEZ.   Wherefore art thou thus?

230   Elmina, my Belov'd!

ELMINA.   No more of love!
Have I not said there's that within my heart
Whereon it falls as living fire would fall
Upon an unclos'd wound?

GONZALEZ.   Nay, lift thine eyes,
That I may read <u>their</u> meaning!

ELMINA.   Never more
With a free Soul—What have I said?—'twas nought

[210]   Take thou no heed!—The words of wretchedness
Admit not scrutiny.—Hath the broken spray
Cast from the torrent in its troubled strife
Object or aim?

GONZALEZ.   I have seen thee in the hour

240   Of thy deep Spirit's joy, and when the breath
Of grief hung chilling round thee; in all change,
Bright Health and drooping Sickness; Hope and fear;
Youth and Decline; but never yet, Elmina,
Ne'er hath thine eye till now, shrunk back, perturb'd
With shame or dread, from mine!

ELMINA.   Thy glance doth search
A wounded heart too deeply.

GONZALEZ.   Hast thou ~~aught~~ there

[220]   [?~~Now~~] Aught to conceal?

ELMINA.   Who hath not?

GONZALEZ.   Till this hour
<u>Thou</u> never hadst!—Yet hear me!—By the free
And unattainted fame which wraps the dust

250   Of thy brave Fathers in their Sepulchres,
And rests upon their Children—

ELMINA.   This to <u>me</u>!
—Bring your inspiring War-notes, and your sounds
Of festal Music round a dying Man!
Will his heart echo them?—But if thy words
Had spells to call up, with each lofty tone,

I can endure it! — But no gentle words!
No words of love! no praise! — Thy sword might slay,
And be more merciful!
GONZALEZ.   Wherefore art thou thus?
Elmina, my beloved!
ELMINA.   No more of love!
— Have I not said there's that within my heart,
Whereon it falls as living fire would fall
Upon an unclosed wound?
GONZALEZ.   Nay, lift thine eyes
That I may read *their* meaning!
ELMINA.   Never more
With a free soul — What have I said? —'twas nought!
Take thou no heed! The words of wretchedness   210
Admit not scrutiny. Wouldst thou mark the speech
Of troubled dreams?
GONZALEZ.   I have seen thee in the hour
Of thy deep spirit's joy, and when the breath
Of grief hung chilling round thee; in all change,
Bright health and drooping sickness; hope and fear;
Youth and decline; but never yet, Elmina,
Ne'er hath thine eye till now shrunk back perturb'd
With shame or dread, from mine!
ELMINA.   Thy glance doth search
A wounded heart too deeply.
GONZALEZ.   Hast thou there
Aught to conceal?
ELMINA.   Who hath not?
GONZALEZ.   Till this hour   220
Thou never hadst! — Yet hear me! — by the free
And unattainted fame which wraps the dust
Of thine heroic fathers —
ELMINA.   This to me!
— Bring your inspiring war-notes, and your sounds
Of festal music round a dying man!
Will his heart echo them? — But if thy words
Were spells, to call up, with each lofty tone,

The Grave's most awful Spirits, they would stand
All powerless in the stern and rigid presence
Of Grief, whose terrible reality
Gives her command o'er Phantoms!

GONZALEZ.   Then, by Her,

[230]   260   Who stands beside thee in the purity
Of her devoted ~~Bosom~~ Youth, and on whose name
No blight must fall, and whose pale cheek must ne'er
Burn with that deeper tinge, caught painfully
From the quick feeling of dishonour; Speak!
Unfold this Mystery!—By thy Sons——

ELMINA.   My sons!
And canst <u>thou</u> name them?

GONZALEZ.   Proudly!—Better far
They died with all the promise of their Youth,
And the bright glory of their House upon them,
Than that with Manhood's high and passionate Soul

[240]   270   To fearful strength unfolded, they should pine,
Barr'd from the lists of crested Chivalry,
And wasting, in the silence of a woe,
Which from the heart shuts daylight; o'er the shame
Of those who gave them birth!—But thou couldst ne'er
Forget their lofty claims!

ELMINA *(wildly).*   'Twas but for them!
'Twas for them only!—Who shall dare arraign
Madness of crime?—And He who made us, knows
There are dark moments of all hearts and lives,
Which bear down reason!

GONZALEZ.   Thou whom I have lov'd
280   With such high trust, as in the proud repose
[250]   Of its security, o'er our Nature threw
A glory, scarce allow'd;—What hast thou done?
—Ximena, go thou hence!

ELMINA.   No, no, my Child!
There's pity in thy look!—All other eyes
Are full of wrath and scorn. Oh! leave me not!

GONZALEZ. ~~That I should live to see~~ [?thee] ~~tremble thus!~~
~~—What e'er~~

The grave's most awful spirits, they would stand
Powerless, before my anguish!

GONZALEZ.   Then, by her,
Who there looks on thee in the purity   230
Of her devoted youth, and o'er whose name
No blight must fall, and whose pale cheek must ne'er
Burn with that deeper tinge, caught painfully
From the quick feeling of dishonour. — Speak!
Unfold this mystery! — By thy sons ——

ELMINA.   My sons!
And canst *thou* name them?

GONZALEZ.   Proudly! — Better far
They died with all the promise of their youth,
And the fair honour of their house upon them,
Than that with manhood's high and passionate soul
To fearful strength unfolded, they should live,   240
Barr'd from the lists of crested chivalry,
And pining, in the silence of a woe,
Which from the heart shuts daylight;— o'er the shame
Of those who gave them birth! — But *thou* couldst ne'er
Forget their lofty claims!

ELMINA *(wildly)*.   'Twas but for them!
'Twas for them only! — Who shall dare arraign
Madness of crime? — And he who made us, knows
There are dark moments of all hearts and lives,
Which bear down reason!

GONZALEZ.   Thou, whom I have loved
With such high trust, as o'er our nature threw   250
A glory, scarce allow'd;— what hast thou done?
— Ximena, go thou hence!

ELMINA.   No, no! my child!
There's pity in thy look! — All other eyes
Are full of wrath and scorn! — Oh! leave me not!

GONZALEZ. ——By every [?blessed] [?——]-and holy thing
But speak i' [?-]—— what hast thou done?

290 GONZALEZ. That I should live to see thee thus abas'd!
Yet speak!—What hast thou done?

ELMINA.   Look to the Gate!
Thou'rt worn with toil—but take no rest to-night!
—The Western Gate!—Its Watchers have been won—
The Christian City hath been bought and sold!
[260] They will admit the Moor!

GONZALEZ.   They have been won!
Brave men and tried so long!—Whose work was this?

ELMINA. Why, what know'st thou of Nature?—If thy heart
Had shut its panoply against her touch,
Were all of such a mould?—Can mothers stand
300 To see their Children perish?

GONZALEZ.   Then the guilt
Was thine?

ELMINA (indignantly). Shall Mortal dare to call it guilt?
I tell thee, Heaven, which made all holy things,
Made nought more holy than the boundless love
Which fills a Mother's heart!—I say, 'tis Woe
Enough, with such an aching tenderness,
To love aught earthly!—And in vain—in vain!
—There's some dark Power in this mysterious World,
Which weighs us down too sorely!

[270] GONZALEZ (in a low deep voice).   —Now my life
Is struck to worthless ashes!—In my Soul
310 Suspicion hath ta'en root!—The nobleness
Henceforth is blotted from all human brows,
And fearful power, a dark and troublous gift,
Almost like Prophecy, is pour'd upon me,
To read the guilty secrets in each eye,
That once look'd bright with truth!
                              —Why then I have gain'd
What men call Wisdom!—a new Sense, to which
All tales that speak of high fidelity,
[280] And holy Courage, and proud Honour, tried,
Search'd, and found stedfast, ev'n to Martyrdom,
320 Are food for Mockery!—Why should I not cast

GONZALEZ. That I should live to see thee thus abased!
 —Yet speak?—What hast thou done?
ELMINA.   Look to the gate!
  Thou'rt worn with toil—but take no rest to-night!
  The western gate!—Its watchers have been won—
  The Christian city hath been bought and sold!
  They will admit the Moor!
GONZALEZ.   They have been won!   260
  Brave men and tried so long!—Whose work was this?
ELMINA. Think'st thou all hearts like thine?—Can mothers stand
  To see their children perish?
GONZALEZ.   Then the guilt
  Was thine?
ELMINA.   —Shall mortal dare to call it guilt?
  I tell thee, Heaven, which made all holy things,
  Made nought more holy than the boundless love
  Which fills a mother's heart!—I say, 'tis woe
  Enough, with such an aching tenderness,
  To love aught earthly!—and in vain! in vain!
  —We are press'd down too sorely!
GONZALEZ (in a low desponding voice). Now my life   270
  Is struck to worthless ashes!—In my soul
  Suspicion hath ta'en root. The nobleness
  Henceforth is blotted from all human brows,
  And fearful power, a dark and troublous gift,
  Almost like prophecy, is pour'd upon me,
  To read the guilty secrets in each eye
  That once look'd bright with truth!
                                    —Why then I have gain'd
  What men call wisdom!—A new sense, to which
  All tales that speak of high fidelity,
  And holy courage, and proud honour, tried,   280
  Search'd, and found stedfast, even to martyrdom,
  Are food for mockery!—Why should I not cast

From my thinn'd locks the wearing Helm at once,
And, in the heavy sickness of my Soul,
Throw the Sword down for ever? — Is there aught
In ~~such~~ all this World of gilded hollowness,
~~Without one heart or [?bosom] to rest our [?faith];~~
Now the bright hues drop off its loveliest things,
Worth striving for again?

XIMENA.   Father! look up!
Turn unto me, thy Child!

GONZALEZ *(in deep dejection).* Thy face is fair!
[290]   And hath been unto me, in other days,
330   As Morning to the Journeyer of the deep!
But now — 'tis too like hers!

ELMINA *(falling at his feet).*   Woe, shame and woe,
Are on me in their might! — forgive, forgive!

GONZALEZ *(suddenly starting).*
Doth the Moor deem that I have ~~put~~ place or share,
Or counsel in this vileness? — Stay me not!
Let go thy hold — 'tis powerless on me now —
I linger here, while Treason is at work!

                              Exit GONZALEZ.

ELMINA. Ximena, dost <u>thou</u> scorn me?

XIMENA.   I have learn'd
To commune with my heart, and there have found,
[300]   Hid, beneath many foldings, from all eyes
340   But <u>One</u>; too much of cherish'd feebleness,
To dare do aught, in this, thy trial's hour,
But pity thee, dear Mother!

ELMINA.   Blessings light
On thy fair head, my gentle Child, for this!
Oh! little, when this cold World's aspect lay
Before me in the sun, I little deem'd
Mercy so rare on Earth! — My Soul is faint,
Worn with long strife! A slumbrous heaviness
Creeps thro' my veins — is there aught else to do,
Or suffer, ere we die? — Oh God! my Sons!

From my thinn'd locks the wearing helm at once,
And in the heavy sickness of my soul
Throw the sword down for ever? — Is there aught
In all this world of gilded hollowness,
Now the bright hues drop off its loveliest things,
Worth striving for again?
XIMENA.   Father! look up!
Turn unto me, thy child!
GONZALEZ.   Thy face is fair;
And hath been unto me, in other days,   290
As morning to the journeyer of the deep;
But now — 'tis too like hers! ←
ELMINA *(falling at his feet)*.   Woe, shame and woe,
Are on me in their might! — forgive, forgive!
GONZALEZ *(starting up)*. Doth the Moor deem that *I* have part or
        share,
Or counsel in this vileness? — Stay me not!
Let go thy hold — 'tis powerless on me now —
I linger here, while treason is at work!

                                        Exit GONZALEZ.

ELMINA. Ximena, dost *thou* scorn me?
XIMENA.   I have found
In mine own heart too much of feebleness,
Hid, beneath many foldings, from all eyes   300
But *His* whom nought can blind; — to dare do aught
But pity thee, dear mother!
ELMINA.   Blessings light
On thy fair head, my gentle child, for this!
Thou kind and merciful! — My soul is faint —
Worn with long strife! — Is there aught else to do,
Or suffer, ere we die? — Oh God! my sons!

350 I have betray'd them!—All their innocent blood
Is on my Soul!
    XIMENA.   How shall I comfort thee?
    —Oh! hark what sounds come deepening on the Wind,
[310]   So full of solemn hope!—Such Melodies
Might float from Heaven around a dying Saint!

*(A procession of Nuns passes across the Scene, bearing relics &c,
and chaunting.)*

Chaunt

A Sword is waving o'er the Land,
Her towers are in the Spoiler's hand,
Red signs of wrath are deepening in her sky;
The Stranger's tread is on her Vines,
The Cross torn rudely from her Shrines;
360   —Hear us! thou God of Armies! hear our cry!

A wail is in the Hall of State,
The Peasant's home is desolate,
The City's grass-grown streets untrodden lie!
But in the chambers of the Tomb,
The gathering Dwellers scarce find room;
—Hear us! thou God of chastening! hear our cry!

The old Man's brow is pale with thought,
The Youth's high heart with bodings fraught,
Wild fear is darkening in the Mother's eye;
370   For there is that gone forth in power,
Which bows young Tree and glorious Flower;
—Hear us! thou God of Suffering! hear our cry!

The weeper sits at Bridal-feast,
The Vintage-melodies have ceas'd;
The ~~Summer~~ Winds come loaded, wafting dirge-notes by!
Is our blood voiceless on the plains?
Where sleeps th'Avenger of our Fanes?
—Hear us! thou God of Judgement! hear our cry!

—I have betray'd them!—All their innocent blood
Is on my soul!
XIMENA.   How shall I comfort thee?
—Oh! hark! what sounds come deepening on the wind,
So full of solemn hope!   310

(*A procession of Nuns passes across the Scene,
bearing relics, and chanting.*)

CHANT

A sword is on the land!
He that bears down young tree and glorious flower,
Death is gone forth, he walks the wind in power!
          —Where is the warrior's hand?
Our steps are in the shadows of the grave,
Hear us, we perish! Father, hear, and save!

If, in the days of song,
The days of gladness, we have call'd on thee,
When mirthful voices rang from sea to sea,
          And joyous hearts were strong;   320
Now, that alike the feeble and the brave
Must cry, "We perish!"—Father! hear, and save!

The days of song are fled!
The winds come loaded, wafting dirge-notes by,
But they that linger soon unmourn'd must die;
          —The dead weep not the dead!
—Wilt thou forsake us midst the stormy wave?
We sink, we perish!—Father, hear, and save!

Woe, for the Children of the Dead!
380 Woe, for the mail'd heart and crested head!
And arm struck down that held our Banners high!
The shield is cleft, the Lance is dust!
On Thee we pour our Spirit's trust!
—Hear us! thou God of Battles! hear our cry!

HERNANDEZ *enters.*

ELMINA. Why com'st thou, man of Vengeance? What have I
To do with thee?—Am I not bow'd enough?
Thou art no Mourner's Comforter!
HERNANDEZ.   Thy lord
Hath sent me unto thee. Till this day's task
Be clos'd, thou Daughter of the feeble heart!
[340] 390 He bids thee seek him not, but lay thy Woes
Before Heaven's Altar, and in penitence
Make thy Soul's peace with God.
ELMINA.   Till this Day's task
Be clos'd!—there is strange triumph in thine eyes—
Is it that I have fall'n from that high place
Whereon I stood, in fame?—But I can feel
A stern delight, a wild and bitter pride
Which doth exult in thus being past the power
Of thy ~~proud~~ dark searching eye! My spirit now
Is wound about by one sole mighty grief,
400 Within whose circle bides no meaner woe!
Thy scorn hath lost its sting. Thou mayst reproach—
[350] HERNANDEZ. I come not to reproach thee! Heaven doth work
By many Agencies; and in its hour,
There is no worm upon the tenderest bud,
No, not an insect which the summer-gale
From the green leaf shakes trembling, but may serve
Its deep unsearchable purposes as well
As the great Ocean, or the eternal fires,
Pent in Earth's Caves!—Thou hast but speeded that,
410 Which, in the ~~passionate~~ infatuate blindness of thy heart,
Thou wouldst have trampled o'er all holy ties,

Helmet and lance are dust!
Is not the strong man wither'd from our eye?   330
The arm struck down that held our banners high?
— Thine is our spirit's trust!
Look through the gathering shadows of the grave!
Do we not perish? — Father, hear, and save!

HERNANDEZ *enters.*

ELMINA. Why comest thou, man of vengeance? — What have I
To do with thee? — Am I not bow'd enough?
Thou art no mourner's comforter!
HERNANDEZ.   Thy lord
Hath sent me unto thee. Till this day's task
Be closed, thou daughter of the feeble heart!
He bids thee seek him not, but lay thy woes   340
Before Heaven's altar, and in penitence
Make thy soul's peace with God.
ELMINA.   Till this day's task
Be closed! — there is strange triumph in thine eyes —
Is it that I have fallen from that high place
Whereon I stood in fame? — But I can feel
A wild and bitter pride in thus being past
The power of thy dark glance! My spirit now
Is wound about by one sole mighty grief;
Thy scorn hath lost its sting. — Thou mayst reproach —
HERNANDEZ. I come not to reproach thee. Heaven doth work   350
By many agencies; and in its hour
There is no insect which the summer breeze
From the green leaf shakes trembling, but may serve
Its deep unsearchable purposes, as well
As the great ocean, or th' eternal fires,
Pent in earth's caves! — Thou hast but speeded that,
Which, in th' infatuate blindness of thy heart,
Thou wouldst have trampled o'er all holy ties,

Aye, rooted up the glory of a life,
A Hero's life, to shun!

ELMINA. Thou saidst — thy words rung strangely in mine ears —
[360]   I could not catch their sense —

HERNANDEZ.   E'en now thy Lord
Hath sent our foes defiance. On the walls
He stands in conference with the boasting Moor,
And awful Strength is with him! — Thro' the blood
Which this day must be pour'd in Sacrifice
420   Shall Spain be free. On all her Olive-hills
From ~~dark~~ wild Morena to th'Asturian Rocks
Shall Men set up the Battle-sign of fire,
And round its blaze, at Midnight, keep the sense
Of Vengeance wakeful in each other's hearts;
Aye, call from Earth the Might of buried Hosts
To pour itself upon the Winds of Spain,
E'en with thy Children's tale.

[370]   XIMENA.   Peace, Father! peace.
Behold she sinks! — the storm hath done its work
Upon the feeble reed. Oh! lend thine aid
430   To bear her hence.

They lead her away.

But to avert one day!

ELMINA.   My senses fail—
Thou saidst—speak yet again!—I could not catch   360
The meaning of thy words.

HERNANDEZ.   E'en now thy lord
Hath sent our foes defiance. On the walls
He stands in conference° with the boastful Moor,   *confrontation*
And awful strength is with him. Through the blood
Which this day must be pour'd in sacrifice
Shall Spain be free. On all her olive-hills
Shall men set up the battle-sign of fire,
And round its blaze, at midnight, keep the sense
Of vengeance wakeful in each other's hearts
E'en with thy children's tale!

XIMENA.   Peace, father! peace!   370
Behold she sinks!—the storm hath done its work
Upon the broken reed. Oh! lend thine aid
To bear her hence.

They lead her away.

[The reputation of Hemans as "political" only on behalf of conservative ideologies is complicated by *1823*'s scene 6, and even more so by the more fully developed MS scenario of class discontent. At the same time, Hemans's hesitation is legible in her giving Ximena a fuller stage as warrior-daughter rallying the citizenry to fight for the honor of the city and its ruling dynasty. And because Ximena's loss has been revealed in the MS's opening ballad, her work in this scene carries an emotional burden as well as ideological agenda. Even more than in *1823*, Ximena emerges as a Hemans-ideal of how the heart's passions can turn to national legend (in this case, El Cid) to give poetry a political force in reconciling private grief and public purpose.]

SCENE [6]

A Street in the City, before a Church. Several groups of Citizens and Soldiers. Many of them lying on the steps of the Church. Arms scattered on the ground around them.

AN OLD CITIZEN. This air is sultry, as with thunder-clouds.
    I left my desolate Home, that I might breathe
    More freely in Heaven's face, but my heart feels
    With this hot gloom o'erburthen'd. I have now
    No Sons to tend me. Which of you, kind friends,
    Will bring the old Man water from the fount,
    To moisten his parch'd lip?

Some of the Citizens go out

[?CITIZENS]   The days are few,
    That he hath yet to linger, cumbering Earth,
    With Age and Sickness.
2nd CITIZEN.   Aye, this wasting Siege
10   Good Father Lopez, hath gone hard with you!

SCENE [6]

[The scene opens with the ordinary citizens and laborers of Valencia discussing the wasting effects of the extended siege and the war of resistance in which their sons are ceaselessly sacrificed in the name of honor and the fame of the ruling class. Bitterly commenting on their luxuries and privileges, one citizen notes the perverse democratic leveling (shared misery) in the extremity of the siege—a phenomenon that in the 1790s Mary Wollstonecraft, Thomas Paine, and Charlotte Smith noted, in similar tones, about the plight of displaced French aristocracy after the Revolution. With this cataclysm a fairly recent memory (only a generation or so old), Hemans evokes the potential for class rebellion that focused anxieties and hopes in the 1790s, and she sounds it for the 1820s. If by 1830 it would be clear that some reforms of the most scandalous class privileges were needed to deflect the potential for a domestic "French Revolution," no contemporary review commented on scene 6, let alone its critique of class differences.]

A Street in Valencia. Several Groups of Citizens and Soldiers, many of them lying on the Steps of a Church. Arms scattered on the Ground around them.

AN OLD CITIZEN. The air is sultry, as with thunder-clouds.
  I left my desolate home, that I might breathe
  More freely in heaven's face, but my heart feels
  With this hot gloom o'erburthen'd. I have now
  No sons to tend me. Which of you, kind friends,
  Will bring the old man water from the fount,
  To moisten his parch'd lip?

                                        A citizen goes out.

SECOND CITIZEN.   This wasting siege,
  Good Father Lopez, hath gone hard with you!

'Tis sad to hear no Voices thro' the House,

Once peopled with fair Sons!

3rd Citizen.   Why, better thus,

Than to be haunted with their famish'd cries

Even in your very dreams. Oh God! mine ears

Ring with mine Children's yet.

Old Citizen.   Heaven's will be done!

These are dark times. I have not been alone

In my affliction.

3rd Citizen.   Why, we have but this thought

Left for our gloomy comfort! — There's no face

Which, like a cloud, doth pass you silently

Midst the dull, grass-grown street, but tells some tale

In its unsettled eye, or hollow cheek

Or troubled brow, of terror which hath sunk

Pale on the Soul, or Sickness, creeping chill

As a slow poison, thro' the restless blood;

Or of long watchings by the bed of pain,

Or weepings for the dead.

4th Citizen.   We bore it well

And manfully, while yet a hope was left;

But what avails it <u>now</u> to strive against

That which is crushing us?

Old Citizen *(vehemently).*   It <u>doth</u> avail!

If but for this, that far throughout the Land,

Then, when our Sufferings shall be told, may learn

How much Man's heart and courage to endure,

And shame to yield far less! — Aye, for their cause,

Be of good cheer, my Brethren, and bear on!

5th Citizen. I marvel oft how long our Chieftains think

We lowly Men in silence may sustain

The woes that reach not them.

Old Citizen.   Shame on the thought!

Their cup is full as ours. These are no ~~days~~ times

That blight the lowly shrub, but leave the Pine

Unscath'd upon its Hills. The Day of Wrath

Is ~~pressing~~ rushing with its whirlwinds o'er the Land

And well I ween there is no Threshold mark'd

20
30
40

'Tis sad to hear no voices through the house,
Once peopled with fair sons!

THIRD CITIZEN.   Why, better thus,   10
Than to be haunted with their famish'd cries,
E'en in your very dreams!

OLD CITIZEN.   Heaven's will be done!
These are dark times! I have not been alone
In my affliction.

THIRD CITIZEN *(with bitterness).*
                    Why, we have but this thought
Left for our gloomy comfort! — And 'tis well!

To be pass'd over.[1]

6th CITIZEN.   Aye, the hour is come
Which for awhile doth strike the balance even
Between the Noble's Palace and the Hut,
Where ~~Peasants die in silence~~ the worn Peasant sickens. They that
    bear
The humble dead unhonour'd to their home
[20]   Pass in the streets no lordly bridal train,
With its exulting music; and the Wretch
50   Who on the marble steps of some proud Hall
Doth fling himself to die, in his last need
And agony of famine, doth behold
No scornful Guests, with their long purple robes,
To the Banquet sweeping by. Why, this is just!
These are the days when Pomp is made to know
Its human mould!

5th CITIZEN.   Heard you last night the sound
Of Saint Iago's bell? — How sullenly
[30]   From the great Tower it peal'd! — I could not rest
On my lone bed, when once that startling note
60   Had broken my feverish slumber!

7th CITIZEN.   Aye, tis said
No mortal hand was near, when that deep Knell
Lent forth its hollow voice, which almost seem'd
To [?rake] shake the Midnight streets.

OLD CITIZEN.   Too well I know
The sound of coming Fate! — 'Tis ever thus,
When Death is on his way to make it Night
In the Cid's ancient House. — Aye, there are things
In this strange world, around us, and beside,
~~Unseen~~ Viewless, yet darkly felt! — ~~That~~ Yon bell, untouch'd,
(Save by the hands we see not) still doth speak
70   When of that line some stately head is mark'd,
[40]   With a ~~dread~~ wild thrilling peal, at dead of Night,

---

1   A reference to the first Passover (Exodus 12.7-29).

Aye, let the balance be awhile struck even
Between the noble's palace and the hut,
Where the worn peasant sickens! — They that bear
The humble dead unhonour'd to their homes,
Pass now i' th' streets no lordly bridal train,   20
With its exulting music; and the wretch
Who on the marble steps of some proud hall
Flings himself down to die, in his last need
And agony of famine, doth behold
No scornful guests, with their long purple robes,[1]
To the banquet sweeping by. Why, this is just!
These are the days when pomp is made to feel
Its human mould!

FOURTH CITIZEN.   Heard you last night the sound
Of Saint Jago's bell? — How sullenly
From the great tower it peal'd!

FIFTH CITIZEN.   Aye, and 'tis said   30
No mortal hand was near when so it seem'd
To shake the midnight streets.

OLD CITIZEN.   Too well I know
The sound of coming fate! —'Tis ever thus
When Death is on his way to make it night
In the Cid's ancient house.[2]—Oh! there are things
In this strange world of which we have all to learn
When its dark bounds are pass'd. — Yon bell, untouch'd,
(Save by the hands we see not) still doth speak—
—When of that line some stately head is mark'd,—
With a wild hollow peal, at dead of night,   40

---

1 Signifier of royalty. Trade in precious Tyrian purple dye, among other exotic Eastern
   commodities, developed in consequence of the Crusades, also a Christian war against
   so-called "infidels."

2 It was a Spanish tradition, that the great bell of the cathedral of Saragossa always tolled
   spontaneously before a king of Spain died. [FH]
   Named "Caesarae Augustus" for and by the Roman emperor, Saragossa was the leading
   city of Aragón, in northeastern Spain. The Moors took it from the Goths in the 8th
   century; Charlemagne then tried unsuccessfully to reclaim it (778). El Cid fought for
   its Muslim Moorish ruler against the Christian count of Barcelona. It was eventually
   conquered by Alfonso I of Aragón in 1118, who made it his capital. Like Valencia,
   Saragossa was famous for its resistance to Napoleon's invasion; it repulsed the first siege
   in 1808 and succumbed in the second, 1808-9, only after 50,000 of its population died.

Rocking Valencia's towers. I have heard it oft,
Nor known its warning false.

7th CITIZEN.   And will our Chief
Buy with the price of his fair Children's blood
A few more days of pining wretchedness
For this our ~~forsaken~~ wasted City?

OLD CITIZEN.   Doubt it not!
But he may purchase with that glorious ransom
The Land's proud freedom also! — Yet 'tis sad
To think that such a Line, with all its fame

80   Should pass away! The beautful, the brave,
Struck by one shaft! — For she, his Daughter too,

[50]   Moves upon Earth as some bright thing, whose time
To sojourn there is short.

4th CITIZEN.   Then woe for us
When she is gone! — What voice like hers shall wake
The Hope that died within us, till she came
Even like the light of [?~~Dreaming~~] summer [?~~Dreaming~~], on our
      paths,
With smiles and words of cheer? — The very sound
Of her soft step was comfort, as she mov'd
Through the still House of Mourning, till the eyes

90   Which gaz'd, in tearless anguish, on the dead,
Were lifted as she pass'd, and caught from hers,
A gleam of heavenward trust!

OLD CITIZEN.   Be still, she comes!
And with a mien how chang'd! — A hurrying step,
And a flush'd cheek! — What may this bode? — Be still!

XIMENA *enters, with Attendants carrying a Banner.*

XIMENA. Men of Valencia! in an hour like this,
What do ye here?

A CITIZEN.   We die!

XIMENA.   Brave Men die <u>now</u>

[60]   Girt for ~~their~~ the toil, as Travellers suddenly
By the dark Night o'ertaken on their way!

Rocking Valencia's towers. I have heard it oft,
Nor known its warning false.

FOURTH CITIZEN.   And will our chief
Buy with the price of his fair children's blood
A few more days of pining wretchedness
For this forsaken city?

OLD CITIZEN.   Doubt it not!
—But with that ransom he may purchase still
Deliverance for the land!—And yet 'tis sad
To think that such a race, with all its fame,
Should pass away!—For she, his daughter too,
Moves upon earth as some bright thing whose time   50
To sojourn there is short.

FIFTH CITIZEN.   Then woe for us
When she is gone!—Her voice—the very sound
Of her soft step was comfort, as she moved
Through the still house of mourning!—Who like her
Shall give us hope again?

OLD CITIZEN.   Be still!—she comes,
And with a mien how changed!—A hurrying step,
And a flush'd cheek!—What may this bode?—Be still!

XIMENA *enters, with Attendants carrying a Banner.*

XIMENA. Men of Valencia! in an hour like this,
What do ye here?

A CITIZEN.   We die!

XIMENA.   Brave men die *now*
Girt for the toil, as travellers suddenly   60
By the dark night o'ertaken on their way!

Aye, with the corslet brac'd, the sword still grasp'd,
100 Tho' but in failing hands. It is too much
Of Luxury for a time, when all should set
Their Spirits for conflict, as a Warrior's bow
In the Land's Battle not to be unbent,
To fold our mantles round us, and to sink
From Life, as flowers that shut up silently,
When the Sun's heat doth scorch them. Such a death
Were meet for lover-lorn Swain, or Village Girl,
Rear'd amidst founts and pastures—but for you—
A Citizen. Lady! what wouldst thou with us?
Ximena.   Rise and arm!
110 E'en now the Children of your Chief are led
Forth by the Moor to perish! Shall this be,
[70] Shall the high sound of such a name be hush'd,
I' the Land to which for Ages it hath been
A Battle-word; as 'twere some passing note
Of Shepherd's reed, in the dim twilight air
Melting to stillness?—Must this work be done,
And ye lie pining here, as Men, in whom
The pulse which God hath made for noble thought
Can so be thrill'd no longer?
Citizen.   'Tis even so!
120 Sickness, and toil, and grief, have breath'd upon us,
Making it early Winter in our veins;
Our hearts beat faint and low!
Ximena.   Are ye so poor
Of Soul, my Countrymen! that ye can draw
[80] Strength from no deeper source than that which sends
The red blood mantling thro' th' elastic frame,
And gives the fleet step wings?—Why, how have Age
And sensitive Womanhood ere now endur'd,
Thro' pangs of searching fire, in some proud cause,
[Gl-?-ing ?ages] Blessing that Agony?—Think ye the Power
130 Which bore them nobly up, as if to teach
The Torturer where Eternal Heaven had set
Bounds to his sway, was earthy, of this earth,
This dull Mortality?—Nay, then look on me!
[90] Death's mark is on me, and I stand amongst you,

These days require such death!—It is too much
Of luxury for our wild and angry times,
To fold the mantle round us, and to sink
From life, as flowers that shut up silently,
When the sun's heat doth scorch them!—Hear ye not?

A CITIZEN. Lady! what wouldst thou with us?

XIMENA.   Rise and arm!
E'en now the children of your chief are led
Forth by the Moor to perish!—Shall this be,
Shall the high sound of such a name be hush'd,   70
I' th' land to which for ages it hath been
A battle-word, as 'twere some passing note
Of shepherd-music?—Must this work be done,
And ye lie pining here, as men in whom
The pulse which God hath made for noble thought
Can so be thrill'd no longer?

CITIZEN.   'Tis even so!
Sickness, and toil, and grief, have breath'd upon us,
Our hearts beat faint and low.

XIMENA.   Are ye so poor
Of soul, my countrymen! that ye can draw
Strength from no deeper source than that which sends   80
The red blood mantling through the joyous veins,
And gives the fleet step wings?—Why, how have age
And sensitive womanhood ere now endured,
Through pangs of searching fire, in some proud cause,
Blessing that agony?—Think ye the Power
Which bore them nobly up, as if to teach
The torturer where eternal Heaven had set
Bounds to his sway, was earthy, of this earth,
This dull mortality?—Nay, then look on me!
Death's touch hath mark'd me, and I stand amongst you,   90

As one whose place, i' th' Sunshine of your World,
Shall soon be void! — A Being, unto whom
Each Wind ~~hath~~ bears ~~voice~~ Language from the ~~Land~~ shore
    unknown,
Heard by no other ear! — I say, the breath
Of th' incense, floating thro' yon Fane, shall scarce
140   Pass from your path before me! — But ev'n now,
I have that within me, kindling thro' the dust,
Which from all time hath made high deeds its Voice
And token to the Nations. — Look on me!
— Why hath Heaven pour'd forth Courage, as a flame,
Wasting the Womanish heart, which must be still'd
[100]   Yet sooner for its swift consuming brightness,
If not to shame your doubt, and your despair,
And your Soul's torpor? — Yet, arise and arm!
It may not be too late!

A Citizen.   Why, what are we,
150   To cope with Hosts? — Thus faint, and worn, and few,
O'ernumber'd and forsaken, is't for us
Alone to breast the Mighty?

Ximena.   And for whom
Hath he, who shakes the Mighty, with a breath
From their high places, made the fearfulness,
And ever-wakeful presence of his power,
[110]   To the pale startled Earth most manifest,
But for the weak? — Was't for the crown'd and helm'd,
And sceptered of the World, that foaming Seas
As a Mountain-rill were parted? — Noonday suns
160   In their mid-path of glory staid?
Ramparts laid prostrate, mail'd Archangels sent
To wither up the Arm of Hosts with death?
I tell you, if these Marvels have been done,
'Twas for the friendless and the scorn'd of Men,
The Captain and the slave! — They needed them!
And Faith, by her undoubting spirit e'en yet
~~Shall~~ May work deliverances, whose tale shall live
~~Scarce less in silent Wonder~~
Scarce less embalm'd in Wonder, than those things
[120] 170   Of the great elder Time! — Be of good heart!

As one whose place, i' th' sunshine of your world,
Shall soon be left to fill!—I say, the breath
Of th' incense, floating through yon fane, shall scarce
Pass from your path before me! But even now,
I have that within me, kindling through the dust,
Which from all time hath made high deeds its voice
And token to the nations;—Look on me!
Why hath Heaven pour'd forth courage, as a flame
Wasting the womanish heart, which must be still'd
Yet sooner for its swift consuming brightness,   100
If not to shame your doubt, and your despair,
And your soul's torpor?—Yet, arise and arm!
It may not be too late.

A CITIZEN.   Why, what are we,
To cope with hosts?—Thus faint, and worn, and few,
O'ernumber'd and forsaken, is't for us
To stand against the mighty?

XIMENA.   And for whom
Hath He, who shakes the mighty with a breath
From their high places, made the fearfulness,
And ever-wakeful presence of his power,
To the pale startled earth most manifest,   110
But for the weak?—Was't for the helm'd and crown'd
That suns were stay'd at noonday?—Stormy seas
As a rill parted?—Mail'd archangels sent
To wither up the strength of kings with death?[1]
—I tell you, if these marvels have been done,
'Twas for the wearied and th' oppress'd of men,
They needed such!—And generous faith hath power
By her prevailing spirit, e'en yet to work
Deliverances, whose tale shall live with those
Of the great elder time!—Be of good heart!   120

---

1 Referring to various miracles of divine intervention recorded in the Bible.

<u>Who</u> is forsaken? — He, that doth unfold
His bosom to the thought! — Aye, its dull weight
Hangs on the Soul of Manhood like the first
Cold chain wherewith a free-born Arm is bound.
⌐ — The chain! — but what have you to do with chains? ⌐
— Know ye this banner?
CITIZENS *(murmuring to each other).*

                  Is she not inspired?
Doth not Heaven call us by her fervent Voice?
XIMENA. Know ye this Banner?
A CITIZEN.   'Tis the Cid's.
XIMENA.   The Cid's!
Who breathes that name but in th' exulting tone
180   Which the heart rings to? — Why, the very wind
As it swells out the noble Standard's fold
Hath a triumphant sound! And could Heaven's air
On its clear viewless fields retain a trace
Of things which have pass'd o'er them, ye would see
A Sun-line bursting from on high to mark
[130]   The glorious track of that which thro' the land,
Mov'd as a sign of victory! from its place
In the free skies ne'er stooping to a foe.
OLD CITIZEN. Can ye still pause, my Brethren? — Oh! that Youth
190   Thro' this worn frame were kindling once again!
XIMENA. Ye linger ~~yet~~ still? — Upon this very air
He that was born in happy hour for Spain,
Pour'd his immortal Spirit brightly forth,
Which burns around us yet! — 'Twas the light breeze
From your own Mountains, which came down to wave
This Banner of his Battles, as it droop'd
Above the Champion's death-bed. Nor ev'n then,
[140]   Its tale of glory clos'd! — They made no moan
O'er the dead Hero, and no dirge was sung,
200   But the ~~wild~~ deep Trumpet and shrill Horn of War
Sent up high Music, as with all his fame,
The Mighty pass'd from Earth! — They wrapt <u>him</u> not
~~In~~ With the pale shroud, but [?round] brac'd the Warrior's form
~~Brac'd him~~ / ~~array'd in~~ [?mail]
In War-array, and on his noble steed,

Who is forsaken? — He that gives the thought
A place within his breast! — 'Tis not for you.
— Know ye this banner?
CITIZENS *(murmuring to each other).*
                    Is she not inspired?
Doth not Heaven call us by her fervent voice?
XIMENA. Know ye this banner?
CITIZENS.   'Tis the Cid's.
XIMENA.   The Cid's!
Who breathes that name but in th' exulting tone
Which the heart rings to? — Why, the very wind
As it swells out the noble standard's fold
Hath a triumphant sound! — The Cid's! — it moved
Even as a sign of victory through the land,   130
From the free skies ne'er stooping to a foe!
OLD CITIZEN. Can ye still pause, my brethren? — Oh! that youth
Through this worn frame were kindling once again!
XIMENA. Ye linger still? — Upon this very air,
He that was born in happy hour for Spain[1]
Pour'd forth his conquering spirit! — 'Twas the breeze
From your own mountains which came down to wave
This banner of his battles, as it droop'd
Above the champion's death-bed. Nor even then
Its tale of glory closed. — They made no moan   140
O'er the dead hero, and no dirge was sung,[2]
But the deep tambour and shrill horn of war
Told when the mighty pass'd! — They wrapt him not
With the pale shroud, but braced the warrior's form
In war-array, and on his barbed[3] steed,

---

1 "El que en buen hora nasco"; he that was born in a happy hour. An appellation given
   to the Cid in the ancient chronicles. [FH]
2 For this, and the subsequent allusions to the Spanish legends, see *The Romances and
   Chronicle of the Cid.* [FH]
   A reference to Southey's *Chronicle* and some of the sources cited therein.
3 This may be a misprint of "barded," to which the word was changed in posthumous
   editions, with a footnote definition (perhaps by Hemans): "caparisoned for battle"
   (from Old Spanish *barda*, ornamental armor for a horse). But Hemans may have meant
   "barbed," to evoke both armament and the barb horse, a breed related to the Arab that
   the Moors introduced into Spain; cf. Ximena's "Battle-Song" (222).

As for the triumph, rear'd him, marching forth
In the ~~still~~ hush'd Midnight, from Valencia's Walls,
Beleaguer'd then, as now. All silently
The stately Funeral moved, but o'er its van
210   Still the good Banner floated! — Who was He
That ~~rush'd before it~~ follow'd, charging on the tall white Steed,
And with the solemn Standard, broad and pale,
Waving in sheets of snow-light? — And the Cross,
The bloody Cross, far-blazing from his shield,
And on his cuirass burning fearfull,
And the fierce meteor-sword? — They fled, they fled,
The Kings of Afric, with their countless hosts,
They of the Forest and the Wilderness,
Were dust in his red pathway! Earth and Sea
220   Were cumber'd with their dead; the Scymetar
Was shiver'd as a reed! for in that hour
The Warrior Saint that keeps the watch for Spain,
Was arm'd betimes! — And o'er that fiery field
The Cid's high Banner stream'd all joyously,
For still its Lord was there!

CITIZENS *(rising tumultuously).* Even unto death
Again it shall be follow'd!

XIMENA.   Will he see
The noble Stem hewn down, the Beacon light
Which his House for Ages o'er the Land
Hath shone thro' cloud and storm, thus quench'd at once,
230   As some poor Goatherd's Watch-fire on the Hills?
Will he not aid his Children in the day
Of this, their uttermost peril? — Awful power
Is with the holy Dead, and there are times
When the Tomb hath no chain they cannot burst!
Is it a thing forgotten, how he woke
From that deep rest of old, ~~remb~~ remembering Spain
In her great danger? — At the Night's Mid-watch
How Leon started, when the sound was heard
That shook her dark and hollow-echoing Streets,
240   As with the heavy tramp of steel-clad Men,
By Thousands marching through! — For he had risen,

As for a triumph, rear'd him; marching forth
In the hush'd midnight from Valencia's walls,
Beleaguer'd then, as now. All silently
The stately funeral moved: —but who was he
That follow'd, charging on the tall white horse,   150
And with the solemn standard, broad and pale,
Waving in sheets of snow-light? —And the cross,
The bloody cross, far-blazing from his shield,
And the fierce meteor-sword? —They fled, they fled!
The kings of Afric, with their countless hosts,
Were dust in his red path! —The scimetar°   *scimitar*
Was shiver'd as a reed! —for in that hour
The warrior-saint that keeps the watch for Spain,
Was arm'd betimes! —And o'er that fiery field
The Cid's high banner stream'd all joyously,   160
For still its lord was there![1]
CITIZENS *(rising tumultuously).* Even unto death
Again it shall be follow'd!
XIMENA.   Will he see
The noble stem hewn down, the beacon-light
Which his house for ages o'er the land
Hath shone through cloud and storm, thus quench'd at once?
Will he not aid his children in the hour
Of this their uttermost peril? —Awful power
Is with the holy dead, and there are times
When the tomb hath no chain they cannot burst?
—Is it a thing forgotten, how he woke   170
From its deep rest of old, remembering Spain
In her great danger? —At the night's mid-watch
How Leon started, when the sound was heard
That shook her dark and hollow-echoing streets,
As with the heavy tramp of steel-clad men,
By thousands marching through![2]— For he had risen!

---

1   A famous legend; see *The Cid's Rising.*
2   This strategically located city in northwest Spain, reconquered from the Moors in the
    9th century, became the center of a Christian kingdom in the 10th century, and
    flourished from the 11th century through the 12th century. See the legend represented
    in *The Cid's Rising.*

The Campeador was on his way again
And in his arms, and follow'd by his Hosts
Of shadowy Spearmen! — He had left the World
[180] From which we are dimly parted, and gone forth,
And call'd his buried Warriors from their sleep,
Gathering them round him to deliver Spain,
For Afric was upon her! — Morning broke,
Day rush'd thro' clouds of Battle, for the Moor
250 Came with the strength of Nations; but at Eve
Our God had triumph'd, and the rescued Land
Sent up a shout of victory from the field
That rock'd her ancient Mountains!
THE CITIZENS.   Arm! to arms!
On to our Chief! — We have strength within us yet
To die with our blood rous'd. Now, be the Word,
[190] For the Cid's House!

They begin to arm themselves.

XIMENA.   Ye know his Battle-song?
The old rude strain wherewith his Bands march'd forth
To strike down Paynim swords! *(She sings)*

The Moor is on his way!
260 With the tambour-peal and the tecbir shout,
And the Horn o'er the blue seas pealing out,
He hath marshall'd his proud array!

Shout thro' the vine-clad Land!
That her Sons on all their Hills may hear,
And sharpen the point of the red Wolf spear,
[200] And the Sword for the brave Man's hand!

(The CITIZENS *join in the song; whilst they continue arming).*

Banners are in the field!
The Chief must rise from his joyous board,

The Campeador was on his march again,
And in his arms, and follow'd by his hosts
Of shadowy spearmen!—He had left the world
From which we are dimly parted, and gone forth,   180
And call'd his buried warriors from their sleep,
Gathering them round him to deliver Spain;
For Afric was upon her!—Morning broke—
Day rush'd through clouds of battle;—but at eve
� Our God had triumph'd, and the rescued land
Sent up a shout of victory from the field,
That rock'd her ancient mountains.
THE CITIZENS.   Arm! to arms!
On to our chief!—We have strength within us yet
To die with our blood roused!—Now, be the word,
For the Cid's house!

                              They begin to arm themselves.

XIMENA.   Ye know his battle-song?   190
The old rude strain wherewith his bands went forth
To strike down Paynim° swords!   (*She sings*)   *Pagan*

                THE CID'S BATTLE SONG

        The Moor is on his way!
    With the tambour-peal and the tecbir-shout,
    And the horn o'er the blue seas ringing out,
        He hath marshall'd his dark array!

        Shout through the vine-clad land!
    That her sons on all their hills may hear,
    And sharpen the point of the red wolf spear,
        And the sword for the brave man's hand!   200

(*The* CITIZENS *join in the song, while they continue arming themselves*).

        Banners are in the field!
    The chief must rise from his joyous board,

And turn from the Feast ere the Wine be pour'd,
270   And take up his Father's shield!

        The Moor is on his way!
Let the peasant leave his Olive-ground,
And the Goats roam wild thro' the Pine-woods round,
        There is nobler work to-day!

            Send forth the Trumpet's call!
[210]   Till the Bridegroom cast the Goblet down,
And the Marriage-robe and the flowery crown,
        And arm in the Banquet-Hall!

            And stay the Funeral train!
280   Bid the chaunted mass be hush'd awhile,
And the Bier laid down in the Holy Aisle,
        And the Mourners girt for Spain!

(They take up the Banner, and follow XIMENA *out, Till their Voices are
heard gradually dying away at a distance).*

        Ere night, must swords be red!
It is not an hour for Knells and tears,
But for Helmets brac'd, and serried Spears!
[220]   — To-morrow for the Dead!

        The Cid is in array!
His steed is barbed, his crest waves high,
His banner is up in the sunny sky,
290   Now, joy for the Cross to-day!

And turn from the feast ere the wine be pour'd,
    And take up his father's shield!

    The Moor is on his way!
Let the peasant leave his olive-ground,
And the goats roam wild through the pine-woods round!
    — There is nobler work to-day!

    Send forth the trumpet's call!
Till the bridegroom cast the goblet down,   210
And the marriage-robe and the flowery crown,
    And arm in the banquet-hall!

    And stay the funeral-train!
Bid the chanted mass be hush'd awhile,
And the bier laid down in the holy aile,[1]
    And the mourners girt for Spain!

(They take up the banner, and follow XIMENA *out. Their voices are heard
gradually dying away at a distance).*

    Ere night, must swords be red!
It is not an hour for knells and tears,
But for helmets braced, and serried spears!
    To-morrow for the dead!   220

    The Cid is in array!
His steed is barbed, his plume waves high,
His banner is up in the sunny sky,
    Now, joy for the Cross to-day!

---

1 Middle French for *wing* and the root for *aisle* (cf. MS), to which the word was emend-
   ed in posthumous editions.

SCENE 7

The Walls of the City.

GONSALVO— GARCIAS—HERNANDEZ.

The Plain beneath, with the Moorish Camp and Army.

(A wild sound of Moorish Music heard below).

HERNANDEZ. What notes are these, in their deep mournfulness
So strangely wild?
GARCIAS.   'Tis the shrill melody
Of the Moor's ancient death-song. Well I know
The rude barbaric sound, but, till this hour,
It seem'd not fearful. Now, a shuddering chill
Comes o'er me with its tones. Lo! from yon Tent,
They lead the noble Boys!
HERNANDEZ.   The young, and pure,
And beautiful Victims!—'Tis on things like these
We cast our hearts in wild idolatry,
Sowing the winds with Hope!—Yet this is well.
Thus brightly crown'd with Life's most gorgeous flowers,
And all unblemish'd, Earth should offer up
Her treasures unto Heaven!
GARCIAS *(to* GONSALVO*).*   My Chief, the Moor
Hath led your Children forth.
GONSALVO *(starting).*   Are my sons there?
I knew they could not perish, for yon Heaven
Would ne'er behold it!—Where is He that said
I was no more a Father?—They look chang'd—
Pallid and worn, as from a Prison-house!
Or is't mine eye sees dimly?—But their steps
Seem heavy, as with pain—I hear the clank—
—Oh God! their limbs are fetter'd!
ABDULLAH *(from beneath).*   Christian! look
Once more upon thy Children. There is yet
One moment for the trembling of the sword;
Their doom is still with thee.

SCENE [7]

The Walls of the City. The Plain beneath,
with the Moorish Camp and Army.

GONZALEZ, GARCIAS, HERNANDEZ.

(A wild Sound of Moorish Music heard from below).

HERNANDEZ. What notes are these in their deep mournfulness
So strangely wild?
GARCIAS.   'Tis the shrill melody
Of the Moor's ancient death-song. Well I know
The rude barbaric sound; but, till this hour,
It seem'd not fearful. —Now, a shuddering chill
Comes o'er me with its tones. —Lo! from yon tent
They lead the noble boys!
HERNANDEZ.   The young, and pure,
And beautiful victims! —'Tis on things like these
We cast our hearts in wild idolatry,
Sowing the winds with hope! —Yet this is well.   10
Thus brightly crown'd with life's most gorgeous flowers,
And all unblemish'd, earth should offer up
Her treasures unto Heaven!
GARCIAS (*to* GONZALEZ).   My chief, the Moor
Hath led your child forth.
GONZALEZ (*starting*).   Are my sons there?
I knew they could not perish; for yon Heaven
Would ne'er behold it! —Where is he that said
I was no more a father? —They look changed—
Pallid and worn, as from a prison-house!
Or is't mine eye sees dimly? —But their steps
Seem heavy, as with pain. —I hear the clank—   20
Oh God! their limbs are fetter'd!
ABDULLAH (*coming forward beneath the walls*).
                        Christian! look
Once more upon thy children. There is yet
One moment for the trembling of the sword;
Their doom is still with thee.

GONSALVO.   Why should this Man
So mock us with the semblance of our kind?
—Moor! Moor! thou dost too daringly provoke,
In thy bold cruelty, th' all-judging One,
Who visits for such things!—Hast thou no sense
Of thy frail Nature?—'Twill be taught thee yet,
[30]   30   And darkly shall the anguish of my Soul,
Darkly and heavily, pour itself on thine,
When thou shalt cry for mercy from the dust,
And be denied!
ABDULLAH.   Nay, is it not thyself,
That hast no mercy and no love within thee?
These are thy Sons, the nurslings of thy House,—
Speak, must they live or die?
GONSALVO *(in violent emotion)*.   Is it Heaven's will
To try the dust it kindles for a day,
With infinite agony?—How have I drawn
This chastening on my head?—They bloom'd around me,
[40]   40   And my heart grew too fearless in its joy,
Glorying in their bright promise!—If we fall,
Is there no pardon for our feebleness?

(HERNANDEZ, *without speaking, holds up* ~~the~~ *a Cross before him*).

ABDULLAH. Speak!
GONSALVO *(snatching the Cross & lifting it up)*.
                    Let the Earth be shaken thro' its depths,
But this must triumph!
ABDULLAH *(coldly)*.   Be it as thou wilt.
(To his Guards.) Unsheath the Scymetar!
GARCIAS *(to* GONSALVO*)*.   Away, my Chief!
This is your place no longer. There are things,
No human heart, though battle-proof as yours,
Unmadden'd may sustain.
GONSALVO.   Be still!—I have now
On Earth place on earth but this.

GONZALEZ.   Why should this man
So mock us with the semblance of our kind?
—Moor! Moor! thou dost too daringly provoke,
In thy bold cruelty, th' all-judging One,
Who visits for° such things!—Hast thou no sense   *avenges*
Of thy frail nature?—'Twill be taught thee yet,
And darkly shall the anguish of my soul,   30
Darkly and heavily, pour itself on thine,
When thou shalt cry for mercy from the dust,
And be denied!
ABDULLAH.   Nay, is it not thyself,
That hast no mercy and no love within thee?
These are thy sons, the nurslings of thy house;
Speak! must they live or die?
(GONZALEZ *in violent emotion*). Is it Heaven's will
To try the dust it kindles for a day,
With infinite agony![1]—How have I drawn
This chastening on my head!—They bloom'd around me,
And my heart grew too fearless in its joy,   40
Glorying in their bright promise!—If we fall,
Is there no pardon for our feebleness?

          HERNANDEZ, *without speaking, holds up a Cross before him.*

ABDULLAH. Speak!
GONZALEZ *(snatching the Cross, and lifting it up).*
                    Let the earth be shaken through its depths,
But *this* must triumph!
ABDULLAH *(coldly).*   Be it as thou wilt.
—Unsheath the scimetar! *(To his Guards.)*
GARCIAS *(to* GONZALEZ*).*   Away, my chief!
This is your place no longer. There are things
No human heart, though battle-proof as yours,
Unmadden'd may sustain.
GONZALEZ.   Be still! I have now
No place on earth but this!

---

1 Cf. Ximena's language at 6.95.

ALPHONSO *(from beneath).* Men! give me way,

50 That I may speak forth once before I die!

GARCIAS. The princely Boy! how gallantly his brow
Wears its high Nature in the face of death!

ALPHONSO. Father!

GONSALVO. My Son, my Son!—Mine eldest-born!

ALPHONSO. Stay but upon the ramparts!—Fear thou not—
That I shall bring dishonour on thy name!
There is good courage in me, Oh my Father!
I will not shame thee!—Only let me fall
Knowing thine eye looks proudly on thy Child,
So shall my heart have strength.

GONSALVO. Would, would to God,

60 That I might die for thee, my noble Boy,

Alphonso! my fair Son!

ALPHONSO. Could I have liv'd,
I might have been a Warrior!—Now, farewell!
But look upon me still!—I will not blench
When the keen Sabre flashes—Mark me well!
Mine eyelids shall not quiver as it falls,
So thou wilt look upon me.

GARCIAS *(to* GONSALVO*).* Nay, my Lord,
We must begone!—Thou canst not bear it.

GONSALVO. Peace!
Why, of what sensitive dust are Men made now?
—Lend me thine arm—my brain whirls fearfully—

70 How thick the Shades close round!—My Boy, My Boy!

Where art thou in this gloom?

GARCIAS. Let us go hence!
This is a dreadful moment!

GONSALVO. Hush!—what saidst thou?
Now let me look on him!—Dost thou see aught
Thro' the dull mist which wraps us?

GARCIAS. I behold—
Oh! for a thousand Spaniards to rush down—

GONSALVO. Thou seest?—my heart stands still to hear thee speak!
—There seems a fearful hush upon the air
As't were the dead of Night!

ALPHONSO *(from beneath)*.   Men! give me way,
That I may speak forth once before I die!   50
GARCIAS. The princely boy!—how gallantly his brow
Wears its high nature in the face of death!
ALPHONSO. Father!
GONZALEZ.   My son! my son!—Mine eldest-born!
ALPHONSO. Stay but upon the ramparts!—Fear thou not—
There is good courage in me: oh! my father!
I will not shame thee!—only let me fall
Knowing thine eye looks proudly on thy child,
So shall my heart have strength.
GONZALEZ.   Would, would to God,
That I might die for thee, my noble boy!
Alphonso, my fair son!
ALPHONSO.   Could I have lived,   60
I might have been a warrior!—Now, farewell!
But look upon me still!—I will not blench
When the keen sabre flashes—Mark me well!
Mine eyelids shall not quiver as it falls,
So thou wilt look upon me!
GARCIAS *(to* GONZALEZ*)*.   Nay, my lord!
We must begone!—Thou *canst* not bear it!
GONZALEZ.   Peace!
—Who hath told *thee* how much man's heart can bear?
—Lend me thine arm—my brain whirls fearfully—
How thick the shades close round!—my boy! my boy!
Where art thou in this gloom?
GARCIAS.   Let us go hence!   70
This is a dreadful moment!
GONZALEZ.   Hush!—what saidst thou?
Now let me look on him!—Dost *thou* see aught
Through the dull mist which wraps us?
GARCIAS.   I behold—
Oh! for a thousand Spaniards to rush down—
GONZALEZ. Thou seest—My heart stands still to hear thee speak!
—There seems a fearful hush upon the air,
As't were the dead of night!

GARCIAS.   The Hosts have clos'd
Around the spot, in stillness. Thro' the spears,
Rang'd thick and motionless, I see him not,
But now —

GONSALVO.   He bade me keep mine eye upon him,
And all is darkness round me! — Now?

GARCIAS.   A Sword,
A Sword springs upward, like a lightning burst,
Through the dark serried mass! — Its cold blue glare
Is wavering to and fro — 'tis vanish'd — Hark!

GONSALVO. I heard it, yes! I heard the dull dead sound,
That heavily broke the silence! — didst thou speak?
— I lost thy words — come nearer!

GARCIAS.   'Twas — 'tis past! —
The sword fell <u>then!</u>

(Gonsalvo sinks back into his arms)

HERNANDEZ *(with a burst of exultation).*
                         Flow forth, thou noble blood!
Filling the cup of Spain's deliverance, flow
Uncheck'd and brightly forth! — Thou kingly stream!
Blood of our Heroes! ~~bl~~ Blood of Martyrdom!
Which thro' so many Warrior-hearts hast pour'd
Thy fiery currents, and hast made our Hills
Free by thine own free offering, 'tis the hour
Of the prevailing triumph! — Bathe the soil,
But there thou shalt not sink! — Our very Air
Shall take thy colouring, and our loaded skies
O'er th' Infidel hang dark and ominous
With Battle-hues of thee! — And thy deep Voice,
Rising above them to the Judgment-seat
Shall call a burst of gather'd Vengeance down,
As the Wind sweeps the locust-clouds away,
To sweep th' Oppressor from us! For his guilt
Is full! Thy fount swells darkly o'er its bounds,
Rise! and awake the Heavens!

GONSALVO *(raising himself).*   'Tis all a dream!

GARCIAS.   The hosts have closed
  Around the spot in stillness. Through the spears,
  Ranged thick and motionless, I see him not;
  —But now—

GONZALEZ.   He bade me keep mine eye upon him,   80
  And all is darkness round me!—Now?

GARCIAS.   A sword,
  A sword, springs upward, like a lightning burst,
  Through the dark serried mass!—Its cold blue glare
  Is wavering to and fro—'tis vanish'd—hark!

GONZALEZ. I heard it, yes!—I heard the dull dead sound
  That heavily broke the silence!—Didst thou speak?
  —I lost thy words—come nearer!

GARCIAS.   'Twas—'tis past!—
  The sword fell then!

HERNANDEZ (*with exultation*). Flow forth thou noble blood!
  Fount of Spain's ransom and deliverance, flow
  Uncheck'd and brightly forth!—Thou kingly stream!   90
  Blood of our heroes! blood of martyrdom!
  Which through so many warrior-hearts hast pour'd
  Thy fiery currents, and hast made our hills
  Free, by thine own free offering!—Bathe the land,
  But there thou shalt not sink!—Our very air
  Shall take thy colouring, and our loaded skies
  O'er th' infidel hang dark and ominous,
  With battle-hues of thee!—And thy deep voice
  Rising above them to the judgment-seat
  Shall call a burst of gather'd vengeance down,   100
  To sweep th' oppressor from us!—For thy wave
  Hath made his guilt run o'er!

GONZALEZ (*endeavouring to rouse himself*).
                         'Tis all a dream!

There is not one — no hand on Earth would harm
That fair Boy's graceful head! — Heaven doth not breathe
Into such glorious things the breath of Life,
That it should be so quench'd! — Why look you thus?

ABDULLAH (*pointing to* CARLOS).

Christian! e'en yet thou hast a Son!

GONSALVO.   E'en yet!

CARLOS. My Father! take me from these bloody Men!
Wilt thou not save me, Father?

GONSALVO (*attempting to unsheath his sword*).

                                        Is the strength
From mine arm shiver'd? — Garcias, follow me!

GARCIAS. Whither, my Chief?

GONSALVO.   Why, we can die as well
On yonder plain, — aye, a spear's thrust will do
The little that our misery doth require,
Sooner, than e'en this Anguish. Life is best
Thrown from us in such moments!

Voices heard at a distance.

HERNANDEZ.   Hark! what strain
Swells in the Wind?

GARCIAS.   'Tis the Cid's Battle-song!
What marvel hath been wrought?

Voices approaching, are heard in chorus.

The Moor is on his Way!
With the tambour peal and the tecbir shout,
And the Horn o'er the blue Seas pealing out,
He hath marshall'd his dark array.

XIMENA *enters, followed by the* CITIZENS *in arms, and with the Banner.*

XIMENA. Is it too late? — My father, these are Men
Thro' Life and Death prepar'd to follow thee
Beneath this Banner! — Is their zeal too late?

There is not one — no hand on earth could harm
That fair boy's graceful head! — Why look you thus?
ABDULLAH (*pointing to* CARLOS).
    Christian! e'en yet thou hast a son!
GONZALEZ.   E'en yet!
CARLOS. My father! take me from these fearful men!
    Wilt thou not save me, father?
GONZALEZ (*attempting to unsheath his sword*).
                    Is the strength
    From mine arm shiver'd? — Garcias, follow me!
GARCIAS. Whither, my chief?
GONZALEZ.   Why, we can die as well

He already decides to go fighting

    On yonder plain, — aye, a spear's thrust will do   110
    The little that our misery doth require,
    Sooner than e'en this anguish! Life is best
    Thrown from us in such moments.

                  Voices heard at a distance.

HERNANDEZ.   Hush! what strain
    Floats on the wind?
GARCIAS.   'Tis the Cid's battle song!
    What marvel hath been wrought?

             Voices approaching heard in chorus.

        The Moor is on his way!
    With the tambour peal and the tecbir shout,
    And the horn o'er the blue seas ringing out,
        He hath marshall'd his dark array!

    XIMENA *enters, followed by the* CITIZENS *with the Banner.*

XIMENA. Is it too late? — My father, these are men   120
    Through life and death prepared to follow thee
    Beneath this banner! — Is their zeal too late?

kinda yes?

— Oh! there 's a fearful history on thy brow!
130   What hast thou seen?

GARCIAS.   It is not <u>all</u> too late.

XIMENA. My Brothers!

HERNANDEZ.   All is well. (*To* GARCIAS)
                       Peace! wouldst thou chill
That which hath sprung within them, as a flame
From th' Altar-embers mounts in sudden brightness?
I say, 'tis not too late. Ye Men of Spain!
On to the rescue!

XIMENA.   Bless me, oh my Father!

[130]   And I will hence, to aid thee with my prayers,
Sending my Spirit with thee, thro' the storm,
Lit up by flashing swords.

GONSALVO *(falling upon her neck).*
                      Hath aught been spar'd?
Am I not all bereft? — Thou'rt left me still,
140   My own, my loveliest one, thou'rt left me still!
— Farewell! — thy Father's blessing, and thy God's,
Be with thee, my Ximena!

XIMENA.   Fare thee well!

(She returns and again embraces him)

If, ere thy steps turn homeward from the field,
The voice is hush'd that still hath welcom'd thee,
— Think of me in thy Victory!

HERNANDEZ.   Peace! no more!

[140]   This is no time to melt our Nature down
To a feeble stream of Womanish tears!
Bearing resolve away. — Be of strong heart!
Give me the Banner, swell the song again!

150 CITIZENS.   Ere night, must swords be red!
It is not ~~a time~~ an hour for knells and tears,
But for Helmets braced and serried Spears!
— To-morrow for the Dead!

Exeunt omnes.

—Oh! there 's a fearful history on thy brow!
What hast thou seen?
GARCIAS.   It is not *all* too late.
XIMENA. My brothers!
HERNANDEZ.   All is well.
    (*To* GARCIAS)   Hush! wouldst thou chill
That which hath sprung within them, as a flame
From th' altar-embers mounts in sudden brightness?
I say, 'tis not too late, ye men of Spain!
On to the rescue!
XIMENA.   Bless me, oh my father!
And I will hence, to aid thee with my prayers,   130
Sending my spirit with thee through the storm,
Lit up by flashing swords!
GONZALEZ *(falling upon her neck).*
                        Hath aught been spared?
Am I not all bereft? — Thou'rt left me still!
Mine own, my loveliest one, thou'rt left me still!
Farewell! — thy father's blessing, and thy God's,
Be with thee, my Ximena!
XIMENA.   Fare thee well!
If, ere thy steps turn homeward from the field,
The voice is hush'd that still hath welcomed thee,
Think of me in thy victory!
HERNANDEZ.   Peace! no more!
This is no time to melt our nature down   140
To a soft stream of tears! — Be of strong heart!
Give me the banner! Swell the song again!

He takes the banner. It is passed from noble to noble, allowing them to lead the citizens.

THE CITIZENS.

Ere night, must swords be red!
It is not an hour for knells and tears,
But for helmets braced and serried spears!
    — To-morrow for the dead!

                        Exeunt omnes.

SCENE [8]

The inside of a Gothic Church. ELMINA *rises before the Altar.*

ELMINA. The clouds are fearful that o'erhang thy ways,
　　Oh thou mysterious Heaven! — It cannot be
　　That I have drawn the Vials of thy Wrath,
　　To burst upon me thro' the lifting up
　　Of a proud heart, elate in Happiness!
　　No! in my Day's ~~bright~~ full noon, for me Life's flowers
　　But wreath'd a cup of Trembling; and the love,
　　The boundless Love, my Spirit was form'd to bear,
　　Hath ever, in its place of silence, been

[10]　10　A trouble and a shadow! wearing still
　　Ev'n in its clearest hours, a hue of thought
　　Too deeply ting'd for joy! — I never look'd
　　On my fair Children, in their [?—] ~~springing~~ buoyant Mirth,
　　Or sunny sleep, when all the gentle air
　　Seem'd glowing with their quiet blessedness,
　　But o'er my Soul there came a shuddering sense
　　Of Earth, and its pale changes; even like that
　　Which vaguely mingles with our glorious dreams
　　A restless and disturbing consciousness

　　20　That the bright things must fade! — And still doth pour
　　Thro' all their lovely Music some dull tone,
　　Which warns us it is passing. — How I shrunk

[20]　From the dim warnings of th' unquiet Voice,
　　As from the sudden anguish of a Wound
　　That wakes midst revelry; and vainly strove
　　To lose its memory in their smiles! — Their smiles!
　　— Where are those bright looks now? Could they go down,
　　With all their o'erflowing Soul of light and joy,
　　To the cold grave? — My Children! — Righteous Heaven!

　　30　There floats a dark remembrance o'er my Soul,
　　Of one who told me, with relentless eye,
　　That this should be the hour!

XIMENA *enters.*

SCENE [8]

Before the Altar of a Church. ELMINA *rises from the steps of the Altar.*

ELMINA. The clouds are fearful that o'erhang thy ways,
 Oh, thou mysterious Heaven!—It cannot be
 That I have drawn the vials of thy wrath,
 To burst upon me through the lifting up
 Of a proud heart, elate in happiness! ∽
 No! in my day's full noon, for me life's flowers
 But wreath'd a cup of trembling; and the love,
 The boundless love, my spirit was form'd to bear,
 Hath ever, in its place of silence, been
 A trouble and a shadow, tinging thought   10
 With hues too deep for joy!—I never look'd
 On my fair children, in their buoyant mirth,
 Or sunny sleep, when all the gentle air
 Seem'd glowing with their quiet blessedness,
 But o'er my soul there came a shuddering sense
 Of earth, and its pale changes; even like that
 Which vaguely mingles with our glorious dreams,
 A restless and disturbing consciousness
 That the bright things must fade!—How have I shrunk
 From the dull murmur of th' unquiet voice,   20
 With its low tokens of mortality,
 Till my heart fainted midst their smiles!—their smiles!
 —Where are those glad looks now?—Could they go down,
 With all their joyous light, that seem'd not earth's,
 To the cold grave?—My children!—Righteous Heaven!
 There floats a dark remembrance o'er my brain
 Of one who told me, with relentless eye,
 That *this* should be the hour!

                                          XIMENA *enters.*

XIMENA.   They are gone forth
Unto the rescue! — strong in heart and hope,
[30]   Faithful, tho' few! — My Mother, let thy prayers
Call on the Land's good Saints to lift once more
The Sword and Cross that sweep the field for Spain,
As in old ~~days; and make our Banner's path~~
~~Again triumph;~~ Battle; so thine Arms e'en yet
May clasp thy Sons! — For me, my part is done.
40   The flame which dimly might have linger'd yet
A little while, hath gather'd all its rays
Brightly to sink at once; and it is well.
The shadows are around me; to thy heart
Fold me, that I may die.
ELMINA.   My Child! what dream
[40]   Is on thy Soul? — Why, from thy brow shines forth,
Life's brightest Inspiration!
XIMENA.   Death's!
ELMINA.   Away!
It is not thus! the light that fills thine eye,
Is like a glory, an immortal ray
Of quenchless hope and joy! Ne'er hath it beam'd
50   With such a strong clearness! And thy cheek
Doth glow beneath it with a richer hue
Than ting'd its earliest flower.
XIMENA.   It well may be!
There are far deeper and far warmer hues
Than those which draw their colouring from the founts
Of Youth, or Health, or Hope.
ELMINA.   Nay, speak not thus!
My Child! there's that about thee shining which would send
E'en through <u>my</u> heart a sunny glow of Hope,
[50]   Wer't not for these sad words! — The dim cold air
And solemn light, which wrap these tombs and shrines
60   With a pale stillness, like the hush of grief
Worn down to slumber, seem as kindled up
With a young Spirit of ethereal hope,
Caught from thy radiant mien! — We die not thus!
XIMENA. Why should not He, whose touch doth burst our chain,
Put on his robes of beauty, when he comes

XIMENA.   They are gone forth
 Unto the rescue! — strong in heart and hope,
 Faithful, though few! — My mother, let thy prayers   30
 Call on the land's good saints to lift once more
 The sword and cross that sweep the field for Spain,
 As in old battle; so thine arms e'en yet
 May clasp thy sons! — For me, my part is done!
 The flame, which dimly might have linger'd yet
 A little while, hath gather'd all its rays
 Brightly to sink at once; and it is well!
 The shadows are around me; to thy heart
 Fold me, that I may die.
ELMINA.   My child! — What dream
 Is on thy soul? — Even now thine aspect wears   40
 Life's brightest inspiration!
XIMENA.   Death's!
ELMINA.   Away!
 Thine eye hath starry clearness, and thy cheek
 Doth glow beneath it with a richer hue
 Than tinged its earliest flower!
XIMENA.   It well may be!
 There are far deeper and far warmer hues
 Than those which draw their colouring from the founts
 Of youth, or health, or hope.
ELMINA.   Nay, speak not thus!
 There's that about thee shining which would send
 E'en through *my* heart a sunny glow of joy,
 Wer't not for these sad words. The dim cold air   50
 And solemn light, which wrap these tombs and shrines
 As a pale gleaming shroud, seem kindled up
 With a young spirit of ethereal hope
 Caught from thy mien! — Oh no! this is not death!
XIMENA. Why should not He, whose touch dissolves our chain,
 Put on his robes of beauty when he comes

As a Deliverer? — He hath many forms;
They should not all be fearful! — If his call
Be but our gathering to that distant Land
[60]   For whose sweet Waters we have pin'd with thirst,
70   Why should not its prophetic sense be borne
Into the heart's deep stillness, with a breath
Of summer-winds, a Voice of Melody,
Solemn, yet lovely? — Mother! I depart.
And let it be thy comfort, when my place
On this dull Earth beholdeth me no more,
That thou hast seen me thus!

ELMINA   Distract me not
With such wild fears! — Can I bear on with Life
When thou art gone? — Thy Voice, thy step, thy smile,
Pass'd from my path? — Heaven wills not we should run
80   Our course thro' starless Night! — Alas! thine eye
[70]   Is chang'd, thy cheek is fading!

XIMENA.   Aye, the cloud
Of the dim hour is gathering o'er my sight,
And yet I fear not, for the God of Help
Is in that quiet darkness! — It may soothe
Thy woes, my Mother, if I tell thee now,
With what glad calmness I behold the shades
Falling between me and the World, wherein
My heart so ill hath rested.

ELMINA.   Thine!

XIMENA.   Rejoice
For her, that, when the garland of her Life
90   Was ~~wither'd~~ blighted, and the Springs of Life were dried,
[80]   Receiv'd her summons hence; and had no time,
Bearing the canker at th' impatient heart,
To wither, sorrowing for that gift of Heaven,
Which lent one moment of existence light,
That dimm'd the rest for ever!

ELMINA.   How is this?
My Child, what mean'st thou?

XIMENA.   Mother! I have loved,
And been belov'd! — The sunbeam of an hour,

As a deliverer? — He hath many forms,
They should not all be fearful! — If his call
Be but our gathering to that distant land
For whose sweet waters we have pined with thirst,   60
Why should not its prophetic sense be borne
Into the heart's deep stillness, with a breath
Of summer-winds, a voice of melody,
Solemn, yet lovely? — Mother! I depart!
— Be it thy comfort, in the after-days,
That thou hast seen me thus!
ELMINA.   Distract me not
With such wild fears! Can I bear on with life
When thou art gone? — Thy voice, thy step, thy smile,
Pass'd from my path? — Alas! even now thine eye
Is changed — thy cheek is fading!
XIMENA.   Aye, the clouds   70
Of the dim hour are gathering o'er my sight,
And yet I fear not, for the God of Help
Comes in that quiet darkness! — It may soothe
Thy woes, my mother! if I tell thee now,
With what glad calmness I behold the veil
Falling between me and the world, wherein
My heart so ill hath rested.
ELMINA.   Thine!
XIMENA.   Rejoice
For her, that, when the garland of her life
Was blighted, and the springs of hope were dried,
Received her summons hence; and had no time,   80
Bearing the canker at th' impatient heart,
To wither, sorrowing for that gift of Heaven,
Which lent one moment of existence light,
That dimm'd the rest for ever!
ELMINA.   How is this?
My child, what mean'st thou?
XIMENA.   Mother! I have loved,
And been beloved! — the sunbeam of an hour,

Which gave Life's hidden treasures to ~~mine eyes~~ my sight,
As they lay shining in their secret founts,
100 Went out, and left them colourless! — The drop
Of heavenly dew, which center'd in itself
All glorious hues from Nature's riches caught,
Was shaken from the flower, which, so bereft,
In the fierce Noon-day sicken'd. — I have lov'd,
And been belov'd! — And it is past! — for me
[90] Earth's festal garb hath dropp'd, the rainbow mist,
Thro' which I gaz'd hath melted, and ~~my sight~~ mine ~~eyes~~ eye
~~Are~~ Is clear'd to look on all things as they are.
— But this is far too mournful! and the gift
110 Hath fall'n too early and too cold upon me!
— Therefore I would go hence.
ELMINA.   And thou hast lov'd
Unknown——
XIMENA.   Oh! pardon, pardon that I wrapt
My thoughts from thee! But Thou hadst woes enough,
And mine came o'er me when thy Soul had need
Of more than earthly strength! — For I had scarce
[100] Given to the deep and thrilling consciousness
That I was lov'd, a treasure's place within
My secret heart, when Death (oh! welcome now!)
Swept by me in my path, and left his trace
120 There, like a dried up torrent's!
                                    'Twas at morn,
I saw the Warriors to their field go forth,
And <u>mine</u> was in his place amidst the rest,
And his high mien was lighted, as he pass'd,
With glory and with joy! — I look'd again —
The strife grew dark beneath me, but his Crest
Wav'd free above the Lances! — Yet again —
— It had gone down! and Steeds were trampling o'er
The spot to which mine eyes were riveted,
[110] Till ~~darken'd~~ blinded by th' intenseness of their gaze!
130 And then — at last — I hurried to the Gate,
And met him there! — I met him! — On his shield —
And with his cloven Helm, and shiver'd sword,

Which gave life's hidden treasures to mine eye,
As they lay shining in their secret founts,
Went out, and left them colourless. —'Tis past—
And what remains on earth?— the rainbow mist,   90
Through which I gazed, hath melted, and my sight
Is clear'd to look on all things as they are!
—But this is far too mournful!—Life's dark gift
Hath fallen too early and too cold upon me!
—Therefore I would go hence!
ELMINA.   And thou hast loved
    Unknown—
XIMENA.   Oh! pardon, pardon that I veil'd
My thoughts from thee!—But thou hadst woes enough,
And mine came o'er me when thy soul had need
Of more than mortal strength!—For I had scarce
Given the deep consciousness that I was loved   100
A treasure's place within my secret heart,
When earth's brief joy went from me!
                                        'Twas at morn
I saw the warriors to their field go forth,
And he—my chosen—was there amongst the rest,
With his young, glorious brow!—I look'd again—
The strife grew dark beneath me—but his plume
Waved free above the lances. —Yet again—
—It had gone down! and steeds were trampling o'er
The spot to which mine eyes were riveted,
Till blinded by th' intenseness of their gaze!   110
—And then—at last—I hurried to the gate,
And met him there!—I met him!—on his shield,
And with his cloven helm, and shiver'd sword,

And dark plume steep'd in blood! — They bore him past —
Mother! I saw his face — Oh! such a death
Works fearful changes on the fair of earth,
The pride of Woman's eye!

ELMINA.   Sweet Daughter, peace!
Wake not the dark remembrance; for thy frame —

XIMENA. — There <u>will</u> be Peace ere long. I shut my heart,

[120]   Ev'n as a tomb, o'er that lone silent grief,
140   That I might spare it thee. This is the World
For the luxurious Weeper! — Well I knew
Thou hadst a Hero's ~~lofty~~ glorious toils to share
And shouldst not turn from that majestic task,
To ~~mourn~~ / ~~weep~~ mourn a broken reed! — But now the hour
Is come, when that, which would have pierc'd thy Soul
Shall be its healing balm. Oh! weep thou not,
Save with a gentle sorrow!

ELMINA.   Must it be?
Art thou indeed to leave me?

XIMENA *(with a wild exultation).* Be thou glad,
I say, rejoice above thy favour'd Child!
150   One grief hath fill'd her cup, and she is call'd
To rest from her brief Pilgrimage, when Death
Had thrown his Wing's first shadow o'er the way.
Joy, for the Soldier when his field is fought,
Joy, for the Peasant when his Vintage task
Is clos'd at Eve! But most of all for her,

[130]   Who, when her Life had chang'd its glittering robes
For the dull garb of Sorrow, which doth cling
So heavily around the Journeyers on,
Cast down its weight — and slept!

ELMINA.   Alas! thine eye
160   Is wandering, yet how brightly! — On thy brow
Sits a Triumphant wildness! Is this Death,
Or some high wondrous Vision? — Speak, my Child!
How is it with thee now?

XIMENA *(wildly).*   Hark! heard ye not
The Trumpet of Castile? — I see it still,
'Tis floating, like a glorious cloud on high,

And dark hair steep'd in blood!—They bore him past—
Mother!—I saw his face!—Oh! such a death
Works fearful changes on the fair of earth,
The pride of woman's eye!
ELMINA.   Sweet daughter, peace!
Wake not the dark remembrance; for thy frame—
XIMENA.—There *will* be peace ere long. I shut my heart,
Even as a tomb, o'er that lone silent grief,   120
That I might spare it thee!—But now the hour
Is come when that which would have pierced thy soul
Shall be its healing balm. Oh! weep thou not,
Save with a gentle sorrow!
ELMINA.   Must it be?
Art thou indeed to leave me?
XIMENA *(exultingly).*   Be thou glad!
I say, rejoice above thy favour'd child!
Joy, for the soldier when his field is fought,
Joy, for the peasant when his vintage-task
Is closed at eve!—But most of all for her,
Who, when her life had changed its glittering robes   130
For the dull garb of sorrow, which doth cling
So heavily around the journeyers on,
Cast down its weight—and slept![1]
ELMINA.   Alas! thine eye
Is wandering—yet how brightly!—Is this death,
Or some high wondrous vision?—Speak, my child!
How is it with thee now?
XIMENA *(wildly).*   I see it still!
'Tis floating, like a glorious cloud on high,

---

1   Near the close of *Memorials,* Chorley writes: "it is remarkable and soothing to observe
the calmness and gentle resignation which gathered round [Hemans] as she approached
the close of her life.[...] In the poems, written in her most *chevalresque* mood, some
indication of this sentiment may always be traced. Thus in the 'siege of Valencia,'—
[quotes 55-64 and these lines from 128.] [...] Though the words are Ximena's the
thoughts were her own" (*CM* 2.323-24).

My Father's Banner! — Swells there not a Voice
Of Victory on the Winds? — Praise, praise to Heaven!
The Conqueror comes, and I go forth, array'd
In Joy to meet him, for my Work is done!
[140] 170   — But I must slumber first — Be still! — Who calls
The Night so fearful? ——

                                                    She dies.

ELMINA.   No! — she is not dead!
Ximena, speak to me! — Oh! yet a tone
From that sweet Voice, that I may gather in
One more remembrance of its lovely sound,
Ere Music pass from Earth! — What! is all still'd?
— But no! It cannot be! — We need too much
Beings like her, when evil days are on us,
To chase the dark misgivings of our Souls,
With images of Heaven! — Why 'tis by looks
180   That shine like hers, we learn how bless'd Hope
Doth light pure Spirits up! — But this is not
Her wonted smile — When it hath seem'd so fix'd
[150]   Her life is frozen to it! — Speak, Ximena!
This stillness is too ~~fearful~~ dreadful! — She is gone!
— Gone! — what a dull cold sound is in that word!
My Child, my Child! — What must it henceforth be
Enough to know that <u>once</u> a thing so fair
Had its bright place amongst us? — Is this all
Left for the years to come? — Hush! doth she move?
190   One light lock seem'd to tremble on her brow
As a pulse throbb'd beneath! — 'twas but the Voice
Of my despair that stirr'd it! — She is gone!

(She throws herself on the body. GONSALVO *enters, alone, and wounded.)*

ELMINA *(rising as he approaches).*
I must not <u>now</u> be scorn'd! No! not a look,
A whisper of disdain! — My Sorrow claims
Deep reverence for its fearful majesty!
[160]   — Thou <u>canst</u> not scorn me now!

My father's banner!—Hear'st thou not a sound?
The trumpet of Castile?—Praise, praise to Heaven!
—Now may the weary rest!—Be still!—Who calls   140
The night so fearful?——

                                                    She dies.

ELMINA.   No! she is not dead!
    —Ximena!—speak to me!—Oh! yet a tone
From that sweet voice, that I may gather in
One more remembrance of its lovely sound,
Ere the deep silence fall!—What! is all hush'd?
—No, no!—it cannot be!—How should we bear
The dark misgivings of our souls, if Heaven
Left not such beings with us?—But is this
Her wonted look?—too sad a quiet lies
On its dim fearful beauty!—Speak, Ximena!   150
Speak!—my heart dies within me!—She is gone,
With all her blessed smiles!—My child! my child!
Where art thou?—Where is that which answer'd me,
From thy soft-shining eyes?—Hush! doth she move?
—One light lock seem'd to tremble on her brow,
As a pulse throbb'd beneath;—'twas but the voice
Of my despair that stirr'd it!—She is gone!

She throws herself on the body. GONZALEZ *enters, alone, and wounded.*

ELMINA *(rising as he approaches).*
    I must not *now* be scorn'd!—No, not a look,
A whisper of reproach!—Behold my woe!
—Thou canst not scorn me now!

GONSALVO.   Hast thou heard <u>all</u>?
ELMINA. Thy Daughter on my bosom laid her head,
    And pass'd away to rest! — Behold her there,
    Even such as Death hath made her!
GONSALVO (*bending over* XIMENA).   Thou art gone
200   A little while before me, oh, my Child!
    Why should the Traveller weep to part with those
    That scarce an hour will reach their promis'd Land
    Ere he too cast his Pilgrim staff away,
    ~~In~~ And spread his couch beside them!
ELMINA.   Who will stay,
    Now that each gentle spirit hath been call'd,
    And all the melodies of Life are lost
    In the fierce din of arms? — We need not weep,
[172]   Earth's chain each hour grows weaker!
GONSALVO (*still gazing upon* XIMENA).   And thou'rt laid
    To slumber in the Shadow, blessed Child!
210   Of a yet stainless Altar, and beneath
    A sainted Warrior's tomb! Oh! fitting place
    For thee to yield thy pure heroic Soul,
    Back unto him that gave it! — And thy cheek
    Yet smiles in its bright paleness!
ELMINA.   Hadst thou seen
    The look with which she pass'd!
GONSALVO (*still bending over the body*).
                                    Why, 'tis almost
[180]   Like Joy to view thy beautiful repose!
    The faded image of that perfect calm
    Doth float, as long-forgotten Music back
    Into my weary heart! — No dark wild spot
220   On <u>thy</u> clear brow doth tell of bloody hands
    That quench'd young Life by violence! — We have seen
    Too much of horror in one crowded hour,
    To weep for aught so gently gather'd hence!

GONZALEZ.   Hast thou heard *all?*

ELMINA. Thy daughter on my bosom laid her head,
And pass'd away to rest. — Behold her there,
Even such as death hath made her![1]

GONZALEZ *(bending over* XIMENA's *body).* Thou art gone
A little while before me, oh, my child!
Why should the traveller weep to part with those
That scarce an hour will reach their promised land
Ere he too cast his pilgrim staff away,
And spread his couch beside them?

ELMINA.   Must it be
Henceforth enough that *once* a thing so fair
Had its bright place amongst us? — Is this all,   170
Left for the years to come? — We will not stay!
Earth's chain each hour grows weaker.

GONZALEZ *(still gazing upon* XIMENA*).* And thou'rt laid
To slumber in the shadow, blessed child!
Of a yet stainless altar, and beside
A sainted warrior's tomb! — Oh, fitting place
For thee to yield thy pure heroic soul
Back unto him that gave it! — And thy cheek
Yet smiles in its bright paleness!

ELMINA.   Hadst thou seen
The look with which she pass'd!

GONZALEZ *(still bending over her).* Why, 'tis almost
Like joy to view thy beautiful repose!   180
The faded image of that perfect calm
Floats, e'en as long-forgotten music, back
Into my weary heart! — No dark wild spot
On *thy* clear brow doth tell of bloody hands
That quench'd young life by violence! — We have seen
Too much of horror, in one crowded hour,
To weep for aught, so gently gather'd hence!

---

1 "La voilà, telle que la mort nous l'a faite!" —*Bossuet, Oraisons Funèbres.* [FH]
[There she is, what death has made of her for us!] Jacques Bénigne Bossuet (1627-
1704), *Oraisons Funèbres H. d'Angl.* (1669). The French prelate was famed for his elo-
quent orations, which also supply FH's epigraphs for *Stanzas on the Late National
Calamity: The Death of the Princess Charlotte,* in *Translations* (1818), and the title-page of
The Sceptic (1820).

THE PUBLICATION OF 1823   213

—Oh! <u>Man</u> leaves other traces!

ELMINA *(suddenly starting)*.   It returns
      On my bewilder'd Soul!—Went ye not forth
[190]   Unto the rescue?—And thou'rt here alone!
      Where are my Sons?

GONSALVO *(solemnly)*.   We were too late.

ELMINA.   Too late!
      Hast thou nought else to tell me?

GONSALVO.   I brought back
      From that last field, the Banner of my Sires,
230   And my own death-wound.

ELMINA.   Thine!

GONSALVO.   Another hour
      Shall hush its throbs for ever! I go hence,
      And with me———

ELMINA.   No! Man could not lift his hand—
      —Where hast thou left thy Sons?

GONSALVO.   I have no Sons.

ELMINA. What hast thou said?—Speak forth!

GONSALVO.   There lives not one,
      To wear the glory of mine ancient house,
[200]   When I have sunk to rest.

ELMINA *(throwing herself upon the body of Ximena, & speaking in a low*
      hurried voice).
      In one brief hour, all gone!—and such a death!
      —I see their blood gush forth!—Oh God! to think
      Of those fair features rigidly convuls'd,
240   Those eyes' bright laughter quench'd in Agony!
      —And <u>such</u> a death for them!—I was not there!
      They were but mine in beauty and in joy,
      Not in that mortal anguish!—All, all gone!
      Why should I struggle more?—What <u>is</u> this Power,
      Against whose might, on all sides pressing us,
      We strive with fierce impatience, which but lays
[210]   Our own frail spirits prostrate?
      (After a long pause).
                              Now I know
      Thy hand, my God!—and they are soonest crush'd
      That most withstand it!—I resist no more.

—Oh! *man* leaves other traces!
ELMINA *(suddenly starting)*.   It returns
    On my bewilder'd soul!—Went ye not forth
    Unto the rescue?—And thou'rt here alone!   190
    —Where are my sons?
GONZALEZ *(solemnly)*.   We were too late!
ELMINA.   Too late!
    Hast thou nought else to tell me?
GONZALEZ.   I brought back
    From that last field the banner of my sires,
    And my own death-wound.
ELMINA.   Thine!
GONZALEZ.   Another hour
    Shall hush its throbs for ever. I go hence,
    And with me———
ELMINA.   No!—Man *could* not lift his hands—
    —Where hast thou left thy sons?
GONZALEZ.   I *have* no sons.
ELMINA. What hast thou said?
GONZALEZ.   That now there lives not one
    To wear the glory of mine ancient house,
    When I am gone to rest.   200
ELMINA *(throwing herself on the ground, and speaking in a low hurried
        voice)*.
    In one brief hour, all gone!—and *such* a death!
    —I see their blood gush forth!—their graceful heads—
    —Take the dark vision from me, oh, my God!
    And such a death for *them!*—I was not there!
    They were but mine in beauty and in joy,
    Not in that mortal anguish!—All, all gone!
    —Why should I struggle more?—What *is* this Power,
    Against whose might, on all sides pressing us,
    We strive with fierce impatience, which but lays
    Our own frail spirits prostrate?
(After a long pause).   Now I know   210
    Thy hand, my God!—and they are soonest crush'd
    That most withstand it!—I resist no more.

250   *(She rises).*—A light, a light springs up from Grief and Death,
        Which with its solemn radiance doth reveal
        Why we have thus been search'd!
    GONSALVO.   Then I may still
        Fix my last look on thee in holy Love,
        Parting, but yet with Hope.
    ELMINA *(falling at his feet).*   Canst Thou forgive?
        —Oh! I have driven the Arrow to thy heart,
        That should have buried it within mine own,
        And borne the pang in silence, teaching Thee

[220]   Scarcely to deem it painful! I have cast
        Thy life's fair honour, in my wild Despair,
260   As an unvalued gem upon the Waves,
        Whence thou hast snatch'd it back, to bear from Earth,
        All stainless, on thy breast. —Well hast thou done!
        But I—canst Thou forgive?
    GONSALVO *(raising her).*   Within this hour
        I have stood upon that Verge whence Mortals fall,
        And learn'd how 'tis with One whose sight grows dim,
        And whose foot trembles on the Gulf's dark side.
        Death purifies all feeling—We will part

[230]   In pity and in love!
    ELMINA.   Death!—And thou too
        Art on thy way!—Oh! Joy for thee, high heart!
270   Glory and Joy for thee! The day is clos'd,
        And well and nobly hast thou borne thyself
        Through its long Battle-toils, though many Swords
        Have entered thine own Soul!—But on my head
        Recoil the fierce invokings of Despair,
        And I am left far distanced in the race,
        The lonely One of Earth!—Aye, this is just!
        I am not worthy that upon my breast

[240]   In this, thine hour of Victory, thou shouldst yield
        Thy Spirit unto God!
    GONSALVO.   Thou art! thou art!
280   Oh! a Life's love, a heart's long faithfulness,
        Ev'n in the presence of Eternal things,
        Wearing their chasten'd beauty all undimm'd,

(She rises).—A light, a light springs up from grief and death,
Which with its solemn radiance doth reveal
Why we have thus been tried!
GONZALEZ.   Then I may still
Fix my last look on thee, in holy love,
Parting, but yet with hope!
ELMINA *(falling at his feet).*   Canst thou forgive?
—Oh, I have driven the arrow to thy heart,
That should have buried it within mine own, ←
And borne the pang in silence!—I have cast   220
Thy life's fair honour, in my wild despair,
As an unvalued gem upon the waves,
Whence thou hast snatch'd it back, to bear from earth,
All stainless, on thy breast. — Well hast thou done—— ~
But I—canst thou forgive?
GONZALEZ.   Within this hour
I have stood upon that verge whence mortals fall,
And learn'd how 'tis with one whose sight grows dim,
And whose foot trembles on the gulf 's dark side.
—Death purifies all feeling— We will part
In pity and in love.
ELMINA.   Death!—And thou too   230
Art on thy way!—Oh, joy for thee, high heart!
Glory and joy for thee! — The day is closed,
And well and nobly hast thou borne thyself
Through its long battle-toils, though many swords
Have entered thine own soul!—But on my head
Recoil the fierce invokings of despair,
And I am left far distanced in the race,
The lonely one of earth!—Aye, this is just.
I am not worthy that upon my breast
In this, thine hour of victory, thou shouldst yield   240
Thy spirit unto God!
GONZALEZ.   Thou art! thou art!
Oh! a life's love, a heart's long faithfulness,
Ev'n in the presence of eternal things,
Wearing their chasten'd beauty all undimm'd,

Assert their [?lofty] holy claims, and these are not
For one dark hour to cancel! — We are here,
Before that Altar which receiv'd the Vows
Of our unbroken Youth, and meet it is
For such a Witness, in the sight of Heaven,
[250]   And in the face of Death, whose mighty shadowy arm
Comes dim between us, to record th' exchange
290   Of our tried hearts' forgiveness. — Who are they,
That in one path have journey'd, needing not
Forgiveness at its close.

(A Citizen enters hastily).

CITIZEN. The Moors! the Moors!
GONSALVO.   How! is the City storm'd?
          Oh! righteous Heaven! — for this I look'd not yet!
          Hath all been done in vain? — Why then, 'tis time
          For prayer, and then to rest!
CITIZEN.   The sun shall set,
          And not a Christian voice be left for prayer;
[260]   To-night within Valencia! — Round our Walls
          The Paynim Host is gathering for th' assault,
          And we have none to guard them!
300 GONSALVO *(hastily rising).*   Then my place
          Is here no longer! — I had hop'd to die
          Ev'n by the Altar and the Sepulchre
          Of my brave Sires — but this was not to be!
          Give me my Sword again, and lead me hence
          Back to the ramparts. I have yet an hour,
          And it hath still high duties. — Now, my Wife!
          Thou mother of my Children — of the Dead,
[270]   Whom I name unto thee in solemn hope,
          Farewell!
ELMINA.   No, not farewell! — My soul hath ris'n
310   To mate itself with thine! — And by thy side
          Amidst the hurtling Lances I will stand,
          As one on whom a brave Man's love hath been
          Wasted not utterly!

Assert their lofty claims; and these are not
For one dark hour to cancel! — We are here,
Before that altar which received the vows
Of our unbroken youth, and meet it is
For such a witness, in the sight of Heaven,
And in the face of death, whose shadowy arm
250
Comes dim between us, to record th' exchange
Of our tried hearts' forgiveness. — Who are they,
That in one path have journey'd, needing not
Forgiveness at its close?

                    (A Citizen enters hastily)

CITIZEN.   The Moors! the Moors!
GONZALEZ.   How! is the city storm'd?
    Oh! righteous Heaven! — for this I look'd not yet!
    Hath all been done in vain? — Why then, 'tis time
    For prayer, and then to rest!
CITIZEN.   The sun shall set,
    And not a Christian voice be left for prayer,
    To-night within Valencia? — Round our walls   260
    The paynim host is gathering for th' assault,
    And we have none to guard them.
GONZALEZ.   Then my place
    Is here no longer. — I had hoped to die
    Ev'n by the altar and the sepulchre
    Of my brave sires — but this was not to be!
    Give me my sword again, and lead me hence
    Back to the ramparts. I have yet an hour,
    And it hath still high duties. — Now, my wife!
    Thou mother of my children — of the dead —
    Whom I name unto thee in stedfast hope —   270
    Farewell!
ELMINA.   No, *not* farewell! — My soul hath risen
    To mate itself with thine; and by thy side
    Amidst the hurtling lances I will stand,
    As one on whom a brave man's love hath been
    Wasted not utterly.

THE PUBLICATION OF 1823   219

GONSALVO.   I thank thee, Heaven!
That I have tasted of the awful joy
Which thou hast given to temper hours like this,
With a deep sense of thee, and of thine ends
In these dread visitings!
                (*To* ELMINA).   We will not part,
[280]   But with the Spirit's parting!
ELMINA.   One farewell
To her, that mantled with sad loveliness,
320   Doth slumber at our feet! — My blessed Child!
Oh! in thy Heart's affliction thou wert strong,
And holy Courage did pervade thy woe,
As Light the troubled Waters! — Be at peace!
Thou whose bright Spirit made itself the Soul
Of all that were around thee! — And thy Life
E'en then was struck, and withering at the core!
But thou has now thy guerdon! — Fare thee well!
Farewell! — thy parting look hath on me fall'n,
[290]   E'en as a beam of faith, and I am now
330   More like what thou hast been! — My soul is hush'd;
For a still sense of purer Worlds hath sunk
And settled on its depths with that last smile
Which from thine shone forth! — Thou hast not liv'd
In vain — my Child, farewell!
GONSALVO.   Surely for thee
Death had no sting, Ximena! — We are blest,
To learn one secret of the shadowy pass,
From such an aspect's calmness! — Yet once more,
I kiss thy pale young cheek, my broken flower,
[300]   In token of th' undying Love and Hope,
340   Whose Land is far away.

                                                        Exeunt.

GONZALEZ.   I thank thee, Heaven!
  That I have tasted of the awful joy
  Which thou hast given to temper hours like this,
  With a deep sense of thee, and of thine ends
  In these dread visitings!
  (*To* ELMINA).   We will not part,
  But with the spirit's parting!
ELMINA.   One farewell   280
  To her, that mantled with sad loveliness,
  Doth slumber at our feet!—My blessed child!
  Oh! in thy heart's affliction thou wert strong,
  And holy courage did pervade thy woe,
  As light the troubled waters!—Be at peace!
  Thou whose bright spirit made itself the soul
  Of all that were around thee!—And thy life
  E'en then was struck, and withering at the core!
  —Farewell!—thy parting look hath on me fall'n,
  E'en as a gleam of heaven, and I am now   290
  More like what thou hast been!—My soul is hush'd,
  For a still sense of purer worlds hath sunk
  And settled on its depths with that last smile
  Which from thine shone forth.—Thou hast not lived
  In vain—my child, farewell!
GONZALEZ.   Surely for thee
  Death had no sting, Ximena![1]—We are blest,
  To learn one secret of the shadowy pass,
  From such an aspect's calmness. Yet once more
  I kiss thy pale young cheek, my broken flower!
  In token of th' undying love and hope,   300
  Whose land is far away.

                                            Exeunt.

---

1 "O death, where is thy sting, O grave, where is thy victory?" (1 Corinthians 15.55).

SCENE [9]

The Walls of the City. HERNANDEZ. —
A few Citizens, chiefly Women and old Men.

HERNANDEZ. Why, Men have cast the treasures, which their lives
Had been worn down in gathering, on the pyre,
Aye, at their household Hearths have lit the brand,
Ev'n from that shrine of quiet love to bear
The flame which gave their Temples and their Homes,
In ashes, to the Winds! — They have done this,
Making a blasted Void where once the Sun
Look'd upon lovely Dwellings; and from Earth
Razing all record that on such a spot
[10]   10   Childhood hath sprung, age faded, Suffering wept
And frail Humanity call'd upon her God;
They have done this, in their free nobleness,
Rather than see the Spoiler's tread pollute
Their holy places! — Praise, high praise be theirs,
Who have left Man such lessons! — And these things,
Not on far distant shores have so far wrought,
But your own Land hath witness'd them! — The sky,
Which doth bend o'er us, and the Seas, wherein
Your rivers pour their gold, rejoicing saw
20   The Altar, and the Birth-place, and the Tomb,
[20]   And all memorials of Man's heart and faith,
Thus proudly honour'd! — Be ye not outdone
By the departed! — Tho' the godless foe
Be close upon us, we have power to snatch
The spoils of Victory from him! — Be but strong!
A few bright Torches and brief moments yet
Shall baffle his flush'd hope, and we may die,
And laugh him unto scorn! — Rise, follow me,
And thou, Valencia! triumph in thy fate,
30   The ruin, not the [?——] yoke! — for thou shalt sink
Nobly, and making thy ~~fair~~ rich Palaces,
[30]   A Beacon unto Spain!

SCENE [9]

The Walls of the City.

HERNANDEZ. —*A few Citizens gathered round him.*

HERNANDEZ. Why, men have cast the treasures, which their lives
Had been worn down in gathering, on the pyre,
Aye, at their household hearths have lit the brand,
Ev'n from that shrine of quiet love to bear
The flame which gave their temples and their homes,
In ashes, to the winds! — They have done this,
Making a blasted void where once the sun
Look'd upon lovely dwellings; and from earth
Razing all record that on such a spot
Childhood hath sprung, age faded, misery wept   10
And frail Humanity knelt before her God;
— They have done *this*, in their free nobleness,
Rather than see the spoiler's tread pollute
Their holy places! — Praise, high praise be theirs,
Who have left man such lessons! — And these things,
Made your own hills their witnesses! — The sky,
Whose arch bends o'er you and the seas, wherein
Your rivers pour their gold, rejoicing saw
The altar, and the birth-place, and the tomb,
And all memorials of man's heart and faith,   20
Thus proudly honour'd! — Be ye not outdone
By the departed! — Though the godless foe
Be close upon us, we have power to snatch
The spoils of victory from him. Be but strong!
A few bright torches and brief moments yet
Shall baffle his flush'd hope, and we may die,
Laughing him unto scorn. — Rise, follow me,
And thou, Valencia! triumph in thy fate,
The ruin, not the yoke, and make thy towers
A beacon unto Spain!¹

---

1 When, at the end of Byron's *Sardanapalus*, a play Hemans knew well, the title character
is about to immolate himself and his palace rather than be taken by his enemies, he

CITIZENS.   It shall be thus!
—Alas! for our fair City! and the Homes
Wherein we rear'd [?~~my Children~~] our Children!—But away!
The Moor shall plant no Crescent o'er our shrines!
VOICE *from a Tower above.*
Succour!—Castile, Castile!
CITIZENS *(rushing to the spot).* It is een so!
Now blessing be to Heaven, for we are saved!
Castile, Castile!
VOICE *from the Tower.* Line after Line of Spears,
Lance after Lance upon th' Horizon's verge,
40   Like festal lights from Cities bursting up,
Doth skirt the plain. In faith, a noble Host!
ANOTHER VOICE. The Moor hath turn'd him from our Walls, to
[40]   front
Th' ~~coming~~ advancing might of Spain!
CITIZENS *(shouting).*   Castile! Castile!

         GONSALVO *enters, supported by* ELMINA *and a Citizen.*

GONSALVO. What shouts of Joy are these?
HERNANDEZ.   Hail, Chieftain, hail!
Thus ev'n in Death 'tis given thee to receive
The Conqueror's crown!—Behold, our God hath heard,
And rob'd himself with Vengeance!—Lo! they come!
The ~~Banners~~ Lances of Castile!—The sharp bright sword,
Which makes Earth crimson with the hues of wrath,
50   Leaps from its thunder-clouds!
GONSALVO.   I knew, I knew
Thou wouldst not utterly, my God, forsake
Thy servant in his need!—My blood and tears
Have not sunk vainly to th' attesting Earth!
[50]   Praise to thee, praise and thanks, that I have liv'd
To see this hour!

CITIZEN.   We'll follow thee!
—Alas! for our fair city, and the homes
Wherein we rear'd our children!—But away!
The Moor shall plant no crescent° o'er our fanes!   *emblem of Islam*
VOICE *(from a Tower on the Walls).*
Succours!—Castile! Castile![1]
CITIZENS *(rushing to the spot).*   It is even so!
Now blessing be to Heaven, for we are saved!
Castile, Castile!
VOICE *(from the Tower).* Line after line of spears,
Lance after lance upon the horizon's verge,
Like festal lights from cities bursting up,
Doth skirt the plain!—In faith, a noble host!
ANOTHER VOICE. The Moor hath turn'd him from our walls,
    to front   40
Th' advancing might of Spain!
CITIZENS *(shouting).*   Castile! Castile!

(GONZALEZ *enters, supported by* ELMINA *and a Citizen).*

GONZALEZ. What shouts of joy are these?
HERNANDEZ.   Hail, chieftain! hail!
Thus ev'n in death 'tis given thee to receive
The conqueror's crown!—Behold our God hath heard,
And arm'd himself with vengeance!—Lo! they come!
The lances of Castile!
GONZALEZ.   I knew, I knew
Thou wouldst not utterly, my God, forsake
Thy servant in his need!—My blood and tears
Have not sunk vainly to th' attesting earth!
Praise to thee, thanks and praise, that I have lived   50
To see this hour!

---

exclaims, "My fathers! whom I will rejoin, / ... I would not leave your ancient first
abode / To the defilement of usurping bondmen"; "the light of this / Most royal of
funereal pyres shall be / Not a mere pillar form'd of cloud and flame, / A beacon in the
horizon for a day, / And then a mount of ashes, but a light / To lesson ages" (5.423-
41).

1 *Succors!: Rescue!* Among Hemans's *Songs of Spain* (*New Monthly Magazine* 40 [1834]: 26-
28) is *Old Spanish Battle Song*, its last line: "And shout ye, 'Castile! to the rescue of
Spain!'"

ELMINA.   And I too bless thy name,
Though thou hast prov'd me unto Agony,
Oh God! Thou God of chastening!
VOICE *from the Tower.*   They move on!
I see the royal Banner in the Air,
With its emblazon'd Towers!
GONSALVO.   Go, bring ye forth
60   The Banner of the Cid, and plant it here
To stream above me, for an answering sign
That the good Cross doth hold its lofty place,
Within Valencia still! — What see ye now?
HERNANDEZ *(with enthusiasm).* I see a Kingdom's Might upon its
[60]   way,
Moving, in terrible Magnificence,
Unto Revenge and Victory! — I behold
~~All~~ The things ~~which~~ [?deal] ~~with~~that work on Man's quick fiery
           heart,
As winds on Ocean's slumber! — With the flash
Of knightly swords, up-springing from the ranks,
70   As Meteors from a still and gloomy deep,
And with the waving of ten thousand plumes,
Like a Land's Harvest in the Autumn gale,
And with fierce light, which is not of the Sun,
But flung from sheets of Mail, it comes, it comes!
The vengeance of our God!
GONSALVO.   I hear it now,
[70]   The measur'd tread of steel-clad Multitudes,
Like thunder-showers upon the forest-paths!
HERNANDEZ. Aye, Earth knows well the omen of that sound,
And she hath echoes, like a sepulchre's,
80   Pent in her secret hollows, to respond
Unto the step of Death!
GONSALVO.   Hark! how the Wind
Swells proudly with the Battle march of Spain!

ELMINA.   And I too bless thy name,
    Though thou hast proved me unto agony!
    Oh God! — Thou God of chastening!
VOICE *(from the Tower)*.   They move on!
    I see the royal banner in the air,
    With its emblazon'd towers![1]
GONZALEZ.   Go, bring ye forth
    The banner of the Cid, and plant it here,
    To stream above me, for an answering sign
    That the good cross doth hold its lofty place
    Within Valencia still! — What see ye now?
HERNANDEZ. I see a kingdom's might upon its path,   60
    Moving, in terrible magnificence,
    Unto revenge and victory! — With the flash
    Of knightly swords, up-springing from the ranks,
    As meteors from a still and gloomy deep,
    And with the waving of ten thousand plumes,[2]
    Like a land's harvest in the autumn-wind,
    And with fierce light, which is not of the sun,
    But flung from sheets of steel — it comes, it comes,
    The vengeance of our God!
GONZALEZ.   I hear it now,
    The heavy tread of mail-clad multitudes,   70
    Like thunder-showers upon the forest-paths.
HERNANDEZ. Aye, earth knows well the omen of that sound,
    And she hath echoes, like a sepulchre's,
    Pent in her secret hollows, to respond
    Unto the step of death!
GONZALEZ.   Hark! how the wind
    Swells proudly with the battle-march of Spain!

---

1   The castle towers of Castile, a city named for the many castles built in the region after
    the Christian nobles (among them, one surnamed González) reconquered the area
    from the Moors.
2   Hemans evokes Burke's famous lament in *Reflections on the Revolution in France* (1790)
    over the failure of chivalry in the arrest of Queen Marie Antoinette, a scandal "in a
    nation of gallant men, in a nation of men of honour and of cavaliers. I thought ten
    thousand swords must have leaped from their scabbards to avenge even a look that
    threatened her." Hemans's chivalric-Christian saviors evoke, by their positive presence,
    the related scandal of the French Republic's disestablishment of the Catholic Church.

Now the heart feels its power! — A little while
Grant me to live, my God! — What pause is this?
HERNANDEZ. A deep and dreadful one! — the serried files

[80] Level their spears for combat; now the Hosts
Look on each other in their brooding wrath,
Silent, and face to face.

VOICES HEARD WITHOUT, CHAUNTING

90
Calm on the bosom of thy God,
Fair spirit! rest thee now!
E'en while with us thy footsteps trod,
His seal was on thy brow!

Dust to its narrow House beneath!
Soul to its place on high!
They that have seen thy look in death,

[90] No more may fear to die!

ELMINA (*to* GONSALVO). It is the Death-hymn o'er thy Daughter's
bier!
— But I am calm, and e'en like gentle winds,
~~That strain floats i' th' stillness of my heart,~~

100 That Music, thro' the stillness of my heart,
~~Breathing of~~ [?~~Grace~~]!
Sends mournful peace.
GONSALVO.   Oh! well those solemn tones
Accord with such an hour, for all her Life
Breath'd of a Hero's soul!

(*A sound of Trumpets and shouting from the plain.*)

HERNANDEZ. Now, now they close! — Hark! what a dull, dead ~~tone~~
sound
Is in the Moorish war-shout! — I have known

Now the heart feels its power! — A little while
Grant me to live, my God! — What pause is this?
HERNANDEZ. A deep and dreadful one! — the serried files
Level their spears for combat; now the hosts   80
Look on each other in their brooding wrath,
Silent, and face to face.

VOICES HEARD WITHOUT, CHANTING.

Calm on the bosom of thy God,
        Fair spirit! rest thee now!
E'en while with ours thy footsteps trod,
        His seal was on thy brow.

Dust, to its narrow house beneath!
        Soul, to its place on high!
They that have seen thy look in death,
        No more may fear to die.[1]   90

ELMINA (to GONZALEZ). It is the death-hymn o'er thy daughter's
        bier!
— But I am calm, and e'en like gentle winds,
That music, through the stillness of my heart,
Sends mournful peace.
GONZALEZ.   Oh! well those solemn tones
Accord with such an hour, for all her life
Breath'd of a hero's soul!

            A sound of trumpets and shouting from the plain.

HERNANDEZ. Now, now they close! — Hark! what a dull dead sound
Is in the Moorish war-shout! — I have known

---

1   These verses were soon republished as *A Dirge* in *Lays of Many Lands (Forest Sanctuary*
    &c [1825]) and in collections thereafter, with an additional stanza: "Lone are the paths,
    and sad the bowers, / Whence thy meek smile is gone; / But oh! — a brighter home
    than ours, / In heaven, is now thine own." The first two stanzas are inscribed on a
    tablet above the vault beneath St. Anne's Church in Dublin, where Hemans is interred
    (Hughes, *Memoir* 314).

Such tones prophetic oft. — The shock is given —

[100] Lo! they have placed their shields before their hearts,
And lower'd their lances with the streamers on,
110 ~~The first bright sparks of Battle have been struck~~
And on their steeds bent forward. — God for Spain!
The first bright sparks of Battle have been struck
From Spear to Spear, across the gleaming ~~field~~ / ~~plain~~ field!
(exultingly) There is no sight on which the blue sky looks
To match with this! — 'Tis not the gallant crests,
Nor Banners with their glorious blazonry,
Nor yet proud Knighthood's bearing of command;
The very Nature and high Soul of Man
Doth now reveal itself!

GONSALVO.   Oh! raise me up,
[110] 120 That I may look upon the noble scene!
— It will not be! — That this dull mist would pass
A moment from my sight! Whence rose that shout,
As in fierce triumph?

HERNANDEZ *(clasping his hands).* Must I look on this?
The Banner sinks! — 'tis taken!

GONSALVO.   Whose?

HERNANDEZ.   Castile's!

GONSALVO. Oh, God of Battles!

ELMINA.   Calm thy noble heart!
Thou wilt not pass away without thy meed.
Nay, rest thee on my bosom!

HERNANDEZ.   Cheer thee yet!
Our Knights have spurr'd to rescue! — There is now
A whirl, a mingling of all terrible things,
[120] 130 More strange and awful than the fierce distinctness
Wherewith they mov'd before! — I see tall crests,
All wildly tossing o'er the Battle's gloom,
Sway'd by the wrathful motion and the press
Of desperate Men, like Cedar-boughs by Storms;
Many a white Streamer there is dyed with blood,
Many a false corslet broken; many a shield
Pierced through! — Now, shout for Santiago, shout!

Such tones prophetic oft. — The shock is given —
Lo! they have placed their shields before their hearts,   100
And lower'd their lances with the streamers on,
And on their steeds bent forward! — God for Spain!
The first bright sparks of battle have been struck
From spear to spear, across the gleaming field!
— There is no sight on which the blue sky looks
To match with this! — 'Tis not the gallant crests,
Nor banners with their glorious blazonry;
The very nature and high soul of man
Doth now reveal itself!
GONZALEZ.   Oh, raise me up,
That I may look upon the noble scene!   110
— It will not be! — That this dull mist would pass
A moment from my sight! — Whence rose that shout,
As in fierce triumph?
HERNANDEZ *(clasping his hands).*
                   Must I look on this?
The banner sinks — 'tis taken!
GONZALEZ.   Whose?
HERNANDEZ.   Castile's!
GONZALEZ. Oh, God of Battles!
ELMINA.   Calm thy noble heart!
Thou wilt not pass away without thy meed.
Nay, rest thee on my bosom.
HERNANDEZ.   Cheer thee yet!
Our knights have spurr'd to rescue. — There is now
A whirl, a mingling of all terrible things,
Yet more appalling than the fierce distinctness   120
Wherewith they moved before! — I see tall plumes
All wildly tossing o'er the battle's tide,
Sway'd by the wrathful motion, and the press
Of desperate men, as cedar-boughs by storms.
Many a white streamer there is dyed with blood,
Many a false corslet broken, many a shield
Pierced through! — Now, shout for Santiago,[1] shout!

---

1 St. James, "Santiago, the tutelary Saint of Spain, the God of their battles" (Southey, *Chronicle,* Preface xxx).

~~And~~ Lo! javelins with a moment's brightness cleave
The thickening dust; and barbed steeds go down,
[130]   140   With their helm'd Riders!—Who, but One, can tell
How Spirits part amidst that fearful rush
And trampling on of furious Multitudes?
GONSALVO. Thou'rt silent!—Seest thou more?—My Soul grows
    dark!
HERNANDEZ. And dark and troubled, as an angry Sea,
    Dashing some gallant Armament in scorn
    Against its rocks, is all on which I gaze!
    —I can but tell thee how tall spears are cross'd,
    And Lances seem to shiver, and proud Helms
    To lighten with the stroke!—But round the Spot,
[140]   150   Wherè, like a storm-fell'd Mast, our Standard sunk,
    The heart of Battle burns!
GONSALVO.   Where is that spot?
HERNANDEZ. It is beneath the lonely tuft of Palms,
    That lift their green heads o'er the Tumult still,
    In calm and stately grace.
GONSALVO.   There, didst Thou say?
Then God is with us, and we must prevail!
For on that spot they died!—My children's blood
Calls on th' Avenger thence!
ELMINA.   They perish'd <u>there</u>!
    —And the bright locks that waved so joyously
    To the free Winds, lay trampled and defil'd,
[150]   160   Ev'n on that place of death!—Oh, Merciful!
    Hush the dark thought within me!
HERNANDEZ *(with sudden exultation).* Who is He,
    On the white Steed, and with the castled Helm,
    And the gold-broider'd mantle, which doth float
    E'en like a sunny cloud above the fight,
    And the [p̶l̶] pale Cross, which from his breast-plate gleams
    With star-like radiance?
GONSALVO *(eagerly).*   Didst thou say the Cross?
HERNANDEZ. On his mail'd bosom shines a broad white Cross,
    And his long plumage thro' the ~~dusky~~ sultry air
    ~~Shows~~ / ~~Streams~~ Gleams like a snow-wreath.

Lo! javelins with a moment's brightness cleave
The thickening dust, and barbed steeds go down
With their helm'd riders! — Who, but One, can tell   130
How spirits part amidst that fearful rush
And trampling on of furious multitudes?
GONZALEZ. Thou'rt silent! — See'st thou more? — My soul grows
    dark.
HERNANDEZ. And dark and troubled, as an angry sea,
    Dashing some gallant armament in scorn
    Against its rocks, is all on which I gaze!
    — I can but tell thee how tall spears are cross'd,
    And lances seem to shiver, and proud helms
    To lighten with the stroke! — But round the spot,
    Where, like a storm-fell'd mast, our standard sank,   140
    The heart of battle burns.
GONZALEZ.   Where is that spot?
HERNANDEZ. It is beneath the lonely tuft of palms,
    That lift their green heads o'er the tumult still,
    In calm and stately grace.
GONZALEZ.   *There,* didst thou say?
    Then God is with us, and we *must* prevail!
    For on that spot they died! — My children's blood
    Calls on th' avenger thence!
ELMINA.   They perish'd there!
    — And the bright locks that waved so joyously
    To the free winds, lay trampled and defiled
    Ev'n on that place of death! — Oh, Merciful!   150
    Hush the dark thought within me!
HERNANDEZ *(with sudden exultation).* Who is he,
    On the white steed, and with the castled helm,
    And the gold-broider'd mantle, which doth float
    E'en like a sunny cloud above the fight;
    And the pale cross, which from his breast-plate gleams
    With star-like radiance?
GONZALEZ *(eagerly).*   Didst thou say the cross?
HERNANDEZ. On his mail'd bosom shines a broad white cross,
    And his long plumage through the darkening air
    Streams like a snow-wreath.

GONSALVO. That should be—

HERNANDEZ. The King!

[160] 170 —Was it not told us how he sent, of late,
To the Cid's tomb, e'en for the silver cross
Which he who slumbers there was wont to bind
O'er his brave heart in fight?
GONSALVO *(springing up joyfully)*. My King! my King!
Now all good Saints for Spain!—My noble King!
And thou art there!—That I might look once more
Upon thy face!—But yet I thank thee, Heaven,
That thou hast sent him, from my dying hands
Thus to receive his City!

He sinks back into ELMINA'*s arms.*

HERNANDEZ. He hath clear'd
A pathway ~~thro'~~ midst the Combat, and the Light
[170] 180 Follows his charge thro' yon close living mass,
E'en as the gleam on some proud Vessel's wake
Along the stormy waters!—'Tis redeem'd!
The castled Pennon rises!—It is flung
Once more in joy and glory to the Winds!
—There seems a wavering thro' the Paynim Hosts—
Castile doth press them sore!—Now, now rejoice!
GONSALVO. What hast thou seen?
HERNANDEZ. Abdullah falls—he falls,
The Man of blood, the Spoiler!—He hath sunk
In our King's path!—Well hath that royal sword
[180] 190 Aveng'd thy cause, Gonsalvo!
They give way,
The Crescent's van is scatter'd!—On the Hills,

GONZALEZ.   That should be —
HERNANDEZ.   The king!
— Was it not told us how he sent, of late,   160
To the Cid's tomb, e'en for the silver cross,
Which he who slumbers there was wont to bind
O'er his brave heart in fight?[1]
GONZALEZ *(springing up joyfully).* My king! my king!
Now all good saints for Spain! — My noble king!
And thou art there! — That I might look once more
Upon thy face! — But yet I thank thee, Heaven!
That thou hast sent him, from my dying hands
Thus to receive his city!

                        He sinks back into ELMINA's *arms.*

HERNANDEZ.   He hath clear'd
A pathway midst the combat, and the light
Follows his charge through yon close living mass,   170
E'en as the gleam on some proud vessel's wake
Along the stormy waters! — 'Tis redeem'd —
The castled banner! — It is flung once more
In joy and glory, to the sweeping winds!
— There seems a wavering through the paynim hosts —
Castile doth press them sore — Now, now rejoice!
GONZALEZ. What hast thou seen?
HERNANDEZ.   Abdullah falls! He falls!
The man of blood! — the spoiler! — he hath sunk
In our king's path! — Well hath that royal sword
Avenged thy cause, Gonzalez!
                        They give way,   180
The Crescent's van° is broken! — On the hills   *front line*

---

1   This circumstance is recorded of King Don Alfonso, the last of that name. He sent to
    the Cid's tomb for the cross which that warrior was accustomed to wear upon his
    breast when he went to battle, and had it made into one for himself; "because of the
    faith which he had, that through it he should obtain the victory." — *Southey's Chronicle
    of the Cid* [FH]
    Chronicle Bk. 11.XXX (364-65); see 365. Don Alfonso the Wise (1221-84) became
    King Alfonso X in 1252, the year he crushed a Muslim revolt, but his later policies pro-
    duced much civil discontent.

And the ~~Pine-forrest~~ dark Pine-woods, may the Infidel
Call vainly, in his agony of fear,
To cover him from Vengeance! — Lo! they fly!
They of the Forest and the Wilderness!
Woe to the sons of Afric! to the Lords
Of the wide Desert and Lion-spear!
~~Spain~~ For Spain prevails! — Now let the Harvest-lands,
And the Vine-mountains, and Hesperian Seas,
200   Take their dead unto them! — that blood shall wash
[190]   Our soil from stains of bondage!

GONSALVO *(attempting to raise himself)*. Set me free!
~~Let me go forth, that I may~~
Come with me forth, for I must greet my King,
After his Battle-field! — Why, what is this?
Is't not the hour of Victory, yet a chain
Drags down my weary limbs!

HERNANDEZ.   Oh, blest in death!
Chosen of Heaven, farewell! — Look on the Cross,
And part from Earth in peace!

GONSALVO.   Now, charge once more!
God is with Spain, and Santiago's ~~Cross~~ sword
210   ~~Doth~~ [?-] ~~upon th'~~ Is reddening all the air! — Shout forth
            "Castile!"
The day is ours — I go, but fear ye not!
For Afric's Lance is broken, and my Sons
Have won their first good field! ——— *He dies.*

ELMINA.   Look on me yet!
[200]   Speak one farewell, my Husband! — Must thy Voice
Enter my soul no more? — Thine eye is fix'd —
— Now is my life uprooted — and 'tis well.

(She kneels beside the body of Gonsalvo)

*A Sound of triumphant Music is heard, and several Castilian Knights and
Soldiers enter.*

A CITIZEN. Hush your triumphant sounds, altho' ye come
E'en as Deliverers! But the noble Dead,

And the dark pine-woods may the infidel
Call vainly, in his agony of fear,
To cover him from vengeance! —Lo! they fly!
They of the forest and the wilderness
Are scatter'd, e'en as leaves upon the wind!
Woe to the sons of Afric! —Let the plains,
And the vine-mountains, and Hesperian seas,
Take their dead unto them! —that blood shall wash
Our soil from stains of bondage.

GONZALEZ *(attempting to raise himself)*. Set me free!   190
Come with me forth, for I must greet my king,
After his battle-field!

HERNANDEZ.   Oh, blest in death!
Chosen of Heaven, farewell! —Look on the Cross,
And part from earth in peace!

GONZALEZ.   Now charge once more!
God is with Spain, and Santiago's sword
Is reddening all the air! —Shout forth 'Castile!'
The day is ours! —I go; but fear ye not!
For Afric's lance is broken, and my sons
Have won their first good field!

He dies.

ELMINA.   Look on me yet!
Speak one farewell, my husband! —must thy voice   200
Enter my soul no more! —Thine eye is fix'd—
Now is my life uprooted,—and 'tis well.

*(A Sound of triumphant Music is heard, and many Castilian Knights and
Soldiers enter).*

A CITIZEN. Hush your triumphal sounds, although ye come
E'en as deliverers! But the noble dead,

Gone from us in their fulness of renown,
220   And those that mourn them, claim from human hearts
Deep, silent reverence.
ELMINA *(rising proudly)*. Nay, swell forth, Castile!
Thy Trumpet-music till the Seas and Heavens,
And the crown'd Hills, give every pealing note
Echoes to ring thro' Spain! — How, know ye not
[210]   That all array'd for Triumph, crown'd and rob'd
With the strong Spirit which hath sav'd the Land,
Ev'n now a Conqueror to his rest is gone?
— Fear not to break his Sleep, but let the Winds
Bear up your shouts of Victory! — for this earth
230   Knows not a sound more sad! — Whence mounts it still,
But from the Grave's dark Verge?
HERNANDEZ.   Lift ye the dead,
And bear him with the banner of his ~~Sires~~ race
Waving above him proudly, as it wav'd
O'er the Cid's Battles, to the tomb, wherein
His Warrior-Sires are gather'd. He hath won
His place beside them nobly! *(They lift up the body.)*
ELMINA.   Aye, 'tis thus
[220]   Thou shouldst be honour'd! And I follow thee
With an unfaltering and a lofty step,
To that last home of Glory! — She that wears
240   In her deep heart the memory of thy love
Shall thence draw strength for all things; till the God
Whose hand around her hath unpeopled Earth,
Looking upon her still and chasten'd Soul,
Call it once more to thine!
(To the Castilians).   Awake, I say
Tambour and Cymbal, wake! And let the Land
Thro' all her Mountains hear your funeral peal!
[230]   — So should a Hero pass to his repose.

Exeunt omnes.

And those that mourn them, claim from human hearts
Deep silent reverence.
ELMINA (*rising proudly*). No, swell forth, Castile!
Thy trumpet-music, till the seas and heavens,
And the deep hills, give every stormy note
Echoes to ring through Spain! — How, know ye not
That all array'd for triumph, crown'd and robed   210
With the strong spirit which hath saved the land,
Ev'n now a conqueror to his rest is gone?
— Fear not to break that sleep, but let the wind
Swell on with victory's shout! — *He* will not hear —
Hath earth a sound more sad?
HERNANDEZ.   Lift ye the dead,
And bear him with the banner of his race
Waving above him proudly, as it waved
O'er the Cid's battles, to the tomb, wherein
His warrior-sires are gather'd.   *They raise the body.*
ELMINA.   Aye, 'tis thus
Thou shouldst be honour'd! — And I follow thee   220
With an unfaltering and a lofty step,
To that last home of glory. She that wears
In her deep heart the memory of thy love
Shall thence draw strength for all things, till the God,
Whose hand around her hath unpeopled earth,
Looking upon her still and chasten'd soul,
Call it once more to thine!
(*To the Castilians*).   Awake, I say,
Tambour and trumpet, wake! — And let the land
Through all her mountains hear your funeral peal!
— So should a hero pass to his repose.   230

Exeunt omnes.

Appendix A: Songs of the Cid [1]

[The four songs under this title immediately follow *The Siege of Valencia* in *1823*. Hemans evokes the eighteenth-century ballad revival during an era of emerging nationalism. Such celebrated collections as Thomas Percy's *Reliques of Ancient English Poetry* (3 vols., 1765-94) and Walter Scott's *Minstrelsy of the Scottish Border* (3 vols., 1802-3) were matched by European ones such as Herder's *Volkslieder* (Hemans read them all), and complemented by modern literary imitations.

Hemans took more specific inspiration from the twelfth-century *Poema del Cid* (see below) and a much later tradition, the *Romances del Cid*—balladlike poems in eight-syllable lines, blended with assonance instead of rhyme—believed to be the work of fifteenth-century "Juglares" (Joculars), the Spanish equivalent of twelfth-century French jongleur and troubadours, who sang them at entertainments. Orally preserved, they were "subject to frequent alterations as the language of the country altered," Southey remarks in *Chronicle of the Cid* (Preface, x). They were collected in *Romances neuvamente sacados de historias Antiguas* (Anvers, 1566), then in *Romancero General* (Medina del Campo, 1602), and Juan de Escobar's *Historia del muy valeroso cavallero El Cid Ruy Diez de Bivar, en Romances, en lenguage antiguo* (Seville, 1632), a work Hemans knew. Southey discredited the romances in terms of both historical and literary value (preferring the older *Poema* and chronicles). "Many of these ballads are evidently little older than the volumes in which they are contained; very few of them appear to me to bear any marks of antiquity, and the great part are utterly worthless. Indeed the heroic ballads of the Spaniards have been over-rated in this country: they are infinitely and every way inferior to our own" (Preface, x-xi).

Hemans devoured Southey's *Chronicle* and knew some of the romance sources, such as Escobar's *Historia*, partly translated in 1805 by Johann Gottfried von Herder in *Der Cid:* ... *nach spanischen*

---

1 Originally published in the New Monthly Magazine. [FH]
   The first appeared in *Literary Gazette,* October 1822, the next three in *New Monthly Magazine,* March and April 1823. Significant variants are noted, with the abbreviations *LG* and *NMM.*

romanzen and the original republished in 1818. Of the "proud *clarion music*" of Herder's "beautiful ballads," she said these "carry us more completely back to the very heart of the proud olden time—the days of the lance—than any other poetry I know" (letters, late 1828; Chorley, *Memorials* 1.225-56, 285). In 1817 Georg Bernhard Depping edited and arranged another source used by Southey, *Romancero General*, which John Gibson Lockhart excerpted and translated in his *Ancient Spanish Ballads: Historical and Romantic* (1823). English ballads are traditionally in quatrains (4-line stanzas) of tetrameter lines (4 stressed syllables), sometimes alternating with trimeter (3 stresses), with at least one rhyme. Hemans uses these forms as well as a quintain variation and a septain lyric. Her scenes trace El Cid's exile, his death, his funeral, the routing of the Moors, and his supernatural resurrection.]

The following ballads are not translations from the Spanish, but are founded upon some of the "wild and wonderful" traditions preserved in the romances of that language, and the ancient poem of the Cid.

THE CID'S DEPARTURE INTO EXILE[1]

With sixty knights in his gallant train,
Went forth the Campeador of Spain;
For wild sierras and plains afar,
He left the lands of his own Bivar.[2]

---

1   First published *Literary Gazette*, 12 October 1822 (p. 649), signed "H." and titled BALLAD: *The Cid's departure into exile*, with this note immediately after: [See Southey's Chronicle of the Cid.]. Variants involve minor punctuation, and a capital for "Knights" (1).

Europe's most famous exile, Napoleon, died in 1821. Hemans uses a standard ballad stanza, a tetrameter quatrain, alternating iambic and anapestic feet, rhymed *aabb*, to imitate a heavy, relentless march. The anapests increase in frequency after the third stanza, as if to underscore the acceleration of the departure. The final rhyme (*far / Bivar*) frames the whole by repeating the rhyme that closes the first stanza.

2   Bivar, the supposed birth-place of the Cid, was a castle, about two leagues from Burgos. [FH] See Southey, *Chronicle*, bk. 1.II (p. 2). A league is about 3 miles.

To march o'er field, and to watch in tent,
From his home in good Castile he went;
To the wasting siege and the battle's van,
— For the noble Cid was a banish'd man!

Through his olive-woods the morn-breeze play'd,
And his native streams wild music made,   10
And clear in the sunshine his vineyards lay,
When for march and combat he took his way.

With a thoughtful spirit his way he took,
And he turn'd his steed for a parting look,
For a parting look at his own fair towers;
— Oh! the Exile's heart hath weary hours!

The pennons° were spread, and the band array'd,   *banners*
But the Cid at the threshold a moment stay'd;
It *was* but a moment — the halls were lone,
And the gates of his dwelling all open thrown.   20

There was not a steed in the empty stall,
Nor a spear nor a cloak on the naked wall,
Nor a hawk on the perch, nor a seat at the door,
Nor the sound of a step on the hollow floor.[1]

Then a dim tear swell'd to the warrior's eye,
As the voice of his native groves went by;

---

1   Tornaba la cabeza, e estabalos catando:
            Vio puertas abiertas, e uzos sin cañados,
            Alcandaras vacias, sin pielles e sin mantos:
            E sin falcones, e sin adtores mudados.
            Sospirò mio Cid.   *Poem of the Cid.* [FH]
["He turned his head, and gazed upon them: / He saw gates open and doors without
locks, / Hooks empty without furs and without cloaks: / And without falcons or
moulted hawks. / My Cid sighed."] *Poema,* canto 1 (2-6), describing El Cid's depar-
ture from Castile, his exile commanded by Alfonso; see Southey, *Chronicle,* bk. 3.XIX-
XX. The locks have stricken from doors and gates to signal that his dwelling is no
longer secure; his valuables have already been confiscated—furs, cloaks, and trained
hunting birds (a moulted hawk is mature).

And he said—"My foemen their wish have won—
—Now the will of God be in all things done!"

But the trumpet blew, with its note of cheer,
30   And the winds of the morning swept off the tear,
And the fields of his glory lay distant far,
—He is gone from the towers of his own Bivar!

THE CID'S DEATH-BED[1]

It was an hour of grief and fear
    Within Valencia's walls,
When the blue spring-heaven lay still and clear
    Above her marble halls.

There were pale cheeks and troubled eyes,
    And steps of hurrying feet,
Where the Zambra's[2] notes were wont to rise,
    Along the sunny street.

It was an hour of fear and grief,
10   On bright Valencia's shore,
For Death was busy with her chief,
    The noble Campeador.

ships / sea   The Moor-king's barks° were on the deep°,
    With sounds and signs of war,
For the Cid was passing to his sleep,
fortress   In the silent Alcazar.°

---

1 First published in *NMM* 7.8 (March 1823) as SONGS OF THE CID. NO. I. / *The Cid's Death-bed: a Ballad,* signed "Mrs. Hemans." For sources, see Southey, *Chronicle,* bk. 11.V-VI (pp. 331-33) and romance 95 in de Escobar's *Romancero.* Hemans's quatrain stanza is another standard ballad form, rhymed tetrameter lines (*a*) alternating with rhymed trimeters (*b*).

2 The zambra, a Moorish dance. When Valencia was taken by the Cid, many of the Moorish families chose to remain there, and reside under his government. [FH]

No moan was heard through the towers of state,
  No weeper's aspect seen,
But by the couch Ximena° sate,   *his wife*
  With pale, yet stedfast mien.[1]   20

Stillness was round the leader's[2] bed,
  Warriors stood mournful nigh,
And banners, o'er his glorious head,
  Were drooping heavily.

And feeble grew the conquering[3] hand,
  And cold the valiant breast;
— He had fought the battles of the land,
  And his hour was come to rest.

What said the Ruler[4] of the field?
  — His voice is faint and low;   30
The breeze that creeps o'er his lance and shield
  Hath louder accents now.

"Raise ye no cry, and let no moan
  Be made when I depart;
The Moor must hear no dirge's tone,
  Be ye of mighty[5] heart!

Let the cymbal-clash and the trumpet-strain
  From your walls ring far and shrill,
And fear ye not, for the saints[6] of Spain
  Shall grant you victory still.   40

---

1 The calm fortitude of Ximena is frequently alluded to in the romances. [FH]
2 *NMM*] conqueror's
3 *NMM*] mighty
4 *NMM*] leader
   The epithet translates El Cid's nickname, "Campeador."
5 *NMM*] dauntless
6 *NMM*] Saints

full armor   And gird my form with mail-array,°
                       And set me on my steed,
                    So go ye forth on your funeral-way,
                       And God shall give you speed.

                    Go with the dead in the front of war,
                       All arm'd with sword and helm,[1]
                    And march by the camp of King Bucar,
                       For the good Castilian realm.

                    And let me slumber in the soil
50   Which gave my fathers birth;
                    I have closed my day of battle-toil,
                       And my course is done on earth."

                    —Now wave, ye glorious banners, wave![2]
                       Through the lattice a wind sweeps by,
                    And the arms, o'er the death-bed of the brave,
                       Send forth a hollow sigh.

                    Now wave, ye banners of many a fight!
                       As the fresh wind o'er you sweeps;
                    The wind and the banners fall hush'd as night,
60   The Campeador—he sleeps!

                    Sound the battle-horn on the breeze of morn,
                       And swell out the trumpet's blast,
                    Till the notes prevail o'er the voice of wail,
                       For the noble Cid hath pass'd!

---

1   Banderas antiguas, tristes   [Banners ancient, sad
    De victorias un tiempo amadas,   Of victories at one time dear,
    Tremolando estan al viento   Were fluttering in the wind
    Y lloran aunque no hablan, &c.   And they weep but do not speak, &c.]
    Herder's translation of these romances are remarkable for their spirit and scrupulous
    fidelity. [FH]
    In *NMM* Hemans cites the Spanish ballad in a footnote to line 53.
2   "And while they stood there they saw the Cid Ruy Diez coming up with three hun-
    dred knights; for he had not been in the battle, and they knew his *green pennon.*" —
    Southey's Chronicle of the Cid. [FH, her italics] See bk. 2.XIII (47-48).

THE CID'S FUNERAL PROCESSION[1]

The Moor had beleaguer'd Valencia's towers,
And lances gleam'd up through her citron-bowers,
And the tents of the desert had girt her plain,
And camels were trampling the vines of Spain;
    For the Cid was gone to rest.

There were men from wilds where the death-wind sweeps,
There were spears from hills where the lion sleeps,
There were bows from sands where the ostrich runs,
For the shrill horn of Afric had call'd her sons
    To the battles of the West.   10

The midnight bell, o'er the dim seas heard,
Like the roar of waters, the air had stirr'd;
The stars were shining o'er tower and wave,
And the camp lay hush'd, as a wizard's cave;
    But the Christians woke° that night.   *stayed awake*

They rear'd the Cid on his barbed° steed,   *dressed for battle*
Like a warrior mail'd for the hour of need,
And they fix'd the sword in the cold right hand,
Which had fought so well for his father's land,
    And the shield from his neck hung bright.   20

There was arming heard in Valencia's halls,
There was vigil kept on the rampart walls;
Stars had not faded, nor clouds turn'd red,
When the knights had girded the noble dead,
    And the burial-train moved out.

---

1 First published paired with *The Cid's Rising* in *NMM* 7.28 (April 1823) in SONGS OF
THE CID, "By Mrs. Hemans"; subtitled "No. II—*The Cid's Funeral Procession.*" To the
tetrameter quatrain stanza used in *Departure*, Hemans slows the march with an added
5th trimeter line, paired in meter and rhyme with the same line in the following
stanza.
Footnote to the title] See the Legends recorded in Southey's Chronicle of the Cid.
[FH]
See bk. 11.VIII (335-36) and romance 98 in Escobar's *Romancero*.

With a measured pace, as the pace of one,
Was the still death-march of the host begun;
With a silent step went the cuirass'd[1] bands,
Like a lion's tread on the burning sands,
30   And they gave no battle-shout.

When the first went forth, it was midnight deep,
In heaven was the moon, in the camp was sleep.
When the last through the city's gates had gone,
O'er tent and rampart the bright day shone,
            With a sun-burst from the sea.

There were knights five hundred went arm'd before,
And Bermudez the Cid's green standard bore;[2]
To its last fair field, with the break of morn,
Was the glorious banner in silence borne,
40   On the glad wind streaming free.

And the Campeador came stately then,
Like a leader circled with steel-clad men!
The helmet was down o'er the face of the dead,[3]
But his steed went proud, by a warrior led,
            For he knew that the Cid was there.

He was there, the Cid, with his own good sword,
And Ximena following her noble lord;
Her eye was solemn, her step was slow,
But there rose not a sound of war or woe,
50   Not a whisper on the air.

The halls in Valencia were still and lone,
The churches were empty, the masses done;
There was not a voice through the wide streets far,

---

1   *Cuirasse*: a piece of body armor originally made of leather (French, *cuir*).
2   In *1823*, FH's note to *Death-Bed* 53 is also keyed here with the same superscript number. Southey reports, "Pero Bermudez went first with the banner of the Cid, and with him five hundred knights who guarded it" (bk. 11.VIII [336]; cf. bk. 4.VIII [113]). *NMM* 36] Knights
3   *NMM*] Dead

Nor a foot-fall heard in the Alcazar,
　—So the burial-train moved out.

With a measured pace, as the pace of one,
Was the still death-march of the host begun;
With a silent step went the cuirass'd bands,
Like a lion's tread on the burning sands;
　—And they gave no battle-shout.　　　　　　　60

But the deep hills peal'd with a cry ere long,
When the Christians burst on the Paynim° throng!　　*Pagan*
　—With a sudden flash of the lance and spear,
And a charge of the war-steed in full career,
　It was Alvar Fañez came![1]

He that was wrapt with no funeral shroud,
Had pass'd before, like a threatening cloud!
And the storm rush'd down on the tented plain,
And the Archer-Queen,[2] with her bands lay slain,
　For the Cid upheld his fame.　　　　　　　70

Then a terror fell on the King Bucar,
And the Libyan kings who had join'd his war;
And their hearts grew heavy, and died away,
And their hands could not wield an assagay,°　　*slender spear, lance*
　For the dreadful things they saw!

---

1 Alvar Fañez Minaya, one of the Cid's most distinguished warriors. [FH]
　NMM] … one of the Cid's bravest warriors.
　Alvar was Cid's nephew and faithful companion; see Southey, bk. 11.IX (p. 336).
2 A Moorish Amazon, who, with a band of female warriors, accompanied King Bucar
　from Africa. Her arrows were so unerring, that she obtained the name of the Star of
　archers.

Una Mora muy gallarda,	[A very gallant Mooress,
Gran maestra en el tirar,	Great master in archery,
Con Saetas del Aljava,	With Arrows from her Quiver,
De los arcos de Turquia	With bows from Turkey
Estrella era nombrada,	She was named the Star,
Por la destreza que avia	For the skill that she had
En el herir de la Xára. [FH]	In wounding with the dart.]

From romance 98 in Escobar's *Romancero*; see Southey, Bk. 11.IX (337).

For it seem'd where Minaya[1] his onset made,
There were seventy thousand knights[2] array'd,
All white as the snow on Nevada's steep,
And they came like the foam of a roaring deep;
80   —'Twas a sight of fear and awe!

And the crested form of a warrior tall,
With a sword of fire, went before them all;[3]
With a sword of fire, and a banner pale,
And a blood-red cross on his shadowy mail,[4]
He rode in the battle's van!

There was fear in the path of his dim white horse,
There was death in the Giant-warrior's course!
Where his banner stream'd with its ghostly light,
Where his sword blazed out, there was hurrying flight,
90   For it seem'd not the sword of man!

The field and the river grew darkly red,
As the kings and leaders of Afric fled;
There was work for the men of the Cid that day!
—They were weary at eve, when they ceased to slay,
As reapers whose task is done!

The kings and the leaders of Afric fled!
The sails of their galleys in haste were spread;
But the sea had its share of the Paynim-slain,
And the bow of the desert[5] was broke in Spain;
100   —So the Cid to his grave pass'd on!

---

1   A title meaning "my brother," applied to Alvar Fañez in the lore of El Cid; see Southey,
    bk. 11.IX (336) and his excerpts from *Poema* (438, 442-43).
2   *NMM* 77] Knights
3   See Hemans's note to *Siege of Valencia* scene 4.51, and Southey, bk. 8.VIII (259).
4   The symbol of Christian Spain.
5   Both the archer's bow and the crescent, symbol of Islam. The terrified Moors fled into
    the sea, where many drowned; see Southey, bk. 11.IX (p. 337).

THE CID'S RISING[1]

'Twas the deep mid-watch of the silent night,
    And Leon in slumber lay,
When a sound went forth, in rushing might,
    Like an army on its way![2]
  In the stillness of the hour,
  When the dreams of sleep have power,
    And men forget the day.

Through the dark and lonely streets it went,
    Till the slumberers[3] woke in dread;—
The sound of a passing armament,   10
    With the charger's stony tread.
  There was heard no trumpet's peal,
  But the heavy tramp of steel,
    As a host's, to combat led.

Through the dark and lonely streets it pass'd,
    And the hollow pavement rang,
And the towers, as with a sweeping blast,
    Rock'd to the stormy clang!
  But the march of the viewless° train   *invisible*
  Went on to a royal fane,[4]   20
    Where a priest his night-hymn sang.

There was knocking that shook the marble floor,
    And a voice at the gate, which said—

---

1 In *NMM* this title is preceded by "No. III." Hemans's septain stanza was a popular
    troubadour verse form, usually (as here) heterometric.
2 See Southey's Chronicle of the Cid, p. 352. [FH, referring to bk. 11.XXI]
    This note was attached to line 3 in *NMM*. León was a medieval Christian kingdom
    northwest of Castile. We correct an apparent printer's error in line 3 of the *1823* text
    ("night") to "might"; cf. *NMM, 1839* (5.119), and Southey: "a mighty sound was heard
    in the whole city of Leon, as if it were the tramp of a great army passing through."
3 *NMM*] sleepers
4 The church of San Isidro is the burial place of Fernando I of León (ruled 1035-65),
    whose assimilation of Castile and Galicia into his kingdom paved the way for the
    unification of Christian Spain in 1492.

"That the Cid Ruy Diez, the Campeador,
    Was there in his arms array'd;
And that with him, from the tomb,
    Had the Count Gonzalez come,[1]
        With a host, uprisen to aid!

And they came for the buried king that lay
At rest in that ancient fane;
For he must be arm'd on the battle-day,
    With them, to deliver Spain!"
—Then the march went sounding on,
And the Moors, by noontide sun,
        Were dust on Tolosa's plain.[2]

1   Fernán González was a military leader under Fernando I and hero of another medieval
    Spanish romance. See *Siege of Valencia*, scene 1.
2   This was the site of the battle of Navas de Tolosa in 1212, when the forces of Alfonso
    VIII of Castile defeated the Almoravid Moors, securing the future of the Christian
    kingdoms in Spain. In *NMM*, only 29-32 are in quotation marks.

Yes, it is ours! — the field is won,
    A dark and evil field!
Lift from the ground my noble son,
And bear him homewards on his bloody shield!

Let me not hear your trumpets ring,
    Swell not the battle-horn!
Thoughts far too sad these notes will bring,
When to the grave my glorious flower is borne!

Speak not of victory! — in the name,
    There is too much of woe!   10
Hush'd be the empty voice of Fame —
Call me back *his* whose graceful head is low.

Speak not of victory! — from my halls
    The sunny hour is gone!
The ancient banner on my walls
Must sink ere long — I had but him — but one!

Within the dwelling of my sires
    The hearts will soon be cold,
With me must die the beacon-fires   19
That stream'd at midnight from the mountain-hold.°   *fortress*

And let them face, since *this* must be,
    My lovely and my brave!
Was thy bright blood pour'd forth for me,
And is there but for stately youth a grave?

Speak to me once again, my boy!
    Wilt thou not hear my call?

---

1 Text: *1823*, pp. 277-79. The *Literary Gazette's* review of the volume ended with a full quotation of this poem, with the effect of giving even fuller credit to Gonzalez's sorrow, with which it was noticeably sympathetic.

Thou wert so full of life and joy,
I had not dreamt of *this*—that thou couldst fall!

Thy mother watches from the steep
30   For thy returning plume;
How shall I tell her that thy sleep
Is of the silent house, th' untimely tomb?

Thou didst not seem as one to die,
              With all thy young renown!
— Ye saw his falchion's[1] flash on high,
In the mid-fight, when spears and crests went down!

Slow be your march! — the field is won!
              A dark and evil field!
Lift from the ground my noble son,
40   And bear him homewards on his bloody shield.

---

1 *falchion*: a broad-bladed sword.

Appendix C: From Songs of Spain

New Monthly Magazine 40 (January 1834): 26-28

I

THE RIO VERDE SONG[1]

Flow, Rio Verde!
   In melody flow;
Win her that weepeth
   To slumber from woe!
Bid thy wave's music
   Roll through her dreams;
Grief ever loveth
   The kind voice of streams.

Bear her lone spirit
   Afar on the sound,   10
Back to her childhood,
   Her life's fairy ground:
Pass like the whisper
   Of love that is gone. —
Flow, Rio Verde,
   Softly flow on!

Dark glassy waters,
   So crimson'd of yore,   20
Love, Death, and Sorrow

---

1   The name of the Rio Verde (the "Gentle River" of Percy's ballad) will be familiar to
every Spanish reader, as associated in song and story with the old romantic wars of the
Peninsula. [FH]
   Reliques of Ancient English Poetry (1765), by Thomas Percy (1729-1811), was an influen-
tial collection. His ballad begins, "Gentle river, gentle river, / Lo, thy streams are stain'd
with gore! / Many a brave and noble captain / Floats along thy willow'd shore." The
Spanish ballad opens: "Rio verde, rio verde, / Quanto cuerpo en ti se baña / De Chris-
tianos y de Moros / Muertos por la dura espada!" [Green river, green river, / In you
have bathed so many bodies / Of Christians and of Moors / Killed by the harsh
sword!]

Know thy green shore.
Thou should'st have Echoes
For Grief's deepest one. —
Flow, Rio Verde!
Softly flow on!

VI
OLD SPANISH BATTLE SONG[1]

Fling forth the proud banners of Leon again;
Let the high word—*Castile*— go resounding through Spain!
And thou, free Asturias, encamp'd on the height,
Pour down thy dark sons to the vintage of fight.
Wake! wake! the old soil where our warriors repose
Rings hollow and deep to the trampling foes.

The voices are mighty that swell from the past,
With Aragon's cry on the shrill mountain-blast;
The ancient sierras give strength to our tread,
Their pines murmur song where bright blood hath been shed.
Fling forth the proud banner of Leon again,
And shout ye, "Castile! to the rescue for Spain!"

---

1   The Roman Empire secured its conquest of Spain in the first century with the fall of
    Numantia, then fell itself to Germanic tribes in the fifth century. The Visigoths pre-
    vailed and Christianity of one kind or another was established. When the Moors
    invaded the Peninsula early in the eighth century, Christian nobles sought refuge in the
    mountains of Asturias in NW Spain and created the first Christian kingdom, under
    Pelayo (Elmina's ancestor in *The Siege of Valencia*). It was from Asturias that the Christ-
    ian reconquest proceeded. In the tenth century Asturias united with León to consoli-
    date a Christian hold in NW Spain. Castile, in north central Spain, derives its name
    from the several castles built by Christians in the war against the Moors (eighth-ninth
    centuries). Its gestures of union with León began in the eleventh century and were
    secured in 1230. Leading the fight against the Moors, the confederation of Castile
    added Aragón in 1479 with the marriage of Ferdinand and Isabella, whose conquest of
    Grenada in 1492 completed the Christian conquest of Spain.

Appendix D: *From* Poema del Cid

(Translated by John Hookham Frere for Southey's *Chronicle of the Cid*)

[Also known as *Cantar del mio Cid* and *Poema del mio Cid*, *Poema* is "unquestionably the oldest poem in the Spanish language," reports Southey, deeming it "beyond all comparison the finest" (Preface ix). He dubbed its anonymous twelfth-century Castilian bard "the Homer of Spain" (xi). Known in English as *The Song of the Cid*, *Poema* survived in one copy made by Per Abbat in 1307, rediscovered in El Cid's reputed native town, Vivar, and published in the first volume of Tomás Antonio Sánchez's *Coleccion de Poesias Castellanas Anteriore al Siglo XV* (1779-90). Lacking several pages of Per Abbat's copy, this fragment still presented some 3744 lines. To Southey, *Poema* claims greater historical and documentary value than the idealizing legends advanced in the popular "romances" (ballads) collected in the sixteenth and seventeeth centuries, in the plays by de Castro and Corneille so inspired, and even in the earlier chronicles. "I have preferred it to the chronicles sometimes in point of fact, and always in point of costume" and "manners" (Preface xi).

Poema eschews the later legends of supernatural intervention and depicts the Moors as worthy opponents rather than mere villains. It gives three chief episodes of El Cid's career: his exile from Castile by Alfonso VI and ensuing life as outlaw and free-lancer; his conquest of Valencia from the Moors and his subsequent reaffiliation with Alfonso; and his retribution for the abuse of his daughters by their new husbands (princes recommended by Alfonso) who beat them and left them for dead as they journeyed from Valencia toward their new homes. Hemans may have read all of *Poema*, surely Southey's excerpts. In addition to invoking the general legend, *The Siege* visibly refracts its Valencian and domestic episodes. Hemans intensifies the militaristic zeal of the Bishop of Valencia, Don Jerónimo, in the character of Hernandez, a warmonger for whom national honor is more important than children's lives. And she bends the narrative to more tragic effect. In *Poema*, El Cid does not himself avenge the abuse of his daughters, but relies on a medieval "trial of justice," a combat of champions for each party, presided over by the king. In *The Siege*, the Governor, a descendant of El Cid, will not (then cannot) save his sons from execution by the besieging, hostage-taking Moors. Vengeance comes as he dies, when the King of Castile arrives to rescue the city; the sole survivor of the ruling family is Elmina, now widowed and bereft of all her children. In *Poema*, El Cid is survived by his children and his wife, Doña Jimena (Ximena), but she is unable to defend Valencia, and has to be rescued by Alfonso, as the city is lost to the Moors.

In an appendix (435-68), Southey supplies three "extracts," in Spanish and English, prefaced by an "Argument" (brief plot summary) in order "to give an idea of the style of the language and metre, and of the species of poetical merit which belongs to the Poem. They have been obligingly communicated to me by a Gentleman well acquainted with the Spanish language. I have never seen any other translation which so perfectly represents the manner, character, and spirit of its original" (436). The translator is Southey's friend, John Hookham Frere, who writes in hexameter (six-beat) couplets, marked by a medial caesura (pause), typographically advertised by a blank space in the midst of the line — a structure that enhances dramatic oppositions, complementarities, paradoxes, and parallelism. The measure is called "alexandrine," so named for its use in French romances (epic sagas) about Alexander the Great. It is the meter used by Corneille in *Le Cid*. The three extracts present the defeat of the Moors who are trying to regain a castle wrested from them by El Cid and his followers into exile (our selection); El Cid's challenge of honor to his abusive sons-in-law; the ensuing combat-trial of justice by El Cid's champions.]

ARGUMENT

The Cid being driven into banishment by the intrigues of his enemies, is accompanied by several of his friends and followers; for whom he undertakes to provide by carrying on a predatory war against the Moors. In the course of their adventures they surprize the Castle of Alcocer, but are soon after surrounded and besieged by a superior army.

After some difference of opinion, the Cid yields to the wishes
of his followers, and determines upon a sally, which is success-
ful.[1]

They fain would sally forth,   but the noble Cid
Accounted it as rashness,   and constantly forbid.
The fourth week was beginning,   the third already past,
The Cid and his companions   they are now agreed at last.
"The water is cut off,   the bread is well nigh spent,
To allow us to depart by night   the Moors will not consent.
To combat with them in the field   our numbers are but few,
Gentlemen tell me your minds,   what do you think to do?"
Minaya Alvar Fañez   answer'd him again,   10
"We are come here from fair Castile   to live like banish'd men.
There are here six hundred of us,   beside some nine or ten;
It is by fighting with the Moors   that we have earned our bread,
In the name of God that made us,   let nothing more be said,
Let us sally forth upon them   by the dawn of day."
The Cid replied, "Minaya,   I approve of what you say,
You have spoken for the best,   and had done so without doubt."
The Moors that were within the town   they took and turn'd them
          out,
That none should know their secret;   they labour'd all that night,
They were ready for the combat   with the morning light.   20
The Cid was in his armour   mounted at their head,
He spoke aloud amongst them,   you shall hear the words he said:
"We must all sally forth!   There can not a man be spar'd,
Two footmen only at the gates   to close them and keep guard;
If we are slain in battle   they will bury us here in peace,
If we survive and conquer,   our riches will increase.

---

1   Southey recounts the successful capture of this Moorish Castle, early in the career of El
     Cid's exile, in *Chronicle*, Book IV.III-IV (pp. 110-11). A league of Moorish kings,
     including the King of Valencia, join to retake the castle, laying siege to it, trapping El
     Cid and his followers, exhausting their food and water at the end of three weeks.
     With no chance of a safe escape, El Cid and company decide to fight, however out-
     numbered, "and either defeat them or die an honourable death" (IV.VI). The battle
     represented in this selection from *Poema* (circa lines 650-800) is narrated in *Chronicle*,
     Book IV.VII-IX (pp. 112-16).

And you, Pero Bermuez,   the standard you must bear,
Advance it like a valiant man,   evenly and fair;
But do not venture forward   before I give command."
Bermuez took the standard,   he went and kist his hand.
30 The gates were then thrown open,   and forth at once they rush'd,
The outposts of the Moorish host   back to the camp were push'd;
The camp was all in tumult,   and there was such a thunder
Of cymbals and of drums,   as if earth would cleave in sunder.
There you might see the Moors   arming themselves in haste,
And the two main battles   how they were forming fast;
Horsemen and footmen mixt,   a countless troop and vast.
The Moors are moving forward,   the battle soon must join,
"My men stand here in order,   rang'd upon a line!
40 Let not a man move from his rank   before I give the sign."
Pero Bermuez heard the word,   but he could not refrain.
He held the banner in his hand,   he gave his horse the rein;
"You see yon foremost squadron there,   the thickest of the foes,
Noble Cid, God be your aid,   for there your banner goes!
Let him that serves and honours it   shew the duty that he owes."
Earnestly the Cid call'd out,   "For heaven's sake be still!"
Bermuez cried, "I cannot hold,"   so eager was his will.
He spurr'd his horse, and drove him on   amid the Moorish rout;
They strove to win the banner,   and compast him about.
rescue Had not his armour been so true   he had lost either life or limb;
51 The Cid called out again,   "For heaven's sake succour° him!"
        Their shields before their breasts,   forth at once they go,
Their lances in the rest   levell'd fair and low;
Their banners and their crests   waving in a row,
Their heads all stooping down   toward the saddle bow.
The Cid was in the midst,   his shout was heard afar,
"I am Rui Diaz,   the Champion of Bivar;
Strike amongst them, gentlemen,   for sweet mercies sake!"
There where Bermuez fought   amidst the foe they brake,
60 Three hundred banner'd knights,   it was a gallant show:
Three hundred Moors they kill'd,   a man with every blow;
When they wheel'd and turn'd,   as many more lay slain,
You might see them raise their lances   and level them again.
There you might see the breastplates,   how they were cleft in twain,

And many a Moorish shield   lie shatter'd on the plain.   *banners*
The pennons° that were white   mark'd with a crimson stain,
The horses running wild   whose riders had been slain.
The Christians call upon St. James,   the Moors upon Mahound,
There were thirteen hundred of them slain   on a little spot of
    ground.
Minaya Alvar Fanez   smote with all his might,   70
He went as he was wont,   and was foremost in the fight.
There was Galin Garcia,   of courage firm and clear,
Felez Munioz,   the Cid's own Cousin dear;
Antolinez of Burgos,   a hardy knight and keen,
Munio Gustioz,   his pupil that had been.
The Cid on his gilded saddle   above them all was seen.
There was Martin Munioz,   that rul'd in Montmayor,
There were Alvar Fanez   and Alvar Salvador:
These were the followers of the Cid,   with many others more,
In rescue of Bermuez   and the standard that he bore.   80
Minaya is dismounted,   his courser has been slain,
He fights upon his feet,   and smites with might and main.
The Cid came all in haste   to help him to horse again;
He saw a Moor well mounted,   thereof he was full fain,
Thro' the girdle at a stroke   he cast him to the plain:
He called to Minaya Fanez   and reach'd him out the rein,
"Mount and ride Minaya,   you are my right hand,
We shall have need of you to day,   these Moors will not disband!"
Minaya lept upon the horse,   his sword was in his hand.
Nothing that came near him   could resist him or withstand;   90
All that fall within his reach   he dispatches as he goes.
The Cid rode to King Fariz,   and struck at him three blows;
The third was far the best,   it forc'd the blood to flow:
The stream ran from his side,   and stain'd his arms below;
The King caught round the rein   and turn'd his back to go,
The Cid has won the battle   with that single blow.

Appendix E: From Robert Southey's Chronicle of the Cid, from the Spanish

(London: Longman, Hurst, Rees, and Orme, 1808)

[As she was working on *The Siege*, Hemans recalled her impatience as a teenager "for the entire perusal" of Southey's *Chronicle* when it was published in 1808 (letter, 31 January 1823). For this epic eleven-book compendium — "wholly translation," Southey says at the top of his Preface (iii) — he assembled two kinds of sources. One was the poetic literature, the old *Poema* and the later "romances." The other was the prose chronicles. The chief one, which Hemans knew, is *Chronica del Famoso Cavallero Cid Ruy-Diez Campeador* (Burgos, 1593), first published in 1552 by Abbot Don Fr. Juan de Velorado, by order of Infante Don Fernando, afterwards Emperor. Velorado worked from an inaccurate copy of an undated manuscript, based on Arabic documents, at Cardeña, where there was a cult of El Cid. "The Abbot performed his task very carelessly and very inaccurately," Southey reports, "giving no account of the manuscript, and suffering many errors to creep into the text" (iii). Other chronicles include *Coronica General,* which included a history of El Cid differing in some aspects from Velorado's, and *La Chronica de España,* published by Florian de Ocampo, Chronicler to the King of Castile. Ocampo not only relied on a "remarkably faulty" manuscript, omitting words, sentences, even entire chapters, but also made matters worse with his own modernizations and mutilations (vi-vii). Southey refers to two more faulty manuscripts, mentioned by de Ocampo, guessing that these are part of *Coronica General.* These contribute to the third version of the *Chronica* (1604), a "very curious work," Southey remarks in his Preface, even as he admits his reliance on it (viii).

We offer some of the episodes that bear on Hemans's *Siege* and *Songs of the Cid,* by direct reference, with thematic alliance or divergence, and with descriptive details, especially of bloody battles, and the misery of a city under siege. Southey and his sources delineate El Cid and the chief events of his life with patent Christian iconography, but also with a remarkable balance of attention between his chivalric honor and his cruel rigor. Our editorial interpolations are in italics, in brackets.]

[from the *Introduction* (pp. xxxviii-xxxix, xli).]

In the beginning of the eleventh century, Navarre, Aragon, and Castille, were united under Sancho the Great. But experience had not taught the Christian Kings good policy, and when accident had joined the separate states, the possessor divided them at his death, desirous that his sons should all be Kings, though thereby they inevitably became enemies. Sancho left Navarre to his eldest son Garcia, Aragon to his bastard son Ramiro, and Castille to Fernando. [...] The elder brother regarded with impatience the division of his father's kingdoms. Fernando had excited some dispute respecting their boundary, and though no enmity was yet avowed, no fraternal affection existed. [*Intrigues and open war follow, in which Garcia is slain.*] In consequence of this victory Fernando became the most powerful of all the Kings of Spain, Moor or Christian. It was in his days that the Cid began to distinguish himself.

[*Origins and lineage.* Book I.II (p. 2).]

In those days arose Rodrigo of Bivar,[1] who was a youth strong in arms and of good customs; and the people rejoiced in him, for he bestirred himself to protect the land from the Moors. [...] In the year of the Incarnation 1026 was Rodrigo born, of [a] noble lineage.

[*Avenging an insult to his father.* Book I.III (pp. 3-4).]

At this time it came to pass that there was strife between count Don Gomez the Lord of Gormaz, and Diego Laynez the father of Rodrigo; and the Count insulted Diego and gave him a blow. Now Diego was a man in years, and his strength had passed from him, so that he could not take vengeance, and he retired to his home to dwell there in solitude and lament over his dishonour. And he took no pleasure in his food, neither could he sleep by night, nor would he lift up his eyes from the ground, nor stir out of his house, nor commune with his friends, but turned from them in silence as if the breath of his shame would taint them. Rodrigo was yet but a youth, and the

---

1   He was lord of the town of that name, now a small place about two leagues North of Burgos. [Southey]

Count was a mighty man in arms, […] held to be the best in the war, and so powerful that he had a thousand friends among the mountains. Howbeit all these things appeared as nothing to Rodrigo when he thought of the wrong done to his father, the first which had ever been offered to the blood […]. He asked nothing but justice of Heaven, and of man he asked only a fair field [*for combat*]; and his father seeing of how good heart he was, gave him his sword and his blessing. […] And he went out and defied the Count and slew him, and smote off his head and carried it home to his father. The old man was sitting at table, the food lying before him untasted, when Rodrigo returned, and pointing to the head which hung from the horse's collar, dropping blood, he bade him look up, for there was the herb which should restore to him his appetite: the tongue, quoth he, which insulted you, is no longer a tongue, and the hand which wronged you is no longer a hand. And the old man arose and embraced his son and placed him above him at the table, saying, that he who brought home that head should be the head of the house of Layn Calvo.

[*Marriage to Ximena*. Book I.V-VI (pp. 5-7).]

King Don Ferrando was going through Leon, putting the Kingdom in order, when tidings reached him of the good speed which Rodrigo had against the Moors. And at the same time there came before him Ximena Gomez, the daughter of the Count, who fell on her knees before him and said, Sir, I am the daughter of Count Don Gomez of Gormaz, and Rodrigo of Bivar has slain the Count my father. […] Sir, I come to crave of you a boon, that you will give me Rodrigo of Bivar to be my husband, with whom I shall hold myself well married, and greatly honoured; for certain I am that his possessions will one day be greater than those of any man in your dominions. Certes Sir, it behooves you to do this, because it is for God's service, and because I may pardon Rodrigo with a good will. The King held it good to accomplish her desire; and forthwith ordered letters to be drawn up to Rodrigo of Bivar, where he enjoined and commanded him that […] he had much to communicate to him, upon an affair which was greatly to God's service, and his own welfare and great honour.

When Rodrigo saw the letters of his Lord the King he greatly rejoiced in them, and said to the messengers that he would fulfil the King's pleasure. [...] And he dight [*arrayed*] himself full gallantly and well, and took with him many knights, both his own and of his kindred and of his friends, and he took also many new arms, and came [...] to the King with two hundred of his peers in arms, in festival guise; and the King went out to meet him, and received him right well, and did him honour; and at this were all the Counts displeased. And when the King thought it a fit season, he spake to him and said, that Doña Ximena Gomez [...] had come to ask him for her husband, and would forgive him her father's death; wherefor he besought him to think it good to take her to be his wife, in which case he should show him great favour. When Rodrigo heard this it pleased him well, and he said to the King that he would do his bidding in this, and in all other things which he might command; and the King thanked him much and he sent for the Bishop of Palencia, and took their vows and made them plight themselves each to the other according as the law directs. And when they were espoused the King did them great honour, and gave them many noble gifts, and added to Rodrigo's lands more than he had till then possessed: and he loved him greatly in his heart, because he saw that he was obedient to his commands, and for all that he had heard him say. [*Southey has a long footnote about the doubts about this marriage, a later one to another Ximena, his second cousin Ximena Diaz, being documented in the archives. In ch. VII Rodrigo takes his bride to his mother's household, and leaves her there, pledging to return to her after he wins five battles against the Moors. He departs for the frontier.*]

[*Already knighted "Ruydiez," in honor of victories against the Moors, El Cid receives this name after a successful siege of a Moorish stronghold at Montemor. Book I.XIX-XX (pp. 23-24).*]

[...] Great honour did Ruydiez win at that siege; for having to protect the foragers, the enemy came out upon him, and thrice in one day was he beset by them; but he, though sorely prest by them, and in great peril, nevertheless would not send to the camp for succour [*rescue*], but put forth his manhood and defeated them. And from that day the King gave more power into his hands, and made him head over all his household. [*The King goes to Zamora.*] And while he was there came messengers from the five Kings who were vassals to Ruy-diez of Bivar, bringing him their tribute [*riches, in exchange for protection*]; and they came to him, he being with the King, and called him Cid, which signifyeth Lord, and would have kissed his hands, but he would not give them his hand till they had kissed the hand of the King. And Ruydiez took the tribute and offered the fifth thereof to the King, in token of his sovereignty; and the King thanked him, but would not receive it and from that time he ordered that Ruydiez should be called the Cid, because the Moors had so called him.

[*King Don Ferrando dies and his realm is divided among his three sons. El Cid serves the eldest, King Don Sancho. When he is murdered, El Cid suspects the second son, King Don Alfonso, and although he swears an oath otherwise, El Cid's uncertainties are apparent and public, with the consequence that* "there was no love towards my Cid in the heart of the King" (III.XI). *Even so, El Cid serves him faithfully and successfully for five years. But Alfonso finds it convenient to believe slanders against El Cid's loyalty, and he is "wrongfully banished."* Book III. XVIII-XX, XXIV-XXV (pp. 96-98, 105-6).]

Now my Cid knew the evil disposition of the King towards him, and when he received his bidding, he made answer that he would meet him between Burgos and Bivar. And the King went out from Burgos and came nigh unto Bivar; and the Cid came up to him and would have kissed his hand, but the King withheld it, and said angrily unto him, Ruydiez, quit my land. Then the Cid clapt spurs to the mule upon which he rode, and vaulted into a piece of ground which was his own inheritance, and answered, Sir, I am not in your land, but in my own. And the King replied full wrathfully, Go out of my kingdoms without any delay. And the Cid made answer, Give me then thirty days time, as is the right of the hidalgos [*lower nobility*]; and the King said he would not, but that if he were not gone in nine days time he would come and look for him. The Counts were well pleased at this; but all the people of the land were sorrowful. And the King and the Cid parted. And the Cid sent for all his friends and his kinsmen and vassals, and told them how King Don Alfonso had banished him from the land, and asked of them who would follow him into banishment, and who would remain at home. Then Alvar Fañez, who was his cousin-german, came forward and said, Cid, we will all go with you, through desert and through peopled country, and never fail you. In your service will we spend our mules and horses, our wealth and our garments, and ever while we live be unto you loyal friends and vassals. And they all confirmed what Alvar Fañez had said; and the Cid thanked them for their love, and said that there might come a time in which he should guerdon [*reward*] them.

And as he was about to depart he looked back upon his own home, and when he saw his hall deserted, the household chests unfastened, the doors open, no cloaks hanging up, no seats in the porch, no hawks upon the perches, the tears came into his eyes, and he said, My enemies have done this . . God be praised for all things. And he turned toward the East, and knelt and said, Holy Mary Mother, and all Saints, pray to God for me, that he may give me strength to destroy all the pagans [*Moors; El Cid swindles some Jewish moneylenders, too*], and to win enough from them to requite my friends therewith, and all those who follow and help me. Then he called for Alvar Fañez and said unto him, cousin, the poor have no part in the wrong which the King hath done us; see now that no wrong be done unto them along our road: and he called for his horse. And then an old woman who was standing at her door said, Go in a lucky minute, and make spoil of whatever you wish. And with this proverb he rode on, saying Friends, by God's good pleasure we shall return to Castille with great honour and great gain. [...]

My Cid Ruydiez entered Burgos, having sixty streamers in his company. And men and women went forth to see him, and the men of Burgos and the women of Burgos were at their windows, weeping, so great was their sorrow; and they said with one accord, God, how good a vassal if he had but a good Lord! and willingly would each have bade him come in, but no one dared so to do. For King Don Alfonso in his anger had sent letters to Burgos, saying that no man should give the Cid a lodging; and that whosoever disobeyed should lose all that he had, and moreover the eyes in his head. Great sorrow had these Christian folk at this, and they hid themselves when he came near them because they did not dare speak to him. [...] My Cid Ruydiez, he who in a happy hour first girt on his sword, took up his lodging upon the sands, because there was none who would receive him within their door. He had a good company round about him, and there he lodged as if he had been among the mountains. [*El Cid leaves his wife and young daughters to the care of the Abbot of St. Pedro de Cardeña and prepares for his departure.*] [...] Meantime the tidings had gone through Castille how my Cid was banished from the land, and great was the sorrow of the people. Some left their houses to follow him, others forsook their honourable offices which they held. And that day a hundred and fifteen knights assembled at the bridge of Arlanzon, all in quest of my Cid. [...] And when he of Bivar knew what a goodly company were coming to join him, he rejoiced in his own strength, and rode out to meet them and greeted them full courteously; and they kissed his hand, and he said to them, I pray to God that I may one day requite ye well, because ye have forsaken your houses and your heritages for my sake, and I trust that I shall pay ye two fold. Six days of the term allotted were now gone, and three only remained: if after that time he should be found within the King's dominions, neither for gold nor for silver could he then escape. That day they feasted together, and when it was evening the Cid distributed among them all that he had, giving to each man according to what he was; and he told them that they must meet at mass after matins, and depart at that early hour. Before the cock crew they were ready, and the Abbot said the mass of the Holy Trinity, and when it was done they left the church and went to horse. And my Cid embraced Doña Ximena and his daughters, and blest them; and the parting between them was like separating the nail from the quick flesh; and he wept and continued to look round after them. Then Alvar Fañez came up to him and said, Where is your courage, my Cid? In a good hour were you born of woman. Think of our road now; these sorrows will yet be turned into joy. And the Cid spake again to the Abbot, commending his family to his care;— well did the Abbot know that he should one day receive good guerdon. [...]

That night my Cid lay at Spinar de Can, and people flocked to him from all parts, and early on the morrow he set out. [... *On the eighth night*] when my Cid was fast asleep, the Angel Gabriel appeared to him in a vision, and said, Go on boldly and fear nothing; for every thing shall go well with thee as long as thou livest, and all the things which thou beginnest, thou shalt bring to good end, and thou shalt be rich and honourable. And the Cid awoke and blest himself; and he crost his forehead and rose from his bed, and knelt down and gave thanks to God for the mercy which he had vouch-safed him, being right joyful because of the vision. Early on the morrow they set forth; now this was the last day of the nine. And they went on towards the Sierra de Miedes. Before sunset the Cid halted and took account of his company; there were three hundred lances, all with streamers, beside foot soldiers. And he said unto them, Now take and eat, for we must pass this great and wild Sierra, that we may quit the land of King Alfonso this night. To-morrow he who seeks us may find us. So they passed the Sierra that night. [*This is the end of* Book III.]

[*El Cid's Siege of Valencia. Adeptly playing its Moorish king off against the threat of an invasion by African Almoravides Moors, El Cid tightens the noose around Valencia, laying waste to its support system — the villages, fields, mills, the suburbs (or co-opting them if they cooperated) — and building a castle from which to assail the city. The King despises and tyrannizes the populace, who hope for rescue by the Almoravides. When it is clear that this will not happen, the populace despairs.* Book VI.XIV-XVII (174-180).]

Now came true tidings that the host of the Almoravides was nigh […] and all the people of Valencia were glad and rejoiced, for they thought that they were now delivered from their great misery, and from the oppression of the Cid […] and the joy of the people of Valencia increased, and they went upon the walls and upon the towers to see them come. And when night came they remained still upon the walls for it was dark, and they saw the great fires of the camp of the Almoravides […] and they began to pray unto God, beseeching him to give them good speed against the Christians, and they resolved as soon as the Almoravides were engaged in battle with the Cid, that they would issue forth and plunder his tents. But our Lord Jesus Christ was not pleased that it should be so and he ordered it after another guise; for he sent such a rain that night, with such a wind and flood as no man living remembered, and when it was day the people of Valencia looked from the wall to see the banners of the Almoravides and the place where they had encamped, and behold they could see nothing: and they were full sorrowful, and knew not what they should do, and they remained in such state as a woman in her time of childing, till the hour of tierce, and then came tidings that the Almoravides had turned back, and would not come unto Valencia, for the rains and floods had dismayed them and they thought the waters would have swept them away, and that the hand of God was against them, and therefore they turned back. And when the people of Valencia heard this they held themselves for dead men, and they wandered about the streets like drunkards, so that a man knew not his neighbour, and they smeared their faces with black like unto pitch, and they lost all thought like one who falls into the waves of the sea. And the Christians drew nigh unto the walls, crying out unto the Moors with a loud voice like thunder, calling them false traitors and renegados, and saying, Give up the town to the Cid Ruydiez, for ye cannot escape from him. And the Moors were silent, and made no reply because of their great misery. [...]

And when the Christians began to plunder the suburbs they of the town came out and plundered also those houses which were nearest unto the walls, so that every thing was carried away and nothing but the timbers left; and then the Christians took that to build them lodgments in the camp; and when the Moors saw this they came out, and carried away what timber they could into the city. And the Christians pulled down all the houses, save only such as could be defended, with arrows, and these which they dared not pull down they set fire to by night. And when all the houses had been levelled they began to dig in the foundations, and they found great wealth there, and store of garments, and hoards of wheat; and when the Cid saw this he ordered them to dig every where, so that nothing might be lost. And when all had been dug up the Cid drew nearer to the city, and girt it round about, and there was fighting every day at the barriers, for the Moors came out and fought hand to hand, and many a sword-stroke was given and many a push with the spear. While the Moors were thus beleagered came letters from the Captain of the Almoravides [...] that it was his set purpose at all events to succour them and deliver them from the oppression which they endured, and he was preparing to do this with all diligence. And he bade them take courage, and maintain the city. And when the Moors of Valencia heard these letters they took heart, and [...] their resolve was that they would be firm and maintain the city.

[...] Then the Cid drew nearer to the walls, so that no man could either enter in or issue out, but whosoever attempted it was either slain or taken. [...] Now came true tidings from Denia that the Almoravides had returned into their own country, and that there was no hope of succour at their hands. And when they of Valencia heard this they were greatly troubled. And they who held the Castles round about came humbly to the Cid, to place their love upon him, and besought him that he would accept tribute from them, and have them under his protection; and he gave orders that they might travel the roads in peace; and in this manner his rents increased, so that he had plenty to give. And he sent to them who held the Castles, bidding them provide him with cross-bow men, and foot soldiers, to fight against the city; and there was none who dared disobey his bidding, and they sent him cross-bow men and foot-men in great numbers, with their arms and provisions. Thus was Valencia left desolate and forsaken by the Moorish people; and it was attacked every day, and none could enter in, neither could any come out; and they were sore distressed, and the waves of death compassed them round about.

Then was there a Moor in the city who was a learned man and a wise, and he went upon the highest tower, and made a lamentation, and the words with which he lamented he put in writing, and it was rendered afterwards from the Arabic into the Castillian tongue, and the lamentation which he made was this:

Valencia! Valencia! trouble is come upon thee, and thou art in the hour of death; and if peradventure thou shouldst escape, it will be a wonder to all that shall behold thee.

But if ever God hath shown mercy to any place, let him be pleased to show mercy unto thee; for thy name was joy, and all Moors delighted in thee and took their pleasure in thee.

And if it should please God utterly to destroy thee now, it will be for thy great sins, and for the great presumption which thou hadst in thy pride.

The four corner stones whereon thou art founded would meet together and lament for thee, if they could!

Thy strong wall which is founded upon these four stones trembles, and is about to fall, and hath lost all its strength.

Thy lofty and fair towers which were seen from far, and

rejoiced the hearts of the people, . . little by little they are falling.

Thy white battlements which glittered afar off, have lost their truth with which they shone like the sunbeams.

Thy noble river Guadalaver, with all the other waters with which thou hast been served so well, have left their channel, and now they run where they should not.

Thy water courses, which were so clear and of such great profit to so many, for lack of cleansing are choked with mud.

Thy pleasant gardens which were round about thee; . . the ravenous wolf hath gnawn at the roots, and the trees can yield thee no fruit.

Thy goodly fields, with so many and such fair flowers, wherein thy people were wont to take their pastime, are all dried up.

Thy noble harbour, which was so great honour to thee, is deprived of all the nobleness which was wont to come into it for thy sake.

The fire hath laid waste the lands of which thou wert called Mistress, and the great smoke thereof reacheth thee.

There is no medicine for thy sore infirmity, and the physicians despair of healing thee.

Valencia! Valencia! from a broken heart have I uttered all these things which I have said of thee.

And this grief would I keep unto myself that none should know it, if it were not needful that it should be known to all.

[*Negotiations fail, the war hardens and the siege worsens.* Book VI.XXI-XXII (pp. 185-87).]

And the Cid made war afresh upon the city as cruelly as he could, and the price of bread was now three times as great as it had been at the beginning. [...] and the Cid drew nigh unto the walls, so as to fight hand to hand with the townsmen. And Abenaif [*the king*] waxed proud and despised the people, and when any went to make complaint before him, and ask justice at his hands, he dishonoured them, and they were evil entreated by him. And he was like a King, retired apart, and trobadors and gleemen and masters [*entertainers*] disported before him which could do the gest, and he took his pleasure. And they of the town were in great misery, from the Christians who warred upon them from without, and the famine whereof they died within. Moreover Abenaif oppressed them greatly, and he took unto himself all the goods of those who died, and he made all persons equal, the good and the bad, and took from all that he could; and those who gave him nothing he ordered to be tormented with stripes [*lashings*], and cast into rigorous prisons, till he could get something from them. And he had no respect neither for kinsman nor friend. There was but one measure for all, and men cared nothing now for their possessions, so that the sellers were many and the buyers none. And with all these miseries the price of food became exceeding great. [...] and they were so weak with hunger that the Christians came to the walls and threw stones in with the hand, and there was none who had strength to drive them back.

And the Cid having it at heart to take the town, let make an engine, and placed it at one of the gates, and it did great hurt both to the walls and within the town; and the Moors made other engines, with the which they brake that of the Cid. And the Cid in his anger let make three engines, and placed them at the three gates to the town, and they did marvellous great hurt. And food waxed dearer every day, till at last dear nor cheap it was not to be had, and there was a great mortality for famine; and they eat dogs and cats and mice. And they opened the vaults and privies and sewers of the town, and took out the stones [*pits*] of the grapes which they had eaten, and washed them, and ate them. And they who had horses fed upon them. And many men, and many women, and many children watched when the gates were open, and went out and gave themselves into the hands of the Christians, who slew some, and took others, and sold them to the Moors in Alcudia; and the price of a Moor was loaf and pitcher of wine: and when they gave them food and they took their fill, they died. Them that were stronger they sold to merchants who came there by sea from all parts. And the Moors of Alcudia, and of the town which the Cid had made there, had plenty of all things, and as great as was their abundance, even so great was the misery of those in the town.

[*Abenaif provides for himself and his guards, and his subjects starve.* Book VI.XXIV (p. 189).]

[…] And the famine now waxed so great that there was no food to sell, and many died of hunger. And many for great misery went out to the Christians, recking not whether they should be made captive, or slain, for they thought it better to be slain than to perish for lack of food. And Abenaif searched all the houses in the town for food, and where he found any store, he left only what would suffice for a fortnight, and took the rest. […] and they who had any food left buried it for fear, and for this reason there was none to be bought, neither dear nor cheap. And they who had nothing else, ate herbs, and leather, […] and the poor ate the dead bodies.

[*The "great cruelty which [El Cid] committed upon the Moor."* Book VI.XXVII (pp. 193–95).]

Now there was no food to be bought in the city, and the people were in the waves of death; and men were seen to drop and die in the streets, and the Place of the Alcazar round about the walls thereof was full of graves, and there was no grave which had fewer than ten bodies in it. As many as could fled out of the town, and delivered themselves up to the Christians to be made prisoners. The Cid thought that they who were the Chiefs within the walls, thrust out the poor and feeble that they might be able to hold out longer; and it troubled him, for he thought to take the town by starving it and he feared the coming of the Almoravides. Sometimes it troubled him, and at other times he seemed pleased that the Moors should come out and give themselves prisoners to his people, [*eventually* …] he held that the worst war which he could make upon the men of Valencia was to let them die of hunger. So he ordered proclamation to be made so loud that all the Moors upon the walls could hear, bidding all who had come out from the town to return into it, or he would burn as many as he should find; and saying also that he would slay all who came out from that time forth. Nevertheless they continued to let themselves down from the walls, and the Christians took them without his knowledge. But as many as he found he burnt alive before the walls, so that the Moors could see them; in one day he burnt eighteen, and cast others alive to the dogs, who tore them in pieces. They who could hide any sent them away by sea and by land to be sold; the most whom they sent were young men and girls, for others they would not take; and many virgins they kept for themselves. And if they knew that any who came out, had left kinsmen or friends in the town who would give any thing for them, they tortured them before the walls, or hung them from the towers of the Mosques which were without the city, and stoned them; and when they in the town saw this they gave ransom for them […] This continued for two months, till there were only four beasts left in the town, and one was a mule of Abenaif, and another was horse of his son's; and the people were so wasted that there were but few who had strength to mount the wall.

[*Valencia surrenders; El Cid takes possession.* Book VII.I-II (pp. 204-5).]

And all the people of the town gathered together, like men risen from their graves, . . yea, like the dead when the trumpet shall sound for the day of judgment, and men shall come out of their graves and be gathered together before the Majesty of God. […] On the following day after the Christians had taken possession of the town, the Cid entered it with a great company, and he ascended the highest tower of the wall and beheld all the city; and the Moors came unto him, and kissed his hand, saying he was welcome. And the Cid did great honour unto them […] and he commanded and requested the Christians that they should show great honour to the Moors, and respect them, and greet them when they met: and the Moors thanked the Cid, greatly for the honour which the Christians did them, saying that they had never seen so good a man, nor one so honourable, nor one who had his people under such obedience.

[*After these honorable overtures, El Cid consolidates his power and dwelling, with full military strength, in the Alcazar of Valencia. He allows the Moors to remain, in their houses and with their inheritances, with their customs and Mosques, on the condition that they pledge loyalty and tithe (give one tenth of) their fields, flocks, and herds.* Book VII.VII (pp. 212-13).]

Nine months did the Cid hold Valencia besieged, and at the end of that time it fell into his power, and he obtained possession of the walls, as ye have heard. And one month he was practising with the Moors that he might keep them quiet, till Abenaif was delivered into his hands; and thus ten months were fulfilled, and they were fulfilled on Thursday the last day of June, in [...] the year one thousand ninety and three of the Incarnation of our Lord Jesus Christ. And when the Cid had finished all his dealings with the Moors, on this day he took horse with all his company in good array, his banner being carried before him, and his arms behind: and in this guise, with great rejoicings he entered the city of Valencia. And he alighted at the Alcazar, and gave order to lodge all his men round about it, and he bade them plant his banner upon the highest tower of the Alcazar. Glad was the Campeador, and all they who were with him, when they saw his banner planted in that place. And from that day forth was the Cid possessed of all the Castles and fortresses which were in the kingdom of Valencia, and established in what God had given him, and he and all his people rejoiced.

[*Abenaif's stash of stolen goods is confiscated, and the Moorish nobles determine and enact a judgment of death, stoning him and his cadre. El Cid imposes additional strictures: Moors may not own arms, and own no more than one animal, a mule. If they wish, they may depart the city in safety, but with nothing other than their persons. There is an exodus of Moors and a Christian influx. Soon Christian Valencia suffers a Moorish siege, which it successfully withstands. El Cid enforces his military and Christian authority. Book VII. IX–XIII (pp. 215-18).*]

And the history saith, that so great was the multitude which departed, that they were two whole days in going out. Great was the joy of the Cid and his people that day, and from thenceforward he was called My Cid the Campeador, Lord of Valencia.

Now was it bruited abroad throughout all lands, how the Cid Ruydiez had won the noble city of Valencia. And when Ali Abenaxa the Adelantado of the Almoravides knew it, he sent his son-in-law the King of Seville to besiege him in Valencia, and gave him thirty thousand men at arms. And this king came in great haste to Valencia, and besieged the Cid therein. And the Cid made ready with all his people, and went out to fight him [...] and it was a good battle, and

at length he of the good fortune conquered; and the pursuit contin-
ued as far as Xativa; even so far did the Christians pursue them,
smiting and slaying. [...] They say that fifteen thousand Moors died.
[...] And when the pursuit was ended the Cid returned to the field
of battle, and ordered the spoils of the field and of the tents to be
collected. Be it known that this was a profitable day's work. Every
foot soldier shared a hundred marks of silver that day. And the Cid
returned full honourably to Valencia. Great was the joy of the Chris-
tians in the Cid Ruydiez, he who was born in a good hour. His
beard was grown, and continued to grow a great length. My Cid said
of his chin, for the love of King Don Alfonso, who hath banished me
from his land, no scissars shall come upon it, nor shall a hair be cut
away, and Moors and Christians shall talk of it.

That night the Cid took counsel with Alvar Fañez, who departed
not from his side, and with the other honourable men who were of
his council, concerning what should be done: for now that his peo-
ple were all rich, he feared lest they should return into their own
country, for my Cid saw that if they might go they would. And
Minaya [*Fañez; a nickname meaning "brother"*] advised him that he
should cause proclamation to be made through the city, that no man
should depart without permission of the Cid, and if any one went
who had not dispeeded himself and kist his hand, if he were overtak-
en he should lose all that he had, and moreover be fixed upon a stake
[*impaled alive*]. And that they might be the more certain, he said unto
Minaya that he would take account of all the people who were with
him [...] and there were found a thousand knights of lineage, and
five hundred and fifty other horsemen, and of foot soldiers four
thousand, besides boys and others; thus many were the people of my
Cid, he of Bivar. And his heart rejoiced, and he smiled and said,
Thanks be to God, Minaya, and to Holy Mary Mother!... we had a
smaller company when we left the house of Bivar!

[*The prototype of Hemans's Hernandez*] At this time there came a
crowned one from the parts of the East [...]; his name was the Bish-
op Don Hieronymo, a full learned man and a wise, and one who was
mighty both on horseback and a-foot: and he came enquiring for the
Cid, wishing that he might see himself with the Moors in the field,
for if he could once have his fill of smiting and slaying them, Chris-
tians should never lament him. And when the Cid knew this it

pleased him in his heart, and he took horse and went to visit him, and rejoiced greatly that he was come; and he resolved to make Valencia a bishopric and give it to this good Christian. And they took counsel, and it was that on the morrow the Bishop and his clergy should turn the Mosques into Churches, wherein they might sing masses, and sacrifice the body of Jesus Christ. And rents were appointed for the table of the Bishop and for his Canons, and for all the clergy in the city of Valencia. And nine parish Churches were made. And the greatest was called St. Pedro's, and another was called St. Mary of the Virtues. This was near the Alcazar, and there the Cid went oftenest to hear service. After this manner the Cid ordered his city that it should be a Bishopric, for the honour of the Catholic faith. God! how joyful was all Christendom that there was a Lord Bishop in the land of Valencia!

Now the Cid bethought him of Doña Ximena his wife, and of his daughters Doña Elvira and Doña Sol, whom he had left in the Monastery of St. Pedro de Cardeña [...] [*El Cid makes reparations to King Don Alfonso, and bestows large sums on the Monastery, on his family "that they might prepare themselves and come in honourable guise" and redeems his deceit on the Jewish moneylenders, with apologies for his desperation. Southey is not so sure about this last act of honor, however; see his note on p. 221.*]

[*In the five years of El Cid's reign, there is a general peace, but then news arrives.* Book XI.I (pp. 326-27).]

[...] King Bucar the Miramamolin of Morocco, holding himself disgraced because the Cid Campeador had conquered him in the field [...] near unto Valencia, where he had slain or made prisoners of all his people, and driven him into the sea, and made spoil of all the treasures which he had brought with him; [...] King Bucar calling these things to mind, had gone himself and stirred up the whole paganism of Barbary [...] to cross the sea again, and avenge himself if he could; and he had assembled so great a power that no man could devise their numbers. When the Cid heard these tidings he was troubled at heart; howbeit he dissembled this, so that no person knew what he was minded to do [...]

[*Death of El Cid. On the heels of this intelligence, El Cid receives a prophe-cy from St. Peter, in a midnight dream vision, that he will die in thirty days, but that God's favor of him guarantees Valencia's victory over Bucar's forces. Gathering his family, friends, and loyal subjects, El Cid tells them of his impending death and their assured victory. Following a final mass, in which he makes a public announcement of his coming death, he gives instructions for the care of his body, makes confession and receives absolution.* Book XI.IV-VI (pp. 330-32).]

[…] Then he arose and took leave of the people, weeping plenteous-ly, and returned to the Alcazar, and betook himself to his bed, and never rose from it again; and every day he waxed weaker and weaker, till seven days only remained of the time appointed. Then he called for the caskets of gold in which was the balsam and the myrrh which the Soldan of Persia had sent him; and […] he bade them bring him the golden cup, of which he was wont to drink; and he took of that balsam and of that myrrh as much as a little spoon-full, and mingled it in the cup with rose-water, and drank of it; and for the seven days which he lived he neither ate nor drank aught else than a little of that myrrh and balsam mingled with water. And every day after he did this, his body and his countenance appeared fairer and fresher than before, and his voice clearer, though he waxed weaker and weaker daily, so that he could not move in his bed.

On the twenty-ninth day, being the day before he departed, he called for Doña Ximena, and for the Bishop Don Hieronymo, and don Alvar Fañez Minaya, and Pero Bermudez, and his trusty Gil Diaz; and when they were all five before him, he began to direct them what they should do after his death; and he said to them, Ye know that King Bucar will presently be here to besiege this city, with seven and thirty Kings whom he bringeth with him, and with a mighty power of Moors. Now therefore the first which ye do after I have departed, wash my body with rose-water many times and well, as blessed be the name of God it is washed within and made pure of all uncleanness to receive his holy body to-morrow, which will be my last day. And when it has been well washed and made clean, ye shall dry it well, and anoint it with this myrrh and balsam, from these golden caskets, from head to foot, so that every part shall be anoint-ed, till none be left. And you my Sister Doña Ximena, and your women, see that ye utter no cries, neither make any lamentation for me, that the Moors may not know of my death. And when the day shall come in which King Bucar arrives, order all the people of Valencia to go upon the walls, and sound your trumpets and tambours, and make the greatest rejoicings that ye can. And when ye would set out for Castille, let all the people know in secret, that they make themselves ready, and take with them all that they have, so that none of the Moors in the suburb may know thereof; for certes ye cannot keep the city, neither abide therein after my death. And see ye that sumpter beasts be laden with all that there is in Valencia, so that nothing which can profit may be left. […] Then saddle ye my horse Bavieca, and arm him well; and ye shall apparel my body full seemlily, and place me upon the horse, and fasten and tie me thereon so that it cannot fall: and fasten my sword Tizona in my hand. And let the Bishop Don Hieronymo go on one side of me, and my trusty Gil Diaz on the other, and he shall lead my horse. You, Pero Bermudez, shall bear my banner, as you were wont to bear it; and you, Alvar Fañez, my cousin, gather your company together, and put the host in order as you are wont to do. And go ye forth and fight with King Bucar; for be ye certain and doubt not that ye shall win this battle; God hath granted me this. And when ye have won the fight, and the Moors are discomfited, ye may spoil the field at pleasure [*plunder the battlefield*]. Ye will find great riches.

[*El Cid's death, King Bucar's siege, the exodus from Valencia, the Christian army's victory over the African forces.* Book XI.VI, VIIII–IX (pp. 333, 335–38).]

[…] the noble Baron yielded up his soul, which was pure and without spot, to God, on that Sunday […] being the twenty and ninth of May, in the year of our Lord one thousand and ninety and nine, and in the seventy and third year of his life. […] Three days after the Cid had departed King Bucar came into the port of Valencia, and landed with all his power [*army*], which was so great that there is not a man in the world who could give account of the Moors whom he brought. And there came with him thirty and six Kings, and one Moorish Queen, who was a negress, and she brought with her two thousand horsewomen, all negresses like herself, all having their hair shorn save a tuft on the top, and this was in token that they came as if upon a pilgrimage, and to obtain the remission of their sins; and they were all armed in coats of mail and with Turkish bows. King Bucar ordered his tents to be pitched around Valencia, and [...] there were full fifteen thousand tents; and he bade the Moorish negress with her archers to take their station near the city. And on the morrow they began to attack the city, and they fought against it three days strenuously; and the Moors received great loss, for they came blindly up to the walls and were slain there. And the Christians defended themselves right well, and every time that they went upon the walls, they sounded trumpets and tambours, and made great rejoicings, as the Cid had commanded. This continued for eight days or nine, till the companions of the Cid had made ready every thing for their departure, as he had commanded. And King Bucar and his people thought that the Cid dared not come out against them, and they were the more encouraged, and began to think of making bastilles and engines wherewith to combat the city, for certes they weened that the Cid Ruydiez dared not come out against them, seeing that he tarried so long.

All this while the company of the Cid were preparing all things to go into Castille, as he had commanded before his death. [...] And the body of the Cid was prepared [...] so that there was not a man who would have thought him dead if he had seen him and not known it. And on the second day after he had departed, Gil Diaz placed the body upon a right noble saddle, and this saddle with the body upon it he put upon a frame [...] and these boards were fastened into the saddle, so that the body could not move. All this was done by the morning of the twelfth day; and all that day the people of the Cid were busied in making ready their arms, and in loading beasts with all that they had, so that they left nothing of any price in the whole city of Valencia, save only the empty houses. When it was midnight they took the body of the Cid, fastened to the saddle as it was, and placed it upon his horse Bavieca, and fastened the saddle well: and the body sate so upright and well that it seemed as if he was alive [...] and they put on it a surcoat of green sendal, having his [*coat of*] arms blazoned thereon, and a helmet of parchment which was cunningly painted that every one might have believed it to be iron;

and his shield was hung round his neck, and they placed the sword Tizona in his hand, and they raised his arm, and fastened it up so subtilly that it was a marvel to see how upright he held the sword. And the Bishop Don Hieronymo went on one side of him, and the trusty Gil Diaz on the other, and he led the horse Bavieca, as the Cid had commanded. And when all this had been made ready, they went out from Valencia at midnight. [...] Pero Bermudez went first with the banner of the Cid, and with him five hundred knights who guarded it, all well appointed. And after these came all the baggage. Then came the body of the Cid with an hundred knights, all chosen men, and behind them Doña Ximena with all her company, and six hundred knights in the rear. All these went out so silently, and with such a measured pace, that it seemed as if there were only a score. And by the time that they had all gone out it was broad day.

Now Alvar Fañez Minaya had set the host in order, and [*during the exodus*], he fell upon the Moors. First he attacked the tents of that Moorish Queen the Negress, who lay nearest to the city; and this onset was so sudden, that they killed full a hundred and fifty Moors before they had time to take arms or go to horse. But that Moorish Negress was so skilful in drawing the Turkish bow, that it was held for a marvel, and it is said that they called her [...] the Star of the Archers. And she was the first that got on horseback, and with some fifty that were with her, did some hurt to the company of the Cid; but in fine [*the end*] they slew her, and her people fled to the camp. And so great was the uproar and confusion, that few there were who took arms, but instead thereof they turned their backs and fled toward the sea. And when King Bucar and his Kings saw this they were astonished. And it seemed to them that there came against them on the part of the Christians full seventy thousand knights, all as white as snow: and before them a knight of great stature upon a white horse with a bloody cross, who bore in one hand a white banner, and in the other a sword which seemed to be of fire, and he made a great mortality among the Moors who were flying. And King Bucar and the other Kings were so greatly dismayed that they never checked the reins till they had ridden into the sea; and the company of the Cid rode after them, smiting and slaying and giving them no respite; and they smote down so many that it was marvellous, for the Moors did not turn their heads to defend themselves.

And when they came to the sea, so great was the press among them to get to the ships, that more than ten thousand died in the water. And of the six and thirty Kings, twenty and two were slain. And King Bucar and they who escaped with him hoisted sails and went their way, and never more turned their heads. Then Alvar Fañez and his people, when they discomfited the Moors, spoiled the field, and the spoil thereof was so great that they could not carry it away. And they loaded camels and horses with the noblest things which they found, and [*caught up to the exodus train*]. And so great was the spoil of that day, that there was no end to it: and they took up gold, and silver, and other precious things as they rode through the camp, so that the poorest man among the Christians, horseman or on foot, became rich with what he had won that day. And when they were all met together, they took the road toward Castille.

[*The stunned local Moors, believing they had seen El Cid leave the city with a procession, suspected some trick, and so dared not plunder the tents left by King Bucar and his allies. The next day they go to the city and find it deserted.* Book XI.X (pp. 339).]

[…] they went into the Alcazar, and looked through all the halls and chambers, and they found neither man nor living thing; but they saw written upon a wall in Arabic characters by Gil Diaz, how the Cid Ruydiez was dead, and that they had carried him away in that manner to conquer King Bucar, and also to the end that none might oppose their going. And when the Moors saw this they rejoiced and were exceeding glad, and they opened the gates of the town, and sent to tell these tidings to those in the suburbs. And they came with their wives and children in the town, each to the house which had been his before the Cid won it. And from that day Valencia remained in the power of the Moors till it was won by King Don Jayme of Aragon, he who is called the Conqueror, which was an hundred and seventy years. But though King Don Jayme won it, it is alway called *Valencia del Cid*.

[*The Cid's rising.* Book XI.XXI (p. 352).]

[…] when the Miramamolin brought over from Africa against King

Don Alfonso, the eighth of that name, the mightiest power of the misbelievers that had ever been brought against Spain since the destruction of the Kings of the Goths, the Cid Campeador remembered his country in that great danger. For the night before the battle was fought at the Navas de Tolosa, in the dead of the night, a mighty sound was heard in the whole city of Leon, as if it were the tramp of a great army passing through. And it passed on to the Royal Monastery of St. Isidro, and there was a great knocking at the gate thereof and they called to a priest who was keeping vigils in the Church, and told him, that the Captains of the army whom he heard were the Cid Ruydiez, and Count Ferran Gonzalez, and that they came there to call up King Don Ferrando the Great, who lay buried in that church, that he might go with them to deliver Spain. And on the morrow that great battle of the Navas de Tolosa was fought, wherein sixty thousand of the misbelievers were slain, which was one of the greatest and noblest battles ever won over the Moors.[1]

[*The Cid's veneration.* Book XI.XXXI (pp. 365-66).]

There is no doubt that the soul of the blessed Cid resteth and reigneth with the blessed in Heaven. And men of all nations and at all times have come from all parts to see and reverence his holy body and tomb, […] especially knights and soldiers, who when they have fallen upon their knees to kiss his tomb, and scraped a little of the stone thereof to bear away with them as a relick, and commended themselves to him, have felt their hearts strengthened, and gone away in full trust that they should speed the better in all battles into which they should enter from that time with a good cause. By reason of this great devotion, and the great virtues of my Cid, and the miracles which were wrought by him, King Philip the Second gave order to his ambassador […] to deal with the Court of Rome concerning the

---

1   This thing, says Yepes [*Chronicle Generale*], God permitted to be heard in Leon, that it might be known how those persons whom the Gentiles in their vanity call Heroes, and the world holds for excellent men, do in Heaven take thought for the things of this world; and though their bodies were not verily and indeed present, yet inasmuch as their souls so vehemently desired to be there, this sound of their march was permitted to be heard, that it might be known how they were still watchful for the good of Spain [Southey].

canonization of this venerable knight Rodrigo Diaz. [...] But before the matter could be proceeded in, [*a local emergency called the ambassador home*]; and thus this pious design could not be brought about. Nevertheless the Cid hath alway been regarded with great reverence as an especial servant of God: and he is called the Blessed Cid, and the Venerable Rodrigo Diaz. Certes, his soul resteth and reigneth with the blessed in Heaven. Amen.

HERE ENDETH THE CHRONICLE OF THAT RIGHT FAMOUS

AND GOOD KNIGHT THE BLESSED CID,

RODRIGO DIAZ DE BIVAR,

THE CAMPEADOR

Appendix F: Letters by Felicia Dorothea Browne (later Hemans), 1808-09, during the Peninsular War

Felicia Browne to her mother's sister in Liverpool, 19 December 1808 (Chorley, *Memorials* 1.30-33)

[...] You have, I know, perused the papers (as I have done,) with <u>anxiety</u>, though, perhaps, without the tremors which I continually experience. The noble Spaniards! surely, surely, they will be crowned with success: I have never given up the cause, notwithstanding the late disastrous intelligence; but I think their prospects begin to wear a brighter appearance, and we may hope that the star of freedom, though long obscured by clouds, will again shine with transcendent radiance. You will smile, my dear aunt, but you know not what an <u>enthusiast</u> I am in the cause of Castile and liberty: my whole heart and soul are interested for the gallant patriots, and though females are forbidden to interfere in politics, yet as I have a dear, dear brother, at present on the scene of action, I may be allowed to feel some ardour on the occasion. [...] You see I am writing on the anniversary of George's birthday;[1] and I know you will pray that every year may see his progress in virtue and true heroism. I am proud that he is at present on the theatre of glory; and I hope he will have an opportunity of signalizing his courage, and of proving an honour to his family and an ornament to his profession. [...] Glorious, glorious Castilians! may victory crown your noble efforts. Excuse me for dwelling so much on this subject; for Spain is the subject of my thoughts and

---

1 Her brother George's regiment sustained heavy losses and injuries at the retreat at Coruña (the action that cost Sir John Moore his life). "He is in a most miserable plight, for he has lost all he possessed in the world, and is worn to a skeleton," their mother wrote to a family friend, even as their sister Harriett wrote to the same correspondent of Felicia's enthusiasm for the campaign: "Felicia is particularly delighted that her hero, Palafox, has gained <u>another</u> victory, and added another <u>laurel</u> to his wreath." George would return from war disillusioned with a military career. See Francis Nicholson, "Correspondence between Mrs. Hemans and Matthew Nicholson," *Memoirs and Proceedings of the Manchester Literary and Philosophical Society* 54 (1910): 1-40; quotations are from page 12. José de Palafox y Melzi, Duke of Saragossa (1775-1847), led the citizens of Saragossa to build barricades and fight off the French in July and again in December 1808.

words— "my dream by night, my vision of the day." Can you be surprised at my enthusiasm? My head is half turned [...]

Felicia Browne to Matthew Nicholson, an elderly family friend living in Richmond Row, near Liverpool, 18 April 1809 (Nicholson, "Correspondence"13-14)

The letter which my Mother has transcribed for your perusal on the other side, we received yesterday from my eldest Brother. You may easily imagine what blended emotions of tenderness, pride, and affection, it has excited in our Bosoms. Deeply as I feel for the sufferings my dearest Brother must have endured, still I can hardly regret that he has received a wound in so glorious a cause, and as a trophy of so brilliant a victory; it will ever be his pride that he has bled in the service of his Country, and like the soldier in the 'Pleasures of Memory,' who 'counts o'er his scars, and tells what deeds were done,'[1] he will ever triumph in a recollection of the perils to which he has been exposed. If, however, he had not written himself to inform us of his convalescence, or if we had imagined he was in any danger from his wound, how different would our feelings have been! I agree with you that my poetic visions of Spanish Freedom are not likely at present to be realized; and I regret that the ardent enthusiasm the cause excited, led my fancy to paint the Spanish people, in colours, which (except in a few instances), have proved only rainbow illusions. [...]

Felicia Browne to the same, 18 April, 1809 (Nicholson, "Correspondence" 14)

[...] I am happy to find that you have not given up the cause of Spain as desperate; had every leader of the Spanish people acted like the illustrious Palafox, and the bravest defenders of Saragossa, they would have deserved the praises and enthusiasm, their energies at first excited, and Spain might have been called the Land of patriot-heroes. [...]

---

1   See Samuel Rogers, *The Pleasures of Memory* (1792), Part II, in which an old veteran entertains a young truant boy: "He counts his scars, and tells what deeds were done" (154).

Appendix G: Reviews and Receptions

1. **From** *The London Literary Gazette, Journal of Belles Lettres, Arts, Sciences, &c.* **no. 335 (21 June 1823): 385–6; no. 336 (28 June 1823): 407–8**

[The *Gazette* was a popular Tory weekly, edited by William Jerdan, also one of the owners. It had a wide readership (around 4000) and drew wide attention in the 1820s when it began publishing passionate, sardonic love poetry by L.E.L. (Letitia Elizabeth Landon).]

[21 June 1823; the front-page review: REVIEW OF NEW BOOKS]

The name of Mrs. Hemans is so well known to the public, and her poetry has been so generally admired, that we are released from the task of introductory criticism or complimentary exordium. The volume now produced is similar in character to its precursors. There are the same sweet thoughts, the same harmonious numbers, the same classical allusiveness, and the same female feeling, grace and pathos. Shall we add that there is also some want of force; and in the first piece, *Constantine,* an inversion of language, carried so far as to render much of its imagery dim, and occasionally its meaning indistinct, without a second perusal? [commentary on *The Last Constantine*]

[28 June 1823, title-line: SIEGE OF VALENCIA, ETC.]

The Siege of Valencia, in a dramatic form, relates to the siege of a city and the extinction of a noble race; and thus far bears a rather close resemblance to 'The Last Constantine,' in the same volume, on which we formed our Review in the preceding *Literary Gazette.* Defended by Gonzalez, a descendant of the Cid, Valencia holds out against the Moors. Alphonzo [*sic*] and Carlos, the two sons of Gonzalez, fall into the hands of the enemy, and an offer is made to spare their lives on the condition of surrendering the place. This, however, the agonized father refuses, though their mother, Elmina, wavers in her resolution; and their sister, Ximena, dies broken-hearted. The boys are put to death; and Gonzalez, mortally wounded, lives but to witness the total defeat of his cruel adversaries by the king of Castile, and the consequent deliverance of Spain. There are some fine lyrical effusions interspersed in the drama, of which we take the first as a specimen: [prints all of Ximena's opening ballad.]

We shall not proceed circumstantially with this drama, but content ourselves with a few quotations to display the character of the sentiments and dialogue. The change from light-heartedness to gloom is happily illustrated in the following allusion: [quotes Ximena 1.81-87, from "I would not" to "awful music"]

A mother's feelings are perhaps rather diffusely (the fault of the drama) drawn in several parts. Elmina says to her husband, [quotes her, 1.340-68, from "I have stood" to "early fate" and 1.429-59, from "There is none" to "Why were ye given me?"]

And finally, near the conclusion, where the fate of the boys is certain, the mother breaks forth in a powerfully natural strain: [quotes 8.1-25, to "My children!"]

The father's distress is pourtrayed with almost equal skill, and there is one brief passage which we cannot but quote as a fine touch of this: [5.178-92, from his "Alas this woe must be!" to Elmina's "one human heart!" but adding italics to his "I do but shake my spirit from its height / So startling it with hope!" (179-80)]

Ximena in vain excites the people to rise and rescue her brothers, and we cite a portion of the scene to complete our examples of the dialogue: [quotes 6.58-78, from her "Men of Valencia!" to Citizen's "Our hearts beat faint and low."]

After the death of the heroine, Gonzalez, wounded to death, enters the temple where her mother is lamenting over the corse. [quotes 8.218-54, from "Elmina *(falling at his feet)*" to Gonzalez, "Forgiveness at its close"]

The last word ["close"], like a catchword, reminds us how much we have filled our paper with this review, and that we must take our leave of Mrs. Hemans. Yet it is not to be done without mentioning that some Spanish traditions, ballads, &c. conclude the volume. Of these we think the very best is *England's Dead*, which (thanks to the author) originally appeared in the *Literary Gazette*.[1] Next to it we

---

1   19 October 1822, p. 664; signed "H." *The Cid's Departure into Exile* had been published in the *Gazette* the week before. *England's Dead* was immediately and widely admired; *New European Magazine* printed it in full in its review of the *The Siege &c* (3 [1823], 122-23).

admire the following, and with its insertion bid a commendatory farewell to a very interesting monument of female genius: [prints all of *The Chieftan's Son*]

2. From *The Literary Museum and Register of the Fine Arts, Sciences, Antiquities, the Drama, &c.* 62 (28 June 1823), 421-22.

[*The Literary Museum*, a London weekly published by John Miller and John Warren, issued several favorable, though not unequivocal, reviews of Lord Byron and Leigh Hunt; the April 26 number had given a mostly praising review of David Douglas's *The Fall of Constantinople*, a likely entry in the aborted Royal Society of Literature prize-competition to which Hemans had submitted the poem eventually titled *The Last Constantine*.]

There is now so much verse of the highest order, rhimed and unrhimed, poured in on the reading public, that few people can find either time or inclination for the perusal of those secondary productions which always ensure an author's fame in the immediate circle of his friends, but are seldom found beyond it. In this respect poetry stands quite alone; one good picture can only belong to one owner, and it therefore still leaves the market open to inferior works, but a single poem when published is the property of whoever chuses to possess it, and as its value is not lessened by the multiplication of copies, it acts as an exclusive barrier against inferior productions. There are now at least six English poets, all indisputably of the highest order of intellect though not of equal reputations, and the rapidity with which they pour out their volumes on the public, leaves the reader neither time nor inclination for the perusal of works that, with much merit, yet want sufficient power to command attention.[1] Independent of this consideration, poetry, unless it be very good indeed, is scarcely tolerable. If it have not the power to excite strongly, it has not the power to excite at all, and to the reader there is no mean between the best and the worst; all that is below excellence is absolute inferiority.

---

1 These six, though not specified, would include Byron, Wordsworth, and Thomas Moore; among other possibilities are Samuel Rogers, Thomas Campbell, and Percy Shelley.

These objections, thus generally stated, apply in their full force to Mrs. Hemans. There is much in her book to praise, much that intitles her to the fame of talent and information, and yet she has written little that any one would wish to read a second time; the gold in the mine is too scantly to recompense the pains of working. Her versification is smooth and flowing, and she has borrowed her images with great taste from a reading that appears to be tolerably extensive, but she has no striking nor original thinking, nothing that evinces power; and without this a name may be forced into a short-lived notoriety, but never can attain a lasting reputation.

The minor poems are the best in the volume; and of these we should give the preference to the song called 'England's Dead.' The leading idea of this little poem is good, though it is beaten out through too many stanzas with an economy of thought that is any thing but praiseworthy: —

[quotes all of *England's Dead*]

[a few dismissive comments on *The Fall of Constantinople*]

'The Siege of Valencia' is a dramatic poem, chiefly founded on two anecdotes of Spanish history: —[quotes the Advertisement's first paragraph, from the second sentence to the end]

This is in blank verse, and the remarks which we have stated as applying to poetry in general, apply more forcibly to this species of poetical composition. We shall however give one extract, and that has been sought out with a view rather to do justice to the author than to our own opinion: —

[quotes 9.194–219]

[concludes with a full quotation of *The Cid's Funeral Procession.*]

3. From *The British Critic* n.s. 20 (July 1823): 50–61.

[Famous for hostile reviews of Godwin, Hunt, and Shelley, this Tory, High-Church monthly was founded to oppose the dissenting, reformist slant of other monthly reviews.]

We heartily abjure Blue Stockings.[1] We make no compromise with any variation of the colour, from sky-blue to Prussian blue, blue

---

1 By the 1820s, this was a derisive term for learned women, having evolved from a more neutral descriptive in the second half of the 18th century.

stockings are an outrage upon the eternal fitness of things. It is a principle with us to regard an Academicienne of this Society, with the same charity that a cat regards a vagabond mouse. We are inexorable to special justifications. We would fain make a fire in Charing-Cross, of all the bas blus [sic] in the kingdom, and albums, and common-place books, as accessaries before or after the fact should perish in the conflagration.[1]

Our forefathers never heard of such a thing as a Blue Stocking, except upon their sons' legs; the writers of Natural History make no mention of the name; it is not to be accounted for by the all-sufficient sensation and reflection of Mr. Locke; it has no place even amongst the phantasms of Bishop Berkeley.[2] Shakspeare, who painted all sorts and degrees of persons and things, who compounded or created thousands, which, perhaps, never existed, except in his own prolific mind, even he, in the wildest excursion of his fancy never dreamed of such an extraordinary combination as a Blue Stocking! No! it is a creature of modern growth, and capable of existing only in such times as the present.

Formerly there were two styles of female education, and consequently two styles of women; the really learned, and the really simple; the first, nurtured in classic lore, and disciplined in scholastic exercises; the second taught to sow [sic] neatly, and read the English Bible distinctly; the one skilful in drawing conclusions, the other in drawing pancakes. You had your Lady Jane Grey with Plato on her breakfast table, or a living Sophia Western with orange marmalade of her own making, and a dozen national tunes on the harpsichord of your own choosing.[3] Both of these were well; they proposed several ends, and adopted several means towards the attaining of them; there was a fitness, and a moral perfection in each. In such times, and under such institution, the anomaly in question *could* not have existed; the ingredients of its composition, and the sphere of its action, were equally wanting.

---

1 Albums are scrapbooks for souvenirs and other miscellaneous items; commonplace books are form of notebook, to record favorite passages from one's reading.

2 Idealist philosopher Bishop Berkeley (1685-1753) disputed the materialist philosophy of John Locke (1632-1704).

3 Lady Jane Gray (1537-54) was queen of England for nine days before she was executed for treason; Sophia Western is loved by the hero of Henry Fielding's *Tom Jones* (1749).

A Blue Stocking is the natural product of an age in which knowledge is lost in accomplishments.[1] It is the vapoury offspring of ignorance, impregnated by conceit. It is the epicene *tertium aliquid* between a fool and a coquette. It is the infallible consequence of the Loves of the Angels fastened upon Conversations on Chemistry, and swallowed according to the prescription of the Mathematical Professor in the University of Lagado.[2] It is the plague and the punishment of a time and nation, in which, as a system, female education is no more understood, than Mr. Payne Knight's Theory of the Iliad, or Mr. Burges's Play on the Troades.[3]

Without being positively criminal, a Blue Stocking is the most odious character in society; nature, sense, and hilarity fly at her approach; affectation, absurdity, and peevishness, follow in her train; she sinks, wherever she is placed, like the yolk of an egg, to the bottom, and carries the filth and the lees with her.

In a drawing-room she is detestable enough, no doubt, but the creature bears a feminine exterior, and we are obliged to refrain ourselves. But when, not contented with infesting private society, she proceeds to outrage public decorum; when satiated with *talking* of books, she advances to the *printing* from books, she leaves the position which ensured to her impunity, and deserts the asylum within the precincts of which alone she could hope to escape the vengeance of insulted literature. Many such fugitives, from sanctuary are rambling about the town and country; their example is evidently contagious;

---

1 The skills acquired for female "finishing": dancing, drawing, needlework, singing, sketching, piano playing, conversational Italian and French.

2 *Tertium aliquid*: a third thing, usually illogical or unnatural. *The Loves of the Angels* (1823), Thomas Moore's poem about three fallen angels enamored of mortal women, was widely translated and very popular. *Conversations on Chemistry, intended especially for the Female Sex,* by Jane Marcet (1769-1858), was published in 1806, and often reprinted. In Jonathan Swift's *Gulliver's Travels* (1726), scholars at the Grand Academy of Projectors at Lagado pursue a variety of fantastic experiments; one master of mathematics writes his lessons on a thin wafer with ink composed of a cephalic tincture and asks his students to swallow it, on the theory that the tincture will rise to the brain as the wafer is digested.

3 Richard Payne Knight (1747-1829), an ardent Hellenist, published *An Inquiry into the Symbolic Language of Ancient Art and Mythology* in 1818. Seneca (first-century Rome) has a play titled *Troades*.

"For they write not, who never wrote before,
And those who always wrote, now write the more!"

We thought it becoming the sound principles, and manly charac-
ter, of our Review, to declare ourselves thus openly upon this sub-
ject; and we hereby give notice to all whom it may concern, that it is
our intention henceforth, to visit enormities of this description, with
the severity they so justly deserve.

We now turn to Mrs. Hemans, and we do so with pleasure and
confidence. She will feel convinced, that whatever we may say, will
be sincere, and though we do not pretend to fix the value of our
advice, yet at all events after the foregoing denunciations, the praises
we bestow, may reasonably be entitled to some consideration at her
hands. Mrs. Hemans is a woman of that undoubted genius, that it is
her legitimate vocation to attend at the altars of the Muses. She has
regularly advanced in intellectual power, from her earliest work,
which was simply blameless, to the present, which contains instances
of a vigour of conception, luxuriance of feeling, and splendor of lan-
guage, which may be compared without disadvantage, to the best
efforts of Mrs. Joanna Baillie. Indeed in point of richness, and fertili-
ty of description, Mrs. Hemans is much superior. She is especially
excellent in painting the strength, and the weaknesses of her own
lovely sex, and there is a womanly nature throughout all her thoughts
and her aspirations, which is new and inexpressibly touching. A
mother *only* could have poured forth the deep and passionate strain
of eloquence which follows. We hardly remember any thing more
exquisitely beautiful. It is conceived in the truest spirit of essential
poetry. The speakers are husband and wife.

[Quotes *Siege of Valencia* 1.421-59.]

When a woman can write like this, she *ought* to write. Her mind
is national property. In the grand scheme of a popular literature,
there are many departments which can alone be filled by the emana-
tions of female genius. There is a fineness of apprehension, and a
subtlety of feeling, peculiar to the weaker sex, and perhaps the result
of that very weakness, which enables them to set some subjects in
such lights, and to paint them in such colours, as the more robust
intellect of men could never have imagined. A woman is so much
more a creature of passion than man; her virtues and her failings flow

so much more directly and visibly from the impulse of affection; her talent and her genius, her thoughts and her wishes, her natural qualities, and her acquired accomplishments are so interchangeably blended, and all but identified with each other, that there results a *wholeness* of conception, and a vividness and reality of colouring in her mental efforts, which advantageously distinguishes them from the most powerful productions of men on the same subjects. Let the golden fragments of Sappho bear testimony to the truth of this remark; let those two mutilated bursts of female passion, be compared with the most happy and finished parts of Ovid or Tibullus, and we may have good reason to wish that envious time had spared to us but a hundred more lines of the Lesbian Lady's, even at the price of one thousand hexameters and pentameters from the pens of the gentlemen of the Augustan age.[1] There have been indeed such things as female translators of Newton, and female interpreters of Kant;[2] but although these, and such like these, have, without doubt, displayed wonderful efforts of intellect, yet there is nothing in them peculiar to the sex; the same things are done as well, and for the most part better, by men; we admire them more for their novelty and strangeness, than for their intrinsic worth; we are surprised, rather than pleased.

It is not our intention to analyse this volume minutely; we dislike the practice generally. It may perhaps be necessary to take a treatise or an essay to pieces, in order to give an adequate representation of the argument contained in it; but to subject a poem, or a book of poems, to the same process, is equally injurious to the author, and useless to the public. A poem is valuable or worthless, according to its poetry; the mere *story* can have little to do with it, and it is the story alone which an analysis of this description affords to the reader. We think it more to the purpose to quote a specimen or two of the poetry comprised in this very delightful volume, and leave the world to judge for itself of the measure, and the strength of the intellectual powers of their author. […]

We are so firmly convinced of the intrinsic power of Mrs.

---

1 The poetry of Sappho (resident of Lesbos) survives only in fragments. Ovid wrote elegant elegiac meters (dactylic hexameter and pentameter); his Augustan contemporary Albius Tibullus was an elegiac poet.

2 Isaac Newton (1642-1727) wrote his treatises in Latin; philosopher Immanuel Kant (1724-1804) wrote in German but was widely translated.

Hemans' genius, that we feel a more than common interest in the success of her writings. We have reason to believe this lady a woman of that modesty and good sense, that she will not disdain to correct errors when temperately pointed out to her, or reject advice, although it comes to her from the suspected pen of a Reviewer. Mrs. Hemans knows very well that a man may reasonably find fault with a bad picture, though he cannot hold a pencil himself, and that habit, study, and observation, may enable a person to judge accurately of a composition, even if nature have denied him the actual capacity of composing himself. There are circumstances relating to this lady, which dispose us to feel much respect for her character, and we can assure her, that what we are about to say, is intended in a spirit of kindness and well-wishing.

Mrs. Hemans has not *studied* the great masters of the English language. Hence her style is not characteristic, her grammar not accurate, and her diction splendid rather than rich. We mean not that Mrs. Hemans is a stranger to the works of Spenser, Shakspeare, and Milton; but she has read them only as an amateur; she has not studied them as an artist. Her acquaintance with foreign literature, has done her indirectly much injury, though it is not irreparable; it has induced her to commence trading before she has amassed a substantial capital. It is a fatal, but a general mistake, to suppose that we acquire our native language, and understand it by the ordinary intercourse of society; a *certain* use of it indeed is acquired by the weakest capacity, and in the lowest stations of life; the degrees of command in language vary infinitely according to the infinite varieties of learning and genius; perhaps no one ever yet obtained *that* mastery over it which *might* be finally won by unremitting and exclusive study of the grand models and treasure-houses of its beauty and its riches. It is no less an error, and a more extended one, to think that to qualify and consummate a poet, the study of poetry *alone* is sufficient. It is *not* sufficient. Great and manifold as are the wealth and splendor of our poetry, yet are they far outweighed by the exhaustless riches of the prose writings of the English language. He who has not seen how this language is managed in the ever-during works of Hooker, Bacon, Milton, Taylor, and Barrow, has not seen the largest and most glorious half of its conquests and the trophies.

It is the profound and reverential study of the great authors of the

Elizabethan, and immediately subsequent ages, that can alone impart an adequate knowledge of the powers of the English language, and can impress a just sense of its genius and idiomatic character. Such a sense is absolutely necessary to a writer in these times, to preserve him from the seduction of the excessively vicious examples which are to be met with on all sides. The danger is greater in proportion to the intellectual power of the modern author. He has thoughts which the imperfection of his acquaintance with his own language, renders it impossible for him to express properly; he has recourse instantly to some one of the thousand extravagances of diction for which he sees abundant authority in the popular writers of the day, and thinks he has given utterance to his conception with energy, when in reality he has given no utterance to it at all. [...] We own we cannot even guess at the meaning of "*night-o'erpeopleing dead;*" but by a fair verbal analogy we shall soon have the "*land dispeopling*" essay of Malthus or the "*land-o'erpeopleing*" answer of Godwin. Surely Mrs. Hemans cannot require to be told that the printer's-devil's hyphen hath not that potent magic in it, that it should make those words one, which logic, and universal grammar, have put asunder. By this process, his Majesty's revenue might be defrauded to a ruinous and indefinite extent; for if an attorney may write seventy-two words in a folio, and he be a bad and ill-disposed subject, he has nothing to do but to fetter ten or twelve substantive words together, like the galley-slaves in Don Quixote, and he may plead stoutly, that they are all but one word. In the-ever-memorable-and-never-to-be-forgotten-pages of the Morning-Post, abundantly-and-forcibly-displayed authority may be found for this practice; but every body knows that the news-papers are not written in English, any more than the Scotch novels, or Mr. Irving's orations.

It requires a fine ear, and an exquisite apprehension of idiom not to err in inventing new compounds; yet there is one plain rule which logic teaches in its rudiments, viz. that the two compounds produce a *tertium aliquid*, the two words make a third word. If the two words retain two senses, what is the use of connecting them together? [...]

"*Sun-burst*" is really an outrage upon the language of this country.
"*Noon-day-night,*" is a bull.[1]

---

1   *The Cid's Funeral Procession* 35.

The sins against technical grammar in this volume are many; the sins against logical grammar are innumerable. Mrs. Hemans must remember, that "*broke*," &c. are solecisms, and that the frequent use of them in our best writers, is an authority, but no reason. 'It *was* Alvar Fañez *came!*" is not only bad grammar, but what is worse, and more extraordinary, a specimen of a very common London vulgarism.[1]

These are blemishes, but they are blemishes only; they obscure and weaken, but do by no means eclipse the light. It is in the belief of the genuine strength of that light, that we have ventured to point out freely a few of the most apparent obstacles to its attaining its full and meridian brightness. Poetry is Mrs. Hemans['] vocation certainly; let it be her study. Let her aim at more concentration of thought, more intenseness of feeling, more austerity of style. Let her before all things check that tendency to extreme diffuseness which enervates the most vigorous conception. Let her be sparing in the use of similes and compounded words, which always indicate real imbecility under the garb of power; in excess they are the epicurism of poetry. [...] In order to leave a sweet savour on the intellectual palates of our readers, we will conclude with a few fine lines from the Siege of Valencia. [Quotes 8.34-64]

4. From *The British Review, and London Critical Journal* 21 (August 1823): 196-202.

[*The British Review*, a quarterly given to support the Evangelical sect of the Church of England, was published by John Hatchard, who also issued the monthly *Christian Observer*. Patriotic and moralizing in tone, pitched toward middle-class readers, it was edited by William Roberts, who also wrote many of the reviews, and was famously lampooned by Byron in *Don Juan*, canto I (1819).]

The writers of poetry may be compared to persons, who lay out plots of ground according to their peculiar taste, and plant them with various trees, shrubs, and flowers; and who, after their labours are finished, invite every passenger, that chooses it, to ramble in their walks, or repose in their arbours; to listen for a moment to the mur-

---

1   *The Cid's Funeral Procession* 65.

mur of a limpid stream, or to pluck a fragrant blossom from the bush; to climb an elevation that commands a diversified and boundless prospect, or to sink into a glen where all is peace and stillness. If passengers attend to every invitation, and inspect every one of these highly decorated spots, they will probably find that some are repulsive for want of taste, that others abound with weeds as well as flowers, that these are so flat as to give no commanding and enlivening view, and that those are planted with productions so familiar that they need not turn out of the beaten road to behold them; while only few are to be found, that merit regard from the choice of place, or from the talent and taste, that have been developed in the cultivation of them.

The province of the critic is to inform the passenger, whether he shall enter on the enchanted ground or not; what he is to expect, if he enters upon it; what he is to guard against; and how he is to take his walk, so as to come away enriched by it. Venerating the dignified oracles of Christian truth, he will only give his cordial permission to explore districts where a due regard has been paid to the welfare of man. It is not the lot of all writers of verse to display the splendour of genius or multifarious stores of knowledge; but all may render a just homage to the sacredness of truth, the dignity of reason, the purity of morals, and the delicacy of taste. If it is the prerogative of a nobleman here and there to conduct us over a large scene, where every variety of magnificence and beauty may be inspected, yet it is within the province of the humblest individual to shew us a garden, where there is no vulgarity to excite disgust, no weed that can injure us, and where there may be some productions that are lovely and fragrant.

In the volume that we are about to examine, two beautiful spots, if we may be permitted to pursue the same illustration, are pointed out to us, in which a lady of genius and taste has worked, and to the inspection of which she now invites her countrymen. It will appear from our present number, that sieges are favorite themes, with both poets and poetesses. Nevertheless, on opening the book, we were rather surprised to find, that it begins with another poem, and not with the Siege of Valencia. We shall review them in the order in which they stand.

The subjects, on which Mrs. Hemans has chosen to employ her

talents and taste, are exceedingly different; the one being taken from the awful transactions of real history, the other from the creations of fancy in connexion with the history of a country, which furnishes an inexhaustible mine of topics to all who love the glittering achievements of chivalry and romance, or the sterner deeds of heroic valour.

[commentary on *The Last Constantine* as pleasing and interesting but not as powerful as its subject could have made it]

[*The Siege*] is a much longer poem than the preceding, dramatic in its form, and tragical in its nature. It will be proper, in the first place, to give a brief outline of the story on which it is founded. Valencia, a city of Spain, is besieged by Abdullah, a Moorish prince. The governor of the city is Gonzalez, who has a wife, Elmina, two sons, Alphonso and Carlos, and a daughter, Ximena, whose constitution is suffering by grief for the loss of one, who was slain in battle, and for whom she cherished a concealed attachment. The two sons are taken prisoners by the Moors, and Abdullah demands the surrender of the city as the only price of their ransom. Gonzalez refuses to be a traitor: but Elmina pleads for his compliance with all the earnestness of a distressed and feeling mother. Not being able to prevail upon her husband, she next unfolds her mind to Hernandez, a priest. But, receiving no encouragement from him, she contrives to get in disguise into the Moorish camp, where she sees her sons, reasons with Abdullah, and withdraws with him to consult in secret about the surrender of the city. This having been arranged, she returns, corrupts the sentinels, and informs Gonzalez of her proceedings in sufficient time for him to adopt preventive measures. Ximena puts forth all her energy, and stirs up the citizens to take arms for the rescue of her brothers: but they come too late, and the boys are beheaded. Ximena reveals her love to her mother, and dies. The Moors attack the city; in the critical moment forces arrive from Castile; Abdullah is slain; the Moors are routed; and Gonzalez breathes his last.

This narrative, with episodes, furnishes nine scenes. Before we make any extracts, we shall mention the characters that are delineated in the poem. In the former poem of the volume there is but one character, Constantine himself; and in our view, it is conceived and portrayed with skill and feeling. He is thoughtful and pensive, but firm, unwavering, and brave. He is calm and collected. There is about him no stormy woe that excites strong emotions of grief. No sudden bursts of heroical ardour absorb the mind in the contemplation of his military prowess. We see him wearing the appearance of forlorn dignity, and entitled to our tenderest regrets. In the 'Siege of Valencia,' there are more. Gonzalez is brave, dignified, faithful, calm, and kind; exhibiting the honour and integrity of a soldier: but his various excellencies are so blended, that it might be difficult to determine which is his predominating virtue. Wherever he appears he obtains our love, esteem, and sympathy. Alphonso, his eldest son, is a boy of high, and unbending spirit, full of pride and impetuosity. In Hernandez we find a total destitution of all kindly feeling. With whomsoever, and on whatsoever subject he converses, he is still severe and vehement, with nothing of the sanctity of affliction, and nothing of the sacredness of a priest. Elmina principally appears in the character of a distressed mother, overwhelmed with grief, and losing, in the prevalence of maternal affection, all sight and sense of rectitude and propriety. But we also see in her a peculiar spirit of pride and loftiness, even after the death of her sons, after her own reconciliation with her husband, and his death. Ximena is a gentle and affectionate daughter: in the sixth Scene, however, she appears with a most unexpected display of courage, tempered with a feeling affectionate earnestness.

After this abstract of the fable, as our limits will not admit of our transcribing a whole scene or dialogue, we shall only quote one passage, which will give a pleasing impression of the style of the authoress. It is from the first scene, where Elmina is pleading with Gonzalez for the rescue of their sons:

[quotes 1.433-77, from "*You* ne'er kept watch" to "above your race."]

The other pieces proceed from the same ardent spirit and elegant pen: but they are not the pieces on which the fame of the authoress will depend. […] In these poems, viewed as a whole, there is much to admire, and much to interest. Still there is too much vehemence, too much effort in our authoress, especially when she enters on scenes that require the exhibition of tender or ardent feeling; but it is in the latter that she puts forth her energy most conspicuously. If we were to judge from the present volume, she has a strong predilection for warlike affairs, for bold, fervid, and daring characters. We must, however, remark that the military spirit that breathes and glows in many of her pages, does not add to their real excellence. We do not like Bellona[1] as a Muse. We would add, that a just taste never suggests thoughts that cannot be easily comprehended; or which, if comprehended, cannot be approved of by a sound judgment. To be full, clear, and equal, as well as dignified and splendid, ought to be the aim of the poet: nor, if wise, will he try to astonish his readers by singular thought, by dazzling imagery, by forced expressions, or by unusual metres. Mrs. Hemans cannot claim entire exemption from the censure, implied in these remarks.

In a moral point of view, the volume can scarcely be said to offend in the least degree: we might make our exceptions at a few exclamations. It may, however, be put into the hands of any one, without any painful apprehension. At the same time we must express our regret, that the volume before us does not contain more in it, that has an immediate reference to the highest interests of man, especially, as in the principal poem one character, and one not the least conspicuous, is a minister of our holy religion [Hernandez], whose appearance in the faithful discharge of his peculiar duties, amidst the calamities of his fellow-citizens, would, by adding a moral dignity to the poem, and by infusing into it the softness and sweetness of religious consolation, have materially aided its effect. Though we are pleased with the blossom whose beauty fades, and whose fragrance evaporates, we dwell with the highest delight on the amaranth steeped in celestial dews; and in conclusion, would simply remind the admirers of harp and song, that they can only weave an imperishable garland for their brows, by frequently visiting a holier hill than Parnassus, and a purer fountain than Aganippe.[2]

5. From *New European Magazine* 3 (August 1823): 120-3.

[*New European*, a short-lived conservative monthly, was published in London by John Letts, Jr., from 1822-24. A deliberate answer to the liberal *European Magazine*, it took a hard line on political progressives

---

1 Roman goddess of War, typically depicted in military armor.
2 The amaranth is a flower said never to fade, and thus associated with immortality and immortal regions. Parnassus, a mountain in Greece, is fabled in mythology to be sacred to Apollo, god of poetry, and the muses, as is Aganippe, a fountain on Mt. Helicon in Boeotia, a district in Greece. The last sentence is an assertion of Christian superiority.

such as Byron and Leigh Hunt, and viciously attacked their journal *The Liberal*, especially its notorious publication of Byron's *The Vision of Judgment* (October 1822), a satirical response to Poet Laureate Robert Southey's epic on the ascension of George III to heaven, a death that also inspired Hemans's reverential *Stanzas to the Memory of the Late King* (London: John Murray, 1820). This notice of *The Siege &c* was the lead article of a section titled "Contemporary Poets."]

It is perhaps the proudest eulogy of the fair Authoress of this elegant little volume, that the lavish praises which have attended the whole of her poetical career, should not have had the too common effect of injuring, instead of improving, her later efforts. For, from her first production down to the present, they have been all distinguished by a purity of taste, a correctness of sentiment, and an elegance of expression, truly feminine; and, with all their alloy of occasional indistinctness of metaphor, and diffusion of feeling, have well merited a large proportion of the Reviewer's unbounded encomiums. When we have stated that the work before us has all the beauties, as well as all the blemishes which we have described as characteristic of Mrs. H.'s former publications, we have said every thing that our present space will allow us to record in the way of criticism; and our few quotations achieve all beside. [comments on and extracts from *The Last Constantine*]
  "*The Siege of Valencia,*" in dramatic form, describes the defeat of *Gonzalez,* by the Moors, and the subsequent deliverance of his city by the King of Castile, at the moment when, mortally wounded, the noble warrior dies a warrior's death. The whole of this Tragedy is admirable; and, with the exception of some few passages in which a single idea is too diluted to be natural, we award it unqualified praise. The following speech of *Elmina,* though partaking of the defect we have noticed, is sweetly poetical. [quotes 1.429-59, from "There is none" to "Why were ye given me?"; cf. *Gazette;* the notice concludes with a full quotation of "her truly beautiful Elegiac Stanzas on England's Dead."]

6. From *Monthly Review, or Literary Journal* 2d ser., 102 (October 1823): 177–81.

[Founded in 1749, this review was known for balance and fair-mindedness, but the newer, more polemical reviews were making it seem tame.]

It is with pleasure that we have remarked in the writings of Mrs. Hemans that gradual and substantial improvement, which is always indicative of high merit and talent; and which, while it makes no rash promises, realizes every honorable anticipation. We well recollect the earliest efforts of her muse, which she gave to the world at a period when her taste was necessarily unformed and her powers immature: but these specimens of juvenile ability encouraged a hope of higher success, which has since been fulfilled. To become a poet has been with Mrs. Hemans, as with almost every other writer, the work of time. She appears, indeed, to have been born with that attachment and predisposition to the art, which is the true foundation of the poetical character: but her genius was not of that over-mastering kind which at once rushes to the high place of its destination. She possessed the germ of poetic inspiration within her breast, but the shoots which it sent forth needed nourishment and cultivation.

In her earlier productions, we had not to complain of false taste, or of perverted feeling, or of extravagance in sentiment or in language: but we were sometimes displeased with the undecided character of the compositions. Mistrusting her powers, she dared not venture on a track of her own, and thus too often contented herself with the common-places of poetry. This defect, it is obvious, could only give way before a more matured judgment, and a more perfect skill in her art; which were necessary to indue [endue] her with confidence in her own strength, and to remit her to the guidance of her own poetical spirit.

Her later productions, however, have manifested this more original tone, and this bolder reliance on her own resources; and the present work is calculated to strengthen their claim to that character, since it exhibits a more strict and intimate acquaintance with poetic feelings than the fair writer has hitherto displayed, and a happier and easier use of poetic diction. In the last of her publications which we noticed [*Tales, and Historic Scenes in Verse*], she confined herself principally to the narrative-style: but she has now ventured on a dramatic attempt, and has added some lyrical specimens, which are exceedingly creditable to her pen.

By the selection of subjects for her muse, Mrs. Hemans has in this volume displayed considerable tact and knowle[d]ge of her own powers of verse. A chivalrous and even a martial strain flows freely from her lyre, which never sends forth nobler sounds than when it celebrates the battles of freedom or the achievements of romance. With such dispositions, the fame of the Cid naturally attracted her regards. Indeed, the history of that hero possesses a singular charm, celebrated as he has been in the rude but fascinating ballads of his country; and we know not any writer by whom the high romantic character of that old poetry has been more successfully caught than by Mrs. Hemans, who has transferred it into her elegant and polished verse with great fidelity and happiness. We would instance the lyrical songs with which the 'Siege of Valencia' is interspersed, as specimens of this kind of composition in which she has been most successful; and which have an air of romantic magnificence and grandeur thrown around them, that is admirably suited to the subject.

'The Cid's Battle-Song,' which we extract, is a very noble effort. [quotes this from scene 6, 193 to the end.] We are induced by the spirit and fine imagination of the piece to give another 'Song of the Cid,' founded on a passage in Southey's Chronicle.

[quotes *The Cid's Rising*]

When we contemplate the achievements of this illustrious hero, whether it be in the rude but splendid ballads of his native land or in the fine imitations of them which Mrs. Hemans has produced, we cannot refrain from expressing a sentiment of degradation and shame at the fate with which Spain is at this moment visited. Is there not, among her nobility or her captains, one unyielding arm or one faithful heart to emulate the heroic virtues of "the Compeador"? Apathy seems to have unnerved the hands of her soldiers, and treason to have corrupted the hearts of her commanders.

As a pure drama, this play cannot receive unqualified praise: but indeed it is rather a dramatic poem, as Mrs. Hemans has properly termed it; full of high chivalric poetry, and fitted not for the stage but for the closet. We cannot afford, nor indeed is it necessary, to give any idea of the plot: but we select from many beautiful passages the following lines, which are full both of thought and poetry. [quotes Hernandez, 2.26-43, from "Thou little know'st" to "Knows no companionship."] We add another singularly pleasing passage, which would do credit to any of our living poets: [quotes Elmina, 1.430-57, from "There is none" to "Steal from her all unmark'd!"]

[...] In conclusion, we can only exhort this fair votary of the muses to persevere in the course which she has hitherto pursued with so much success. When we review the progress which she has made, and more especially when we turn to this last production of her pen, we feel assured that she cannot be under better guidance than that of her own taste and judgment. Let her continue to study, with the same devotion and fervour as heretofore, the works of our great poets: —let her cherish that high moral sense which pervades all her writings;—and we do not doubt that we shall see her assume her merited station among the leading poets of her age.

7. From *North American Review* 24 (ns 15) (April 1827): 443-63.

[This review is by Andrew Norton (1786-1853), man of letters and Biblical scholar, Professor of Sacred Literature at Harvard Divinity School from 1819 to 1830, when he resigned to devote himself to literary and theological pursuits. His most famous work would be *The Evidences of the Genuineness of the Gospels* (1837-44). An enthusiastic admirer of Hemans, he edited *Poems of Mrs Hemans* (Boston, 1826-28), the major U.S. edition of her works and the occasion of this review. His lengthy obituary on Hemans for the *Christian Examiner* (January 1836) was generously excerpted in *1839* (7.299-328), and this review was reprinted entire therein, 3.389-90.]

[454-57] The "Siege of Valencia" is a dramatic poem, but not intended for representation. The story is extremely simple. The Moors, who besiege Valencia, take the two sons of the Governor, Gonzalez, captive, as they come to visit their father; and now the ransom demanded for them is the surrender of the city; they are to die, if the place is not yielded up. Elmina, the mother of the boys, and Ximena, their sister, are the remaining members of a family, to which so dreadful an option is submitted. The poem is one of the highest

merit. The subject is of great dignity, being connected with the defence of Spain against the Moors, and at the same time it is of the greatest tenderness, offering a succession of the most moving scenes that can be imagined to occur in the bosom of a family. The father is firm; the daughter is heroic; the mother falters. She finds her way to the Moorish camp, sees her children, forms a plan for betraying the town, and then is not able to conceal her grief and her design from her husband. He immediately sends a defiance to the Moors; his children are brought out and beheaded, a *sortie*[1] is made from the besieged city; finally the king of Spain arrives to the rescue, the wrongs of Gonzalez[2] are avenged; he himself dies in victory, and the poem closes with a picture of his wife, moved by the strongest grief, of which she is yet able to restrain the expression. The great excellence of the poem lies the delineation of the struggle between the consciousness of duty and maternal fondness. We believe none but a mother could have written it. We will quote a few passages, and leave it to our readers to commend.

Elmina learns of her husband the terrible choices submitted to them. The mother entreats;

[quotes 1.281 (from "I *must* be heard")-308 ("I perish with my race"), but changes *1823*'s 304 to "treasure he recalls"; and 1.411 (from Elmina)-459 (Elmina)]

Elmina meets with a priest, and holds a long discourse with him. She obtains of him no relief for her mind. "Let them die," he answers her questions.

[quotes Hernandez, 2.290-304 ("loved!")]

[Admiring "the scene in which Elmina, after her visit to the Moorish camp, meets her daughter and her husband, the scene in which her daughter expires, and that in which the battle of the king of Spain with the Moors is described," the reviewer regrets that there is "no room" to quote these.]

---

1 A sudden issuing of troops from a defensive position against an enemy.
2 Wrongs of: injuries inflicted upon.

8. From David Macbeth Moir, "Biographical Memoir of the Late Mrs. Hemans."

[Satirist, physician, poet, and critic David Macbeth Moir (1798-1851) wrote under the pseudonym "Delta" (often signed Δ) for *Blackwood's Edinburgh Magazine* and the annuals. His obituary essay on Hemans appeared in *Blackwood's* 38 (July 1835): 96-97. He helped edit the 1839 *Works of Mrs. Hemans* and in 1848 prepared a single volume edition. This "Memoir" introduced *Poetical Remains of the Late Mrs. Hemans* (Edinburgh: William Blackwood and Sons / London: T. Cadell, 1836).]

[T]he genius of Mrs Hemans was not essentially dramatic, yet [*The Siege* and *Vespers*] abound with high and magnificent bursts of poetry. It was not easy to adapt her fine taste and uniformly high-toned sentiment to the varied aspects of life and character, necessary to the success of scenic exhibition; and she must have been aware of the difficulties that surrounded her in that path. If these cannot, therefore, be considered as successful tragedies, they hold their places, as dramatic poems of rich and rare poetic beauty. Indeed it would be difficult, from the whole range of Mrs Hemans's writings, to select any thing more exquisitely conceived, more skilfully managed, or more energetically written, than the Monk's tale in The Siege of Valencia [Hernandez, 2.280-400]. His description of his son, in which he dwells with parental enthusiasm on his boyish beauty and accomplishments—of his horror at that son's renunciation of the Christian faith, and leaguing with the infidel—and of the twilight encounter in which he took the life of his own giving,—are all worked out in the loftiest spirit of poetry (xvi-xvii).

9. From Henry F. Chorley, *Memorials of Mrs. Hemans*, 1836.

[Musician, music critic, journalist, reviewer for the *Athenæum*, and frequent contributor to the annuals, Henry Fothergill Chorley (1808-72) befriended Hemans at Wavertree in 1828. Among his intimate friends were Mary Russell Mitford, Lady Blessington, the Brownings, Dickens, and Thackeray. Chorley adored Hemans and was a strong advocate of women's writing in general. His "Personal Recollections of the Late Mrs. Hemans" appeared in the *Athenæum*, 13 June 1835, then developed into *Memorials*.]

None of her poems contain[s] finer bursts of strong, fervid, indignant poetry than "The Siege of Valencia": its story—a thrilling conflict between maternal love and the inflexible spirit of chivalrous honour—afforded to her an admirable opportunity of giving utterance to the two master interests of her mind [...] though it must be confessed, that [...] somewhat of a monotony of colouring is thrown over its scenes by the unchanged employment of a lofty and enriched phraseology, which would have gained in emphasis by its being more sparingly used. Ximena, too, all glowing and heroic as she is; stirring up the sinking hearts of the besieged citizens, with her battle song of the Cid, and dying, as it were, of that strain of triumph—is too spiritual, too saintly, wholly to carry away the sympathies. Our imagination is kindled by her splendid, high-toned devotion—our tears are called forth by the grief of her mother, the stately Elmina; broken down but not degraded, by the agony of maternal affection, to connive at a treachery she is too noble wholly to carry through. The scenes with her husband are admirable—some of her speeches absolutely startle us with their passion and intensity—the following for instance. [quotes 1.424-59] (*CM* 1.111-12)

10. From William Archer Butler, "Introductory Notice" to Hemans's *National Lyrics, and Songs for Music* (Dublin: William Curry, 1838)

[Hemans's volume was first published in London and Dublin in 1834. Butler (?1814-1848), man of letters, poet and essayist, was appointed as the first professor of moral philosophy at Trinity College, Dublin, in 1837. He was also a much admired clergyman, famous for his eloquent sermons and his exertions on behalf of the poor.]

The graceful powers of Mrs Hemans in the same walk which had been trodden so grandly by Miss Baillie, were manifested in her "Ves-

pers of Palermo," and her "Siege of Valencia."[1] The latter is a noble
work, and as a poem ranks with her highest productions, though it is
filled too uniformly perhaps with the spirit of her own mind, to be
very distinctively dramatic. It has indeed variety, but less of the vari-
ety of human nature, than of a godlike and exalted nature which
belongs to few among mankind, and to them, perhaps, only in
strange and terrible crises. The steadfastness of the paternal chieftain,
the sterner enthusiasm of the priest, the mother's maddening affec-
tion, and the gentle heroism of the melancholy Ximena are drawn
with individuality, but it is the individuality of a common greatness,
the apparent appropriation to many of an essence really the same in
all. In her own heart the poetess found this pure essence; and when
she created her Christian patriots at Valencia, she but translated her-
self into a new dialect of manners and motives. Of this one elevated
material she has, however, made fine dramatic use. The language,
while faultless in its measured music, has passion to swell its cadences;
the loftiness is never languid; and the flow of the verse is skilfully bro-
ken into the animated abruptness suitable to earnest dialogue. There
are many, too, of those sudden glimpses of profound truth in which
the energy of passion seems to force its rude way, in a moment, into
regions of the heart that philosophy would take hours to survey with
its technical language. Thus, when the iron-hearted monk [Hernan-
dez] is telling the story of his son's disgrace. [quotes 2.331-44]

The whole of the scene to which the passage belongs, is moulded
in the highest spirit of tragic verse. The bewilderment of the mother
betrayed into guilt by overpowering affection, and the death of the
beautiful enthusiast Ximena, are sketched in a style of excellence lit-
tle inferior; and the peculiar powers of Mrs Hemans's poetry, less dra-
matic than declamatory, have full scope in the spirit-stirring address
of the latter to the fainting host of Valencia, as she lifts in her own
ancient city the banner of the Cid, and recounts the sublime legend

---

1   Poet and playwright Joanna Baillie was widely admired for her *Plays on the Passions*
    (1798-1812). In 1823 Hemans praised the "gentle fortitude" and "deep, self-devoting
    affection" of her female characters: "so perfectly different from the pretty 'un-idea'd
    girls,' who seem to form the *beau idéal* of our whole sex in the works of some modern
    poets" (*CM* 1.196; cf. *HM* 69). When she wrote to Baillie in 1827 to ask permission to
    dedicate *Records of Woman* (1828) to her, she addressed her as one "of whom my whole
    sex may be proud" (*HM* 127; cf. *CM* 1.146).

of his martial burial. Spain and its romances formed the darling theme of Mrs Hemans's muse; and before leaving the subject, she gives us her magnificent series of ballads, the "Songs of the Cid," which meet us at the close of the drama, as if to form an appropriate chorus to the whole.

11. From Jane Williams, *The Literary Women of England* (London: Saunders, Otley, 1861)

[Historian, poet, essayist, and biographer, Jane Williams (1806-85) initially meant to write "a Critical and Biographical Essay on the subject of Mrs. Hemans and her poetry," but then realized the need for an account of "the general progress of female literature in England" ("Introduction"). *Literary Women* treats over 90 authors in its 564 pages, beginning with the Anglo-Saxons and concluding with a 106-page, three-chapter treatment of Hemans.]

In this drama Mrs. Hemans ventures not only upon the construction of a plot, but also upon the invention of imaginary personages, and the selection of their sphere of action. The opening ballad is too long; the secret grief of Zimena [*sic*] for her lover's death might have been better told in half the number of words. The second scene is also too long; the latter part of it consists of a dialogue between Elmina the heroine and Hernandez a priest, and is distinguished by passages of high poetic merit, and by an ill-managed division and counteraction of scenic interest. No one who has either felt or witnessed the emotions of passionate anxiety can be ignorant that a past and narrated sorrow offers a cold, repelling, and abhorrent contrast to the active, concentrated and absorbing presence of such agony. Yet here the mind of Elmina, bent on one purpose, full of devices for its accomplishment, seeing and feeling nothing but the peril of her children, and the necessity of averting it, is unnaturally interrupted in its course by a tedious and vain attempt to divide the reader's sympathy with the old griefs of a fierce ecclesiastic. Subsiding emotion may be soothed by narratives of kindred trouble, but on the full-swelling tide of effort, in the face of a dire and instantly impending calamity, the dreary frost of such delay is intolerable, and Elmina's patience under it preternatural.

All the characters of the piece are well conceived and well sustained. In that of Elmina, Mrs. Hemans seems to have embodied her idea of how she herself would have felt and acted under similar trials: there is in it such an intensity of life and love, such majesty, such tenderness, such sad reality, that the most vivid imagination must have failed in creating it without the concurrent wear and tear of a fervid heart. The terrible conflict of Elmina between maternal instinct on one side and conjugal love with chivalrous honour on the other, her temporary subjection to evil, her conscious loss of moral dignity under the crushing pressure of temptation, her vacillation, her repentant recognition of the purpose of affliction, her faith and heroic constancy when all is lost, forms one of the finest word-pictures ever drawn by a woman's hand. For such originality the penalty must have been previously paid in tears. [423-24]

12. From W.M. Rossetti, "Prefatory Notice" to *Poetical Works of Mrs. Hemans*, 1878

[Brother of poet and painter Dante Gabriel Rossetti and poet Christina Rossetti, William Michael Rossetti (1829-1919) was part of the original Pre-Raphaelite Brotherhood. His art criticism from the *Spectator* was collected as *Fine Art, Chiefly Contemporary* (1867). He then turned to literary biography, criticism, and editing. An introductory "Memoir" for *The Poetical Works of Percy Bysshe Shelley* (1870) was followed by a critical edition of *Adonais* (1891); a "Biographical Sketch" for *Poems of John Keats* (1872) was expanded to *Life of John Keats* (1887). He wrote memoirs of his family (1895, 1904), and a study of Dante (1910). The essay on Hemans first appeared as a "Critical Memoir" for *Poetical Works of Mrs. Hemans* (1873) and was often republished as an authoritative critical assessment.]

The Siege of Valencia [...] appears to have been written without any view to the stage: a condition of writing which acts detrimentally upon a drama composed by a born dramatist, but which may rather have the opposite effect upon one coming from a different sort of author. In *The Siege of Valencia* the situation is in a high degree tragical—even terrible or harrowing: and there is this advantage,—no small one in the case of a writer such as Mrs. Hemans—that, while the framework is historical, and the crisis and passions of a genuinely heroic type, the immediate interest is personal or domestic. Mrs. Hemans may be credited with a good and unhacknied choice of subject in this drama, and with a well-concerted adaptation of it to her own more special powers: the writing is fairly sustained throughout, and there are passages both vigorous and moving. As the reader approaches the *dénouement*,[1] and finds the authoress dealing death with an unsparing hand to the heroically patriotic Gonzalez and all his offspring, he may perhaps at first feel a little ruffled at noting that the only member of the family who has been found wanting in the fiery trial — wanting through an excess of maternal love — is also the only one saved alive: but in this also the authoress may be pronounced in the right. Reunion with her beloved ones in death would in fact have been mercy to Elmina, and would have left her undistinguished from the others, and untouched by any retribution; survival, mourning, and self-discipline, are the only chastisement in which a poetic justice, in its higher conception, could be expressed [16-17].

---

1 Literally, "unknotting," the resolution of the dramatic conflicts.

Bibliography

The Texts

The Siege of Valencia, A Dramatic Poem; The Last Constantine: With Other Poems. By Mrs. Hemans. London: John Murray, 1823. 91–247.

The Siege of Valencia, ~~or the Race of the Cid~~. Houghton Library MS Eng. 1227 64M-40. The MS is not dated; the catalogue indicates 1823, without explanation. It is inscribed "To Mr. Mackenzie Bell, with Felicia Hemans [sic] compliments April 1899." The catalogue identifies the namesake as the poet's great granddaughter.

Felicia Hemans

Chorley, Henry F. *Memorials of Mrs. Hemans, with Illustrations of her Literary Character from her Private Correspondence.* 2 vols. London: Saunders and Otley, 1836.

Hemans, Felicia. *The Works of Mrs. Hemans.* 7 vols. Edinburgh: Blackwood & Sons; London: T. Cadell, 1839.

[Hughes, Harriett]. *Memoir of the Life and Writings of Felicia Hemans: By Her Sister.* In vol. 1 *Works* (1839).

Feldman, Paula R., ed. *British Women Poets of the Romantic Era.* Baltimore: Johns Hopkins UP, 1997.

Wolfson, Susan J. *Felicia Hemans: Selected Poems, Letters, and Reception Materials.* Princeton: Princeton UP, 2000. Includes a comprehensive bibliography.

Wu, Duncan, ed. *Women Romantic Poets: An Anthology.* Oxford, U.K, and Cambridge Mass.: Blackwell, 1998.

The Siege of Valencia, recent assessments, related issues

Kelly, Gary. "Death and the Matron: Felicia Hemans, Romantic Death, and the Founding of the Modern Liberal State." *Felicia Hemans: Reimagining Poetry in the Nineteenth Century.* Ed. Julie

Melnyk & Nanora Sweet. Houndsmill, UK: Macmillan, 2000.
196-211.

Lootens, Tricia. "Hemans and Home: Victorianism, Feminine 'Internal Enemies,' and the Domestication of National Identity."
PMLA 109 (1994): 238-53.

Mellor, Anne K. *Romanticism & Gender.* New York and London:
Routledge, 1993. 135-40.

Ross, Marlon. *The Contours of Masculine Desire: Romanticism and the
Rise of Women's Poetry.* New York and London: Oxford UP,
1989. 274-85.

Southey, Robert. *Chronicle of the Cid, from the Spanish.* London:
Longman &c, 1808.

Sweet, Nanora. *The Bowl of Liberty: Felicia Hemans and the Romantic
Mediterranean.* Ann Arbor: U of Michigan, 1993; Microfilm
9332173.

Wolfson, Susan J. "Felicia Hemans and the Revolving Doors of
Reception." *Romanticism and Women Poets: Opening the Doors of
Reception.* Ed. Harriet Kramer Linken & Stephen C. Behrendt.
Lexington: U of Kentucky P, 1999. 214-41.

———. "Editing Felicia Hemans." *Romanticism on the Net.* May, 2000.